THE NATURE OF PSYCHOLOGICAL
EXPLANATION

Date Due

⊣ㄴ *Bradford Books*

Edward C. T. Walker, Editor. Explorations in THE BIOLOGY OF LAN-
GUAGE. 1979. The M.I.T. Work Group in the Biology of Language:
Noam Chomsky, Salvador Luria, et alia.

Daniel C. Dennett. BRAINSTORMS. 1979.

Charles Marks. COMMISSUROTOMY, CONSCIOUSNESS AND UNITY
OF MIND. 1980.

John Haugeland, Editor. MIND DESIGN, 1981.

Fred I. Dretske. KNOWLEDGE AND THE FLOW OF INFORMATION.
1981.

Jerry A. Fodor. REPRESENTATIONS. 1981.

Ned Block, Editor. IMAGERY. 1981.

Roger N. Shepard and Lynn A. Cooper. MENTAL IMAGES AND THEIR
TRANSFORMATIONS. 1982.

Hubert L. Dreyfus, Editor, in collaboration with Harrison Hall. HUS-
SERL, INTENTIONALITY AND COGNITIVE SCIENCE. 1982.

John Macnamara. NAMES FOR THINGS. 1982.

Natalie Abrams and Michael D. Buckner, Editors. MEDICAL ETHICS.
1982.

Morris Halle and G. N. Clements. PROBLEM BOOK IN PHONOLOGY.
1983.

Irvin Rock. THE LOGIC OF PERCEPTION. 1983.

Jon Barwise and John Perry. SITUATIONS AND ATTITUDES. 1983.

Elliott Sober, Editor. READINGS IN THE PHILOSOPHY OF BIOL-
OGY. 1983.

Stephen Stich. FOLK PSYCHOLOGY AND COGNITIVE SCIENCE.
1983.

Jerry A. Fodor. MODULARITY OF MIND. 1983.

George D. Romanos. QUINE AND ANALYTIC PHILOSOPHY. 1983.

Robert Cummins. THE NATURE OF PSYCHOLOGICAL EXPLANA-
TION. 1983.

The Nature of
Psychological Explanation

ROBERT CUMMINS

A BRADFORD BOOK

THE MIT PRESS
Cambridge, Massachusetts and London, England

First MIT Press paperback edition, 1985

Library of Congress Cataloging in Publication Data

Cummins, Robert.
    The nature of psychological explanation.

    "A Bradford book."
    Bibliography: p.
    Includes index.
    1. Psychology—Philosophy.   2. Hermeneutics.
3. Cognition.   I. Title.   [DNLM: 1. Psychology.
BF 121 C971n]
BF38.5.C85   1983   150'.1   82–20895
ISBN 0-262-03094-2 (hardcover)
ISBN 0-262-53065-1 (paperback)

Typographic design by David Horne
Composition by Horne Associates, Inc.,
West Lebanon, New Hampshire.
This book was printed and bound
in the United States of America.

Preface

This is a book about the nature of psychological explanation. Psychologists theorize about animals—humans, mainly—in an effort to understand their dispositions and abilities. When the theorizing is good theorizing, it helps us understand such things as your ability to calculate, speak a language, remember your name and way home, and tell your elbow from a hot rock. Good psychological theory explains such things (or tries to). In the following chapters, I theorize about this phenomenon, i.e., about the fact that psychological theory can make us understand such abilities as perception and cognition. How does it do this? What would it take to make us understand the capacity to be operantly conditioned or the capacity to learn French?

The Received Doctrine about scientific explanation is that it consists of subsumption under law. The classic expression of this doctrine is the Deductive Nomological (D-N) model of Hempel and Oppenheim (1948), but it has dominated without serious competition at least since Newton. Yet the Received Doctrine is not without internal difficulties. It is well known that nomic subsumption is not sufficient for explanation (e.g., Kim, 1973), and there are reasons for supposing it isn't necessary, even in mechanics, the domain most often used to illustrate nomic subsumption (Cummins, 1979). Indeed, the literature abounds with well-taken critiques of the Received Doctrine. Nevertheless, scientists and philosophers continue to force scientific explanation into a subsumptive mold. This appears to be due mainly to the lack of any well-articulated alternative to the Received Doctrine. Those who abandon the subsumptive pattern find themselves in a methodological vacuum. If we think of a methodology as a canon for evaluating applications of an explanatory strategy, we can see that the dominance of the Received Doctrine was bound to have the consequence of limiting methodological studies to uncovering and clarifying the canons of nomic subsumption. Scientific explanation was equated with nomic subsumption, hence scientific methodology was equated with the methodology of nomic subsumption.

Nowhere has the Received Doctrine been more influential than in psychology. Yet most "classical" psychological explanation makes little sense as subsumption, as I try to show in Chapter IV. A good theory of psychological explanation therefore requires an alternative to the Received Doctrine. Chapter I attempts to supply such an alternative.

In Chapters II and III I use the machinery developed in Chapter I to investigate a number of issues at the various interfaces between the philosophy of mind on the one hand and cognitive science on the other. What would it take to *really* explain a cognitive capacity? Intelligence? What can we expect cognitive science to tell us about propositional attitudes? These are the issues with sex appeal, and they are currently receiving wide and competent attention, largely thanks to Jerry Fodor (1975) and Daniel Dennett (1978). My task has been mainly to recast familiar points and issues in terms of a theory of explanation that makes them (I hope) more intelligible. Chapter IV uses the analysis of Chapter I to "reconstruct" a number of key historical episodes in psychological explanation.

Section III.2 is something of a digression, written after the rest of the manuscript was completed. There I make an attempt to relate the themes of this book to the pioneering work of Fred Dretske in *Knowledge and the Flow of Information* (1981). The section is short, barely touching on some of the important issues, but anyone interested enough in these kinds of issues to read the rest of this book will surely want to be made aware of Dretske's work, if they are not already familiar with it, and to begin thinking seriously about the connections between the "interpretive" approach to the semantics of psychological states advocated here and the information-theoretic approach developed and advocated by Dretske. The section will have succeeded if it leads those who have not already read *Knowledge and the Flow of Information* to do so.

Finally, a word about Philosophy: this book does not argue for, but simply assumes, an antidualist position on the mind-body problem. This is because it is intended to be a work in the philosophy of science, not in the philosophy of mind. Still, to the extent that it is possible to give a cogent and persuasive account of what psychological explanation *ought to be* from an antidualist perspective, that perspective is vindicated. No more direct form of argument in this area has had any notable success.

ACKNOWLEDGMENTS

In the course of preparing the manuscript, I have benefited from comments and discussion with many colleagues around the country. They are too numerous to name individually, but I would be remiss if I did not acknowledge the special thanks I owe to Pat and Paul Churchland, whose encouragement at an early stage wan critical in getting the project off the ground; to Daniel Dennett, John Haugeland, and William Lycan, who read and commented on various drafts; and especially to Denise DellaRosa, who acted as a critic and sounding board at every stage of the project.

Two parts of the Manuscript appear elsewhere. The section called "Representation and Internal Manuals" (Chapter II, section 3) was published as "The Internal Manual Model of Psychological Explanation" in *Cognition and Brain Theory,* (1982), 5:257–268; and the material on Hull in Chapter IV, section 2, is forthcoming in *Philosophy of Science* as "Analysis and Subsumption in the Behaviorism of Hull."

Work on this book was supported in part by a fellowship from the American Council of Learned Societies, by a Summer Stipend from the National Endowment for the Humanities, and by a grant from the National Science Foundation (SES-8108211). That support is gratefully acknowledged.

Finally, I would like to salute Harry and Betty Stanton at Bradford Books for running an operation that is fun and human as well as first class.

Chicago   R.C.

Contents

THE NATURE OF PSYCHOLOGICAL
EXPLANATION

CHAPTER ONE
Analysis and Subsumption

A major contention of this study is that psychological phenomena are typically not explained by subsuming them under causal laws, but by treating them as manifestations of capacities that are explained by analysis. Thus, a contrast between two explanatory strategies—*subsumption* and *analysis*—is central to what follows. Since the analytical strategy is by no means peculiar to psychology or to the social sciences,[1] and since it has generally been neglected by philosophers and methodologically minded scientists, it will be useful to begin with an abstract characterization of the analytical strategy and its relation to the more familiar subsumptive strategy

In order to see this matter clearly, we need to distinguish between two kinds of theorizing, one of which customarily achieves its goals via causal subsumption, the other one via analysis.

I.1. TRANSITION THEORIES

Many scientific theories are designed to explain change. The point of what I call a *transition theory* is to explain changes of state in a system as effects of previous causes—typically disturbances in the system. The emphasis is on what will happen *when* (i.e., under what conditions). Subsumption under causal law is the natural strategy: one tries to fix on a set of state variables for the system that will allow one to exhibit each change of state as a function of a disturbing event and the state of the system at the time of the disturbance. A transition law therefore requires a systematic way of representing the states of the target system S, and a systematic way of transforming these representations such that, given a representation R of S at t, the (or a) transformation of R will represent S at t'. We can picture the situation this way:

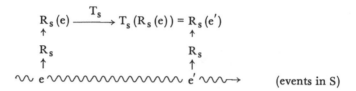

The wavy line represents the temporal sequence of events in S. R_s is a function that maps events in the system S onto the canonical representations licensed by the theory, and T_s is a function that maps the domain of R_s into itself.

A venerable tradition to which I subscribe holds that transition theories are not genuinely explanatory unless the laws appealed to are causal laws—i.e., laws that subsume cause-effect pairs[2]—for the goal of such theories is to explain changes as effects. Subsumption under a generalization that is not causal merely summarizes our reasons for believing the change would occur—it justifies our expectations perhaps—but it doesn't explain why the change occurs.[3] Certain cases of subsumption under noncausal generalization are admittedly called explanations, and I have no desire to arbitrarily restrict use of the word. But it is important to see that the goals of a *transition theory* will not be satisfied by noncausal subsumption. Hence, transition theories are fairly criticized as nonexplanatory when noncausal generalizations are substituted for the genuine article. Throughout this book, I shall mean by "subsumption" *causal subsumption.* Causal subsumption is not, of course, the only sort of explanation that involves logical derivation from laws, but it is the only sort of derivation that achieves the goal of what I am calling transition theories.

The causal character of many standard subsumptive explanations is obscured by the equational form of most physical laws. For example, the pendulum law that tells us that the period of a pendulum, T, is equal to 2π times the square root of the pendulum's length, lh, divided by the constant of gravitation, g.

$$(1) \quad T = 2\pi \sqrt{lh/g}.$$

Here we have no obvious reference to events, nor do standard textbook applications of the law involve such references. Philosophers add to this obscurity when they give the following as an instance of a D–N (deductive-nomological) "explanation."

$$(2) \quad T = 2\pi \sqrt{lh/g} \ ;$$
$$lh = 2 \ ft \ ;$$
$$\overline{\quad T = 1.570 \ sec \ .\quad}$$

Argument (2) is typically offered as a genuine explanation in contrast to (3) which, though it fits the usual D–N schema, is said to be nonexplanatory.

$$(3) \quad T = 2\pi \sqrt{lh/g} \ ;$$
$$T - 1.570 \ sec \ ;$$
$$\overline{\quad lh = 2 \ ft \ .\quad}$$

(2) is univerally preferred to (3) on the grounds that the length isn't two feet because the period is $\pi/2$ seconds: length causes period, not vice versa.

Anyone who shares this and like intuitions should, it seems, abandon the Humean doctrine that to be causally connected is simply to be an instance of a nomological generalization, for (1) will not distinguish between the claim that length causes period and the claim that period causes length. It is useless to reply that once (1) is rewritten as a statement subsuming cause-effect pairs (as below), only the former connection will appear as an instance. That is true, as we shall see shortly, but it begs the question: the decision to represent changes in length in the "cause" slot rather than in the "effect" slot is motivated solely by a prior conviction that changes in length cause changes in period, and not vice versa. Equation (1) exhibits no such asymmetry. A temporal priority condition will not help either: the changes are concomitant. Nor, finally, can we resort to the fact that we can alter ("control") the period by altering (controlling) the length, for this is just a misleading way of saying that the change in length causes the change in period, and not vice versa.

As they stand, it seems to me that (2) and (3) are, in a crucial sense, on a par: neither is a causal explanation. Both are acceptable "problem solutions" ("Given T, find lh; given lh, find T"), hence explanations of why one thinks (or should think) that T = 1.570 sec. or lh = 2 ft. But if we mean by a causal explanation something that explains an effect by citing its cause, then neither (2) nor (3) is a causal explanation, for neither has an effect as explanandum, and neither invokes a causal law. Compare (2) and (3) with (4) and (5):

(4) A change of u to v in lh
   causes a change of
   $2\pi \ (\sqrt{v/g} - \sqrt{u/g})$ in T;[4]
   lh increased from 1 to 2 ft;
   ―――――――――――――――
   T increased from 1.110 sec
   to 1.570 sec .

(5) A change of u to v in T
   causes a change of
   $gv^2/4\pi - gu^2/4\pi$ in lh;[4]
   T increased from 1.110 sec
   to 1.570 sec ;
   ―――――――――――――――
   lh increased from 1 to 2 ft.

Notice that the information in the equational form of the simple pendulum law is neutral as between a construal that has changes in length causing changes in period and a construal that has changes in period causing changes in length. Since whatever supports the equation supports both construals equally, it follows that the equation is not a causal law but, as it were, an abstraction from the causal facts that make it true. This is why schemata like (2) tend to obscure the causal element in the explanation of a state transition: no causal element is present in (2), and it is precisely the reference to causes that is essential to the explanation of a state transition as an effect. (4), on the other hand, is a literal case of causal subsumption, with a change in T explained as an effect of a change in lh. Replacing the causal law in (4) with a noncausal generalization—e.g., an equation—unhinges the explanation while leaving the calculation (the transformation of representations) intact.

Causal laws—laws that do subsume cause-effect pairs—have two roles within transition explanations, both surprisingly limited in explanatory power.

First role: explanation of individual events. Individual events are explained by appeal to individual causes. The law may provide justification, since whatever reasons we have to accept the law will support our choice of cause/effect description in a particular case. Sometimes, especially when these descriptions are quantitative or heavily theoretical, we would not accept the explanation, let alone arrive at it, without this sort of support. But laws are not essential to the causal explanation of individual events. We can often causally explain an individual event with justified confidence even though no subsuming law is known. In any case, we should distinguish the explanation from its justification. Since causal laws play only a justifying role in the explanation of individual effects, they are not the source of explanatory force in such cases.

Often we need no guidance, and theory provides none, in finding causes. Theory will not help choose between (4) and (5)—Newtonian mechanics will simply yield the equation which is neutral between them—nor is it needed to explain why the window broke when I missed the nail and hit the pane with a hammer.

Of course, theory *is* required to explain why strikings cause breakings in glass but not putty. Hence, causal laws can be explananda. We could choose to say, with Hempel (1948), that we haven't "completely explained" a particular breaking by citing its cause unless we also explain how/why breakings—hence this breaking—are caused by strikings hence by this striking. This would be all right were it not for the fact that this way of speaking tempts one to suppose that we don't "really know" what caused the breaking in the absence of this deeper theory. We are likely to be misled in just this way, however, for it is tempting to move from (a) we haven't completely explained the breaking, to (b) we don't really know why it occurred, to (c) we don't really know what caused it. It is only because we do know what caused it that we want a theory to explain the causal link!

Second role: explanation of event-types. More important than the explanation of individual events, which is seldom of scientific interest, is the explanation of event-types. A transition theory provides a recipe for explaining events of the types specified in its effect-descriptions. We have an especially important case of this when a transition theory for a system S can be derived from a transition theory for a more general type of system S* of which S is a special case. But even this last sort of explanation is limited in power. A transition theory for a system S simply specifies a dispositional property of S. Hence, derivation of a transition theory T_s for S from a transition theory T_{s*} for S* exhibits the dispositional property specified by T_s as a special case of the dispositional property specified by T_{s*}. It allows us to see manifestation of the T_s disposition as manifestation of the T_{s*} disposition.

Dispositions want explaining for reasons made famous if not clear by Molière in *Le malade imaginaire*. Asked why opium puts people to sleep, Molière's doctor replies that opium has a *virtus dormitiva*. The prospect of having to take seriously at the most fundamental level what we regard as a joke elsewhere is sufficiently unwelcome to lead us to ask whether there is some explanatory strategy to exploit other than more and more general subsumption of one transition theory to another. In particular, we are led to wonder whether there is some nonregressive way to explain the dispositional properties of a system, for transition theories only *specify* dispositions; they do not explain them. Not surprisingly: transition theories explain events or event-types, and dispositions are not events or event-types. The strategy of causal subsumption cannot stand alone.

Not all laws are causal laws, of course, and even causal laws play roles other than the roles they play in transition theories. To provide perspective, it will be useful to list and briefly identify a number of other sorts of laws, sorts that will loom large in my discussion of the analytical strategy.

1. **CAUSAL LAWS.** These are nomic[5] correlations whose instances are cause-effect pairs. (4) is an example. In addition to the two roles just discussed, causal laws define—or, better, *specify*—dispositional properties of the systems whose state transitions they subsume. They are thus candidate explananda of theories that seek to explain the properties (as opposed to the transitions) of those systems.

2. **NOMIC CORRELATIONS.** An example is the law correlating

thermal and electrical conductivity. Nomic correlations have no explanatory role at all, contrary to what is predicted by the deductive-nomological model of explanation. But they are important nevertheless. First, they serve as predictive rules; they justify expectations by summarizing inductive evidence. As such, they are important to science mainly as aids to experimental design, including devising tests of an uncontrolled sort, as in astronomy. Second, nomic correlations are among the facts that explanatory theories must explain. The law correlating thermal and electrical conductivity is striking and important not as a candidate explanans, but as a candidate explanandum.

3. **NOMIC ATTRIBUTIONS.** These are predications, lawlike statements to the effect that all x's have a certain property P. An example is the statement that photons have gravitational mass. The law of inertia appears to be a nomic attribution in classical mechanics, and the law of gravitation appears to be a nomic attribution in the theory of general relativity. The explanatory role of nomic attributions, along with the roles of laws in the next two categories, will be taken up in the next section.

4. **INSTANTIATION LAWS.** These are lawlike statements specifying how a property is instantiated in a specified type of system. An example is the statement that temperature is instantiated in a gas as the average mean kinetic energy of the molecules in the gas.

5. **COMPOSITION LAWS.** These are lawlike statements specifying the (or an) analysis of a specified type of system. An example (greatly simplified) is the statement that water molecules are made of two hydrogen atoms ionically bonded to one oxygen atom. The most celebrated recent example is the double helix model of DNA.

One of the more unfortunate consequences of the dominance of the deductive-nomological model of explanation is that it has focused attention on causal laws and their associated explanatory roles, i.e., on transition theories, to the exclusion of more important alternatives. This consequence is not surprising: subsumptive explanation of the sort featured in transition theories is the only sort of explanation for which the model is initially plausible. Analytical explanation, as we shall see shortly, can be given a deductive-nomological format, but the result is completely uninformative,

obscuring rather than illuminating the nature of analytical explanation. It is only in the case of causal subsumption that the model
provides any hint as to the nature of explanation, and that hint is
limited by failure to take causation explicitly into account (and
the consequent failure to distinguish (2) and (3)).[6]

Philosophers and methodologically minded scientists have
focused their attention on transition theorizing. As a result, the
methodology of causal subsumption has received a great deal of
attention from scientists and philosophers, and is therefore relatively well understood. As I use the term, a methodology is a set
of adequacy conditions on the application of an explanatory
strategy. One has a methodology for an explanatory strategy when
one has a set of principles for distinguishing legitimate from illegiti-
mate applications of that strategy. A methodology is thus naturally
construed as a canon of criticism. From this point of view, it is
useful to think of a methodology as having two parts corresponding to two sorts of critical questions we can raise about a particular
application of an explanatory strategy: (i) Could the strategy have
any explanatory force in such an application? (ii) What sorts of
evidential considerations would tend to support or undermine an
application of the strategy in this case? Chapter V, section 1, illustrates the methodology of causal subsumption in action against
introspective psychology.

A familiar empiricist ploy is to move from (ii) to (i) by arguing
that a particular application could have no explanatory force because nothing could support or undermine it. No doubt an explanation is unacceptable if it is untestable, but this is quite a different
sort of unacceptability than that intended by (i). Moving from (ii)
to (i) has been a serious source of misunderstanding about explanatory force, for it encourages us to confuse the truth of a theory,
or its justification, with its explanatory value, thus obscuring the
very real difference between description and explanation. It is easy
to overlook the fact that a theory with no chance of being true
can have much greater explanatory force than a well-confirmed
theory about the same phenomena. Contrast, for example, the
theory that molecules are held together by "hooks and eyes" with
the theory that molecules are held together by some unknown
force. By the mid-nineteenth century the former theory was
strongly disconfirmed, while the latter theory turned out to be

true (because molecules *are* held together by a force unknown at the time). Still, the "hook-and-eyes" theory is at least capable of explaining such facts as the occurrence of H_2O but not H_4O, and the occurrence of H_2—e.g., on the hypothesis that each hydrogen atom has one free hook, and each oxygen atom has two free eyes. The "unknown force" theory, however, has no explanatory force whatever, being equivalent to the theory that the molecules that do occur do occur and the ones that don't don't. So explanatory force is quite independent of confirmation and truth.

Perhaps "explanatory potential" would be a better phrase than "explanatory force" or "explanatory value," for saying that T has explanatory potential leaves the door open for the remark that explanatory potential is proportional to how explanatory T would be if it were true. But I'm inclined to take a hard line on this largely verbal issue: false theories can explain things (and have); it's just that the explanations they provide are not true. It seems to me quite mistaken to suppose that one cannot understand something if one has false beliefs about it. The doctrine that only truth can explain would surely rule that much contemporary theory is not explanatory!

It is arguable that an explanatory theory must be testable: if T is explanatory, it must have implications vis-à-vis its explananda, and observations relevant to the latter surely constitute a test of T. Something like this is probably correct, but it establishes only an uninformative connection between testability and explanatory force. Untestable theories fail to be explanatory not because they have no explananda, but because they say the wrong sort of thing about the (purported) explananda that they *do* have. The assumption to avoid is that a theory need only be well confirmed (or true) to explain its target phenomena.

The Methodology of Causal Subsumption

There is, among philosophers at any rate, no generally received account of how transition theories are to be tested, let alone a generally received account of their explanatory force. Still, there are common elements discernible in the many attempts in the tradition of Bacon, Hume, and Mill to articulate canons of "scientific method." These common elements correspond to uniformities in scientific practice, uniformities that evidence agreement on, and adherence to, a tacit methodology that Empiricist writers have sought to make explicit. When one canvasses methodological "casuistry," especially methodological chapters of undergraduate textbooks, one finds, I think, that the great bulk of this effort derives from three fundamental concerns: (i) *causality:* many of the rules and methods are designed to distinguish causal connections from mere correlations, whether these be lawlike or simply accidental; (ii) *determinism:* theory construction is constrained by the idea that one must not countenance uncaused or idle events; (iii) *justification* (Hume's condition): a program of research is regarded as fairly subject to criticism if the causes and effects it appeals to cannot be observed or measured independently of each other. I will briefly discuss each of these. The reader should keep in mind, however, that the point of this exercise is not to advance the discussion of the methodology of causal subsumption, but rather to make plausible the claim that there are commonly accepted canons of "scientific method" (however they should be formulated), and that these are, in fact, canons of causal subsumption.

(i) *Causality.* Does smoking cause cancer, or are smoking and cancer only highly correlated? In introductory social science classes, this example is as familiar as are deductions of Socrates' mortality in introductory logic classes. The practical implications of the problem are obvious: only the causal claim provides an immediate reason to give up smoking. But it is not the practical implication that the example is designed to bring out, but a methodological moral: only the causal claim has the sort of explanatory force for which good theory is valued. Smoking may be a good predictor of cancer and yet tell us nothing about why people get cancer. Hence the standard emphasis on control: if we can control cancer by controlling smoking, we have in smoking more than a good predictor of cancer.

The concern to distinguish genuine causal connections from other correlations is, as I noted above, central to good transition theory, since the point is to explain events as effects of causes. The universality of this concern is therefore a measure of the extent to which scientific methodology was identified with the methodology of causal subsumption. Nowhere is this concern more apparent than in Mill's famous discussion of the "four methods of experimental inquiry" (Bk. III, ch. viii). Like Hume before him, Mill assumes that scientific reasoning—indeed all *a posteriori* reasoning—is causal reasoning. He therefore never seriously questions the assumption that to explain a phenomenon is to subsume it under causal law. At the beginning of the famous chapter entitled "Of the Four Methods of Experimental Inquiry" (in *Philosophy and Scientific Method*) Mill writes:

> The simplest and most obvious modes of singling out from among the circumstances which precede or follow a phenomenon those with which it is really connected by an invariable law are two in number. One is by comparing together different instances in which the phenomenon occurs. The other is by comparing instances in which the phenomenon does occur with instances in other respects similar in which it does not. These two methods may be respectively denominated the method of agreement and the method of difference.
>
> In illustrating these methods, it will be necessary to bear in mind the two fold character of inquiries into the laws of phenomena, which may be either inquiries into the cause of a given effect or into the effects or properties of a given cause.

According to Mill, there are, at bottom, just four methods of experimental inquiry, and all four are concerned with the problem of distinguishing genuine causal connections!

The same concern apparently dominates Hume's work: how are we to tell genuine causal connection from mere constant conjunction? Mill's four methods can be thought of as an expansion of Hume's fourth rule for judging of causes and effects (*Treatise of Human Nature,* I.III.xv): "The same cause always produces the same effect, and the same effect never arises but from the same cause. This principle we derive from experience, and is the source of most of our philosophical [i.e. scientific] reasonings." Indeed, Hume's rules five through eight essentially embody Mill's four methods, and Hume claims that his fifth and sixth rules, at least, are corollaries of rule four. After stating the eight rules by which to judge of causes and effects, Hume remarks, "Here is all the Logic I think proper to employ in my reasoning . . . ," thus confirming (what is obvious anyway) that the rules by which to judge of causes and effects exhaust, for Hume at least, scientific methodology.

(ii) *Determinism*. Refusals to countenance uncaused or idle events in the theoretical treatment of a given domain are, perhaps, familiar enough in explicit methodological writings, but in that context such refusals have always been controversial. In actual practice, however, a theory is always subject to criticism on the grounds that it allows for uncaused or idle events. The motivation here is that a theory designed to explain events as effects of causes is in trouble if it countenances uncaused events or ineffectual causes. (See Cummins, 1976, for further discussion of this principle in the context of a particular historical application.)

A classic example is the critique of behaviorist theories of language on the grounds that linguistic behaviors—i.e., distinct linguistic performances or "outputs"—cannot be predicted on the basis of environmental stimuli. (See, e.g., Chomsky, 1959a, and Fodor, Bever and Garrett, 1974.) Critics and advocates alike agree that a one-many mapping of stimuli to linguistic responses would, if it is the best we can do, refute stimulus-response accounts of linguistic behavior.

There are, of course, cases in which theoretical allowance for uncaused or idle events has not been thought crippling. The quantum theory, on certain interpretations, allows for uncaused events, and epiphenomenalism, popular in psychology in the early part of the century (and in some quarters still), allows for idle events. But both of these cases are controversial, and they are controversial, moreover, precisely because they countenance uncaused or idle events. The controversy generated by these cases is itself a measure of the extent to which the methodology of science *is,* in most minds, just the methodology of causal subsumption. Uncaused or idle events are explanatory lacunae in a transition theory, and since all theory tends to be seen as transition theory, uncaused or idle events are generally regarded as explanatory failures *tout court.* Thus both advocates and critics regard uncaused and idle events as embarrassments to the theories that allow them.

(iii) *Justification (Hume's condition)*. Hume is unjustly famous[7] for the idea that causal claims are unjustified if there is no way to observe or measure the causes independently of the effects they are supposed to produce, and *vice versa*. In Chapter IV I show how this principle was used to great effect against the introspectionist psychology of Wundt and Titchener by their behaviorist critics.

Unlike the substitution of a noncausal correlation for a causal law, or theoretical allowance for uncaused or idle events, violation of Hume's condition does not strike directly at the explanatory power of a transition theory, but it does strike directly at its acceptability. Violation of Hume's condition is generally held to strike indirectly at the explanatory power of a theory, however, and if we examine the reasoning underlying this thought, we see once again that the assumed explanatory strategy is the strategy of causal subsumption.

It is often supposed that galvanic skin responses (gsr—the sort of thing measured by a "lie detector") provide a good measure of anxiety. Indeed, anxiety is sometimes "operationally defined" in terms of gsr. The motivation for this definitional maneuver is this: we cannot really explain gsr by appeal to anxiety because we cannot measure anxiety directly, but must have recourse to gsr or something comparably "external"—hence we shouldn't distinguish anxiety from gsr and the like, for this only encourages "pseudo-explanations." This line of thought is ubiquitous in the behavioral sciences. A (perhaps *the*) classic example is Skinner (1953). If we ask what underlies this line of reasoning, it seems clear that the following assumption is being made: to explain gsr means to explain changes in skin conductivity as effects of some cause. Given this assumption, Hume's condition applies directly: we cannot attribute these effects to changes in anxiety level, for, given that these very effects are our only way to observe or measure changes in anxiety level, we cannot justify the resulting causal claims. Hence, any attempt to explain gsr in terms of anxiety will be vitiated by appeal to an unjustified causal claim.

Whatever one may think of this reasoning, I don't see how one could understand it except on the assumption that all explanation is causal subsumption. One might suppose that it is only being assumed that the sort of explanation at issue in *cases of this sort* is causal subsumption, but in fact this is never even stated, but taken for granted. It could be, of course, that everyone assumes that the sort of explanation in question is causal subsumption because it is *obvious,* and not because there are no alternatives to rule out, but I don't think this can be right: the behaviorist conclusion is so controversial that the assumption would have been widely denied had there been any well-articulated alternative available. But the assumption (viz., that it is causal subsumption that is at issue) has not been widely denied and even when it has been denied, it was not denied because there is some widely recognized alternative explanatory strategy to assert in place of the strategy of causal subsumption. Some philosophers, of course, have argued that mental explanation is not a species of causal explanation, but a kind of rationalization. (See, for example, Meldin, 1961, and Ryle, 1949.) But no one, I think, has taken this line about anxiety, and in any case the doctrine that reasons are not causes has fallen on hard times. (See Davidson, 1963, Alston, 1967, Brandt and Kim, 1963.) What's more, it has fallen on hard times mainly because it seems clear that reasons do explain actions, and the underlying assumption here, once again, is surely that explanation is causal subsumption.

The concern to distinguish causal laws from noncausal correlations, to shun uncaused or idle events, and to make provision for independent access to causes and effects are, of course, not the only methodological concerns to manifest themselves in scientific practice and in writings on scientific method, but they are, perhaps, the most fundamental and pervasive. The universality of these concerns, and their status as *the* fundamental concerns, leaves little doubt that scientific methodology has often been identified (tacitly or explicitly) with the methodology of causal subsumption. It should become clear shortly, however, that these concerns are simply out of place in the context of property theories and the analytic strategy of explanation. This is, I think, something of a scandal: the analytic strategy is as old as atomism, yet its methodology is only now beginning to receive serious attention. Give or take a nicety of formulation, the canons of causal subsumption are widely recognized and honored; they have the status of truisms. None of this can be said concerning the methodology of analysis.

I.2. PROPERTY THEORIES

Many scientific theories are not designed to explain changes but are rather designed to explain properties. The point of what I call a property theory is to explain the properties of a system not in the sense in which this means "Why did S acquire P?" or "What caused S to acquire P?" but, rather, "What is it for S to instantiate P?", or, "In virtue of what does S have P?" Just as we can ask, "Why did the gas get hotter (or expand)?", we can ask, "In virtue of what does a gas have a temperature (volume)?" Understood as an answer to the latter questions, the kinetic theory of heat (and the molecular theory of gases that it presupposes) is not a transition theory but a property theory: it explains temperature in a gas by explaining how temperature is instantiated in a gas; it does not, by itself, explain changes in temperature.

Many of the most pressing and puzzling scientific questions are questions about properties, not about changes. We know a lot about what causes pain, but there is no very good theory of how pain is instantiated. Good property theories are wonderfully satisfying: we know how temperature is instantiated, how inheritance is instantiated, how electricity is instantiated, how solubility is instantiated. I think we are close to knowing how life and intelligence are instantiated, though we are a long way from understanding how consciousness or intentionality are instantiated.

The characteristic question answered by a transition theory is: Why does system S change states from s-1 to s-2? The characteristic question answered by a property theory is: What is it for system S to have property P?[8]

The natural strategy for answering such a question is to construct an analysis of S that explains S's possession of P by appeal to the properties of S's components and their mode of organization. The process often has as a preliminary stage an analysis of P itself into properties of S or S's components. This step will loom large when we come to discuss complex dispositional properties such as information-processing capacities. Analysis of a *system* will be called compositional analysis, to distinguish it from analysis of a *property*, which will be called functional analysis when the property is dispositional, and property analysis when the property is not dispositional. Analysis is "recursive," since a given analysis may appeal to properties or components that themselves require analysis.

Historically, the most important property theories are applications of the doctrine of atomism. In its simplest form, atomism is the claim that all physical objects are collections of elementary parts (a part being elementary if it has no theoretically relevant parts itself). The explanatory interest of this doctrine derives from the further claim that the properties of every object are determined by its microconstitution—i.e., by the properties of its elementary parts and the way those parts are "put together" to constitute the object in question. Thus atomism promises to explain the properties of an object by exhibiting its elementary part constitution— e.g., the shape and density of a crystal is explained by the relative positions of its elementary parts, which, in turn are fixed by the properties of those parts; the temperature of a gas is explained by identifying it with the average kinetic energy of its molecules. Chemistry texts detail an enormous number of applications of the atomist strategy.

Atomism explains property instantiation in S by appeal to property instantiation in S's elementary parts. A crucial assumption of the theory is that all qualitative change is compositional change. Thus an elementary part cannot change in its categorical properties (though it might be created or destroyed); hence no pressure is generated to explain how an elementary part acquires its categorical properties. An elementary part cannot be the object of a transition theory.[9] It might seem, however, that questions about instantiation could arise at the level of elementary parts— e.g., what is it for an elementary part to have a spherical shape? But the question is actually quite different at this level. Whereas we can explain how something made of cubes can be spherical, the corresponding question about an elementary part can only be met with a definition of "spherical"—e.g., surface everywhere equidistant from a single point. It isn't that we cannot *explain* what makes an elementary part spherical: nothing *makes* it spherical. There is just nothing to be explained here, or, rather, there is only a concept to be explained here, not a property.[10]

Thus atomism envisages an end to the explanatory regress by arriving at a case in which state transition does not occur and property instantiation requires no theoretical treatment. The fundamental laws are nomic attributions. This is easily overlooked if one is working within the hypothetical-deductive tradition, for that tradition assimilates explaining p to providing a "scientific" justification for p. Since we can justify any property attribution "scientifically"—e.g., by appeal to inductive evidence or theoretical derivation—it will seem from within the H-D tradition that all property attributions are candidate explananda. This is mistaken: fundamental nomic attributions require justification but not explanation. Hempel (1966) pointed out that "narrow inductivism" fails to distinguish theory construction from theory testing. Since testing is inductive, narrow inductivism left no room in science for theories that were not generalizations of the data. We now require a comparable distinction between theory testing and theoretical explanation. To assimilate the logic of explanation to the logic of testing leaves us no conceptual space to delineate the differences between laws that do and laws that do not require explanation, for all laws require justification. It also forces us to see the explananda of a theory as (among) the data that support it. The pernicious effects of this last consequence are illustrated in the discussion of Clark Hull in section IV.2, below.

Successful analysis yields an explanatory payoff when we come to see that something having the kinds of components specified, organized in the way specified, is bound to have the target property. Unfortunately, the fact that what we come to see is a generalization of this sort encourages an assimilation of the analytical strategy to the subsumptive strategy, for it provides what looks like a deductive nomological schema:

(6i)   Anything having components

$C_1 \ldots C_n$ organized in manner

O—i.e., having analysis

$[C_1 \ldots C_n, O]$ —has property P;

(6ii)   S has analysis $[C_1 \ldots C_n, O]$;

(6iii)   S has property P.

There is nothing wrong with representing analytical explanations in this format provided we avoid the assumption that the explanation is achieved by a state-transition type of subsumption of (6iii) under (6i) given (6ii). Assimilating the analytical strategy to the subsumptive strategy obscures the difference between explaining changes and explaining properties and thereby leads one to misapply the methodology of causal subsumption to analysis.

Let us call "laws" of the form (6i) "instantiation laws," and laws of the form (6ii) "composition laws."[11] We can begin to see

the difference between instances of the schema (6) and causal subsumption [e.g., (4)] by noting that instantiation laws are not
causal laws at all, for they do not have cause-effect pairs as instances. Thus the role of an instantiation law cannot be to explain
S's possession of P as an effect of some cause. Indeed, laws of instantiation need not even be empirical. If the analysandum is a
symbolic capacity—a capacity to manipulate symbols—the instantiation law will typically be a bit of mathematics. For example,
"Anything executing the bubble algorithm sorts numbers into
order; S executes the bubble algorithm; hence S sorts numbers into order."

Instantiation laws are derived principles—or they *should* be in a
full-dress theory—for they obviously call for explanation themselves. There is really only one available strategy for explaining an
instantiation law: it must be derived from laws specifying the
properties of the components. If we can carry out this derivation,
our schema looks like this:

(6a) The properties of $C_1 \ldots C_n$
      are $<$whatever$>$, respectively;

(6ii) S has analysis $[C_1 \ldots C_n, O]$;

(6iii) S has property P.

Instances of this schema will be valid when we can derive (6i) from
(6a). When we can do this, we can understand how P is *instantiated*
in S. Laws like (6a) I call *nomic attributions,* to emphasize that
they do not state correlations or causal connections, but attribute
properties. [12]

The most interesting property theories are aimed at explaining
dispositional properties. To attribute a disposition d to an object
x is to assert that the behavior of x is subject to (exhibits or would
exhibit) a certain lawlike regularity: to say x has d is to say that x
would manifest d (dissolve, shatter) were any of a certain range of
events to occur (x is put in water, x is struck sharply). The regularity associated with a disposition is a regularity that is special to the
behavior of a certain kind of object and obtains in virtue of some
special facts about that kind of object. Not everything is water-
soluble: such things behave in a special way in virtue of certain
(microstructural) features special to water-soluble things. Thus it is
that dispositions require explanation: if s has d, then s is subject

to a law or regularity in behavior special to things having d, and such a fact needs to be explained. When we discover that not everything *is* water-soluble, we are led to ask why the things that *are* dissolve in water, while other things do not. To explain a dispositional regularity, then, we must explain how or why manifestations of the disposition are brought about given the requisite precipitating conditions.

As an example of a property-theoretic explanation, consider Einstein's explanation of the photoelectric effect. When light shines on a metal surface, electrons are emitted from the surface. Five facts are central to the specification of this dispositional property of light.

    a. The number of electrons emitted per unit time is proportional to the intensity of the incident light.

    b. The kinetic energy of an emitted electron does not depend on the intensity of the incident light.

    c. For a given metal, the maximum kinetic energy of an emitted electron is solely a function of the frequency of incident light.

    d. For a given metal, no electrons are emitted if the incident light is below a certain threshold frequency.

    e. Electrons are emitted immediately, regardless of the intensity of incident light.

Facts (b) through (e) are radically at odds with classical conceptions according to which (i) the energy of a light beam is continuously distributed throughout the beam, and (ll) a beam of light may have any amount of energy. For example, (I) implies that a surface irradiated by a very weak beam (say, 10^{-10} w/m^2) should take years to accumulate enough energy to release electrons, contrary to (e). (ii) implies that the kinetic energy of emitted electrons is a function of the intensity of incident light, contrary to (b). (c) and (d) are simply "danglers": classical theory provides no link between frequency and available energy to explain (c) and (d).

Einstein explained the photoelectric effect by assuming that light consists of discrete photons, and that the energy of a photon is quantized, its energy being hv, where h is Planck's constant, and v is the frequency. These assumptions allowed Einstein to treat the photoelectric effect as a straightforward case of energy conservation.

Each photon interacts with at most one electron, providing that electron with as much energy as it will ever get from the beam. Since this is a fixed amount, given by the frequency, the electron will either be emitted immediately (e), or not at all (d), with a maximum kinetic energy less than hv (c). Increase in intensity or duration will increase the number of photons, hence the number of emitted electrons (a), but it will not affect the energy of the photons in the beam, hence will not affect the kinetic energy of emitted electrons (b). Here, we have a simple and elegant explanation of a dispositional property of light—the photoelectric property—a property that is completely mysterious from the point of view of classical wave mechanics. The explanation can be conceived in stages. *Stage one,* corresponding to (6ii), is an analysis of the incident light beam into a stream of particle-like photons. *Stage two,* corresponding to (6a), introduces two fundamental nomic attributions governing the photons: their energy is quantized (NA_1), and is directly proportional to frequency (NA_2).[13] *Stage three* consists in deriving the facts (a) through (e), characterizing the photoelectric property from the assumptions of stages one and two. This evidently amounts to deriving an instantiation law for the photoelectric effect: A system consisting of a light beam— i.e., consisting of photons satisfying (NA_1) and (NA_2)—incident to a metal surface will satisfy (a) through (c).

As a second illustration of analytical explanation, consider the standard derivation of Archimedes' Principle, which specifies the dispositional property of liquids to exert a force on submerged objects in the direction of the surface and equal in magnitude to the weight of displaced liquid.

Consider an object, O. Let v be an arbitrary volume of the liquid having the same size and shape as O. The volume is at rest with respect to the remainder of the liquid, hence the net force on v is zero. Let W_o and W_v be the weights of o and v, respectively. The net force NF_v on v is the upward force UF_v minus the downward force $DF_v = W_v + W_c$, where W_c is the weight of the column of liquid above v:

$$NF_v = UF_v - (W_v + W_c) = 0.$$

Hence,

$$UF_v = W_v + W_c.$$

Now imagine O in place of v. Evidently

$$UF_o = UF_v = W_v + W_e.$$

The force of LF_o exerted by the liquid on O is $UF_o = W_c$. But $LF_o = UF_o - W_c$, so,

$$LF_o = (W_v + W_e) - W_e = W_v.$$

Since we have assumed that the direction of the surface is positive, the fact that LF_o is positive indicates that it is in the direction of the surface.

Here we explain Archimedes' property of liquids by assuming (i) that a liquid consists of a collection of parts (or volumes) free to move with respect to one another, (ii) that a part (or volume) at (relative) rest experiences a net force of zero, (iii) that weight is a downward force, and (iv) that forces are additive. (i) is a composition law. (iv) is a nomic attribution. (That is easier to see if we think of a force on x as a disposition of x to accelerate. It is then a property of masses that these dispositions can be (algebraically) summed.)[14] (iii) is an instantiation law imported from Newtonian mechanics, and (ii) follows from construing forces as dispositions to accelerate. (ii) and (iii) and a clear thought experiment (substituting o for v) suffice to establish an instantiation law: systems satisfying (ii) will have Archimedes' Property.

By now it should be clear that the same equation can appear as part of a property theory and a transition theory—e.g., as part of an instantiation law and as part of a causal transition law. Thus it should come as no surprise that focusing on the role of nomic equations in mathematical derivations should obscure rather than reveal their explanatory functions.

Property theories and transition theories fit together in an important way when target properties are dispositional, for when a system manifests a disposition, we have cause and effect (precipitating event causing manifestation), hence state transition. When we derive an instantiation law for a dispositional property from underlying nomic attributions, what we derive is a (minimal) transition theory for the disposed system—viz., the dispositional regularity. Since what we derive is a transition law for the system, the derivation will often (though not always) invoke transition laws governing components of S. The explanatory theory will not be "complete," of course, until we have discharged all the dispositions. Thus, as emphasized above, transition theories specify explananda for property theories. The pressure for explanation *increases* as more and more general transition theories are devised, for a very general transition theory specifies a dispositional property that a wide variety of systems have. A perfectly general transition theory is suspicious, for it would specify a disposition that every system has. In such a case we should ask whether the property specified is really dispositional—i.e., really supports a distinction between having the property and manifesting it. If not, the theory is not really a transition theory, but a set of nomic attributions. When we notice that everything is subject to gravitation, we are led to notice further that everything gravitates all the time. Thus the law of universal gravitation is a fundamental nomic attribution, not a transition law.

I.3. REDUCTION AND INSTANTIATION

It is important to distinguish the claim that a theory identifies instantiations from the claim that it licenses reductions. As I use the term, reduction requires that the true statements one can make about a domain in a vocabulary v can all be formulated in a different reducing vocabulary v'. For example, physicalistic reductionism in psychology is the claim that the truths of psychology are all formulatable in the language of physics. It is now a commonplace (I hope) that one can hold that everything is physical—has some physical description—without holding that everything worth saying in science can be said in the language of physics. (For example, see Fodor, 1975.) Thus, since systems not satisfying (i) could have Archimedes' Property as well as systems that do, we cannot *reduce* having Archimedes' Property to satisfying (i), for there are truths about Archimedes' Property that are not truths about satisfaction of (i), viz. that systems not satisfying (i) could have Archimedes' Property. I think a whole cluster of problems surrounding the issue of theoretical (property) identifications and reduction can be avoided by substituting the language of instantiation for the language of identity.[15]

It is now commonplace in the philosophy of mind to say that type–type identity theories fail because mental properties can be "realized" (i.e., instantiated) in more than one way. (The idea seems to have begun with Putnam, 1960.) The same point can be made about functional properties: adding is one sort of physical process in a mechanical calculator and another sort in a computer. And about some chemical properties: bonding is one sort of thing in H_2 and another sort of thing in NaCl. Hence, the advent of "token-identity" theories: bonding is identical with one thing in H_2—call it ψH_2—and with another in NaCl—ψNaCl. Is this reduction or not? It *seems* to be, for if bonding *is* ψH_2 (in H_2), then talk about bonds (in H_2) is just talk about ψH_2. But it can't be reduction, for there are truths about bonding that aren't truths about ψH_2 or any other physical kind. And isn't this a strange sort of identity? We have bonding = ψH_2 and bonding = ψNaCl but $\psi H_2 \neq \psi$NaCl. Even if bonding were physically homogeneous—just ψ every time—this would surely be a contingent fact, and hence our physics would license only a "contingent identity." There is, by now, a notorious controversy over whether this notion is coherent, and if it is, whether such an identity would license reductions.

We can begin to make progress in this matter by substituting the language of instantiation for the language of identity. Rather than saying that bonding is identical with one thing in H_2 and something else in NaCl, we can say that bonding is instantiated one way in H_2, another in NaCl. This avoids the logical muddle lately rehearsed while retaining the central point: multiple instantiation blocks reduction because there are truths about the instantiated property that are not truths about the instantiations.

But suppose there aren't multiple instantiations? Suppose bonding were always instantiated as, say, hook-and-eye connection? If we express this in the language of identity, we prejudice the issue of reduction: if bonding is everywhere identical with hook-and-eye connection, how could there be truths about bonding that weren't truths about hook-and-eye connection?

Well, perhaps the identity is "contingent." Then there will be modal truths about bonding that aren't truths about hook-and-eye connection—e.g., "Bonding *could be* something other than hook-and-eye connection." (I take it this is what saying the identity is "contingent" amounts to.) But, perhaps the notion of "contingent identity" doesn't make sense, as Kripke (1972) has argued. And if it doesn't, then it seems we cannot have theoretical identities without reduction.

Once again, identity is a red herring. The question is whether uniform instantiation amounts to reduction. Most of the familiar points carry over, but without the logical and metaphysical problems surrounding identity.

(i) Uniform instantiation is necessary for reduction, since diverse instantiation blocks it.

(ii) Uniform instantiation is not sufficient for reduction, since a variety of modal truths will hold of the target property that do not hold of the instantiation.

(iii) If uniform instantiation is not "accidental" but nomically necessary, then we do have genuine reduction.

A word of caution about (iii) is in order. We can have a law of the form:

(7) S has P iff S has analysis $[C_1 \ldots C_n, O]$,

and yet have no reduction, for something of the form (7) might be true and lawlike yet not give the instantiation of P. Consider (8) and (9):

(8) (E) (n) {E has a valence of n iff [(n is positive and E atoms have n free hooks) or (n is negative and E atoms have n free eyes)]}.

(9) (E) (n) {E has a valence of n iff [(n is positive and E atoms have a mean diameter of cn) or (E is negative and E atoms have a mean diameter of kn)]} (where c and k are distinct constants).

Assume for the sake of argument that (8) and (9) are both lawlike and true. (8) would license a reduction, but (9) would not, because (9) does not give a hint as to how valence is instantiated. To have a valence is to have a disposition to form chemical bonds, *which* disposition depending on *which* valence. Such a disposition could be instantiated as possession of free hooks or eyes but could not be instantiated as possession of a certain mean diameter. (9) would allow us to derive possession of P (a valence of +n) from the analysis (the element consists of atoms with a mean diameter of cn), but (9) itself would not (presumably) be derivable from fundamental nomic attributions, whereas (8) has a painfully obvious derivation (one hook to each eye, hence H_2O but not H_3O, etc.).

I know of no general criterion by which the reductive instances of (7) are to be distinguished from the nonreductive except this: the reductive instances specify how P is instantiated, the details being revealed by a derivation of the instantiation law from underlying nomic attributions. It seems obvious that (8) but not (9) is (or could be) reductive in this sense, because there is no route from attributions of diameter to bonding dispositions and hence (9), but there is a route from attributions of hooks and eyes to bonding dispositions and hence (8).

This seems obvious to me. But to many scientists brought up on a steady diet of hypothetical-deductivism, and to some philosophers of like history, this will seem question-begging at best: If (9) were true, well confirmed, and lawlike, why wouldn't it explain bonding?

(9) itself cries out for explanation: Why/how do different diameters lead to different bonding capacities? Perhaps when atoms bond, they fit into a kind of "frame"—a local property of the electromagnetic field, say—and "fit" is determined by diameter. An explanation of this sort would give (9) a status on a par with (8). Failure to explain (9) [or a nonreductive law used in "explaining" (9)] leaves us with a brute correlation—i.e., a correlation that holds for no reason at all (so far as our theory goes). This might be the best we could do, but to call it "explanation" (rather than "discovery of a brute correlation") is to make a virtue of necessity at the price of obscuring the very real difference in understanding achieved by deriving correlations from noncorrelational nomic attributions that are not themselves candidate explananda (though they require justification, of course).

Once it is clear that we can explain how a chemical property is instantiated in a physical system without identifying chemical and physical properties, the pressure to reduce chemistry to physics evaporates. Chemical properties need to be explained—presumably they don't figure in fundamental nomic attributions. If we mistakenly suppose that the only way to explain a property that doesn't figure in a fundamental nomic attribution is to identify it with a property that does, we will be committed to identifying chemical properties with physical properties. We have reduction just in case we have genuine property identification. Hence reduction will appear the only alternative to leaving chemical properties unexplained. But since we *can* explain how chemical properties are instantiated in a physical system without identifying chemical properties with physical properties, a physical explanation of chemical properties need not be reductionist.

I.4. CONCLUSION

In this chapter I have presented a characterization of two distinct explanatory strategies. And, although that characterization is rough and incomplete at many points, and probably just wrong in places, enough has been said, I think, to establish that the methodology of analysis is bound to be quite different from the methodology of causal subsumption. Indeed, we are now in a position to discern some rough analogues to the illustrative methodological canons mentioned in connection with causal subsumption. Corresponding to the basic requirement that subsumptive laws be causal, we have the requirement that instantiation laws should be derivable from nomic attributions specifying properties of components. Just as causal subsumption fails to get off the ground if the laws appealed to are not causal, so analysis fails to get off the ground if analyzing properties are not derivable from properties of the elements of the analyzed system, for in such a case we have no reason to think we have analyzed the target property as it is instantiated in the target system.

Corresponding to the requirement that transition theories must not countenance uncaused or idle events, we have the requirement (emphasized by Dennett, 1978, 123-124) that the analyzed property should not reappear in the analysis. Appealing to the analyzed property, or something comparable, in the analysis defeats the explanatory point of a property theory in the same way that uncaused or idle events defeat the explanatory point of a transition theory: in each case, the offending theory reintroduces the very thing it is supposed to explain.

Finally, corresponding to the principle that causes and effects must be observable or measurable independently of one another, we have the requirement that attributions of analyzing properties should be justifiable independently of the analysis that features them. If, for example, we analyze the capacity of a child to solve division problems into the capacity to copy numerals, to multiply, and to subtract, we must know, or be able to find out, that the child can copy numerals, multiply, and subtract without simply inferring this from the capacity to divide, and we must know, or be able to find out, that these capacities are in fact organized as the analysis specifies.

The trick to providing a good property theory is generally to manage to satisfy this requirement and the first one simultaneously. The hook-and-eye theory of chemical bonding satisfies the first requirement, but there is no other reason to believe that elementary parts (i.e., atoms, for the theory of bonding) have hooks and eyes. There is plenty of independent evidence that they have mean diameters, but no hint as to how diameters could produce bonds.

Sometimes the problem is making the first requirement mesh with the requirement that the analyzed property not reappear in the analysis. This is (notoriously) *the* problem in cognitive psychology: how to explain intelligence without recourse to equally intelligent components.

A full exposition and defense of the claims I have made here concerning analysis and subsumption would require a book by itself. My topic, however, is psychological explanation. This chapter has been included because it seems to me that most psychological explanation makes no sense when construed as causal subsumption but makes a great deal of sense construed as analysis. Hence, an understanding of the analytic strategy is essential to an understanding of psychological explanation. Equally important, however, is the realization that analysis is an important and generally applicable explanatory strategy, a strategy that is both common and of fundamental importance outside psychology and the life sciences. To appreciate this point is to see that psychological explanation is not anomolous—a special case—but continuous with the rest of science. Forcing psychological explanation into the subsumptivist mold made it continuous with the rest of science only at the price of making it appear trivial or senseless.

CHAPTER TWO
Functional Analysis

A property theory may explain a dispositional property by system analysis—i.e., analyzing the system that has it, as in the example of section I.2—or it may proceed instead by property analysis—i.e., analyzing the disposition itself. I call the application of property analysis to dispositions/capacities[1] functional analysis. In the context of science, to ascribe a function to something is to ascribe a capacity to it that is singled out by its role in an analysis of some capacity of a containing system. When a capacity of a containing system is appropriately explained via analysis, the analyzing capacities emerge as functions.[2]

Functional analysis consists in analyzing a disposition into a number of less problematic dispositions such that programmed manifestation of these analyzing dispositions amounts to a manifestation of the analyzed disposition. By "programmed" here, I simply mean organized in a way that could be specified in a program or flow-chart. Assembly-line production provides a transparent illustration. Production is broken down into a number of distinct and relatively simple (unskilled) tasks. The line has the capacity to produce the product in virtue of the fact that the units on the line have the capacity to perform one or more of these tasks, and in virtue of the fact that when these tasks are performed in a certain organized way—according to a certain program—the finished product results. Schematic diagrams in electronics provide a familiar example of this sort of analysis in a physical science context. Since each symbol represents any physical object whatever having a certain capacity, a schematic diagram of a complex device constitutes an analysis of the electronic capacities of the device as a whole into the capacities of its components. Such an analysis allows us to explain how the device as a whole exercises the analyzed capacity, for it allows us to see exercises of the analyzed capacity as programmed exercises (i.e., organized) of the analyzing capacities.

Physiological analysis in biology is essentially similar. The biologically significant capacities of an entire organism are explained by analyzing them into a number of "systems"—the circulatory system, the digestive system, the endocrine system—each of which is defined by its characteristic capacities. These capacities are in turn analyzed into capacities of component organs and structures. We can easily imagine biologists expressing their analyses in a form analogous to the schematic diagrams of electronics, with special symbols for pumps, conduits, filters, and so on. Indeed, if transplants and implants ever become commonplace, this is the only sort of description that would achieve real generality.

In all of these examples, analysis of the disposition goes together in a fairly obvious way with componential analysis of the disposed system, analyzing dispositions being capacities of system components. This sort of direct form-function correlation is fairly common in artifacts because it facilitates diagnosis and repair of malfunctions. Form-function correlation is certainly absent in many cases, however, and it is therefore important to keep functional analysis and componential analysis conceptually distinct. Componential analysis of computers, and probably brains, will typically yield components with capacities that do not figure in the analysis of capacities of the whole system. A cook's capacity to bake a cake analyzes into other capacities of the "whole cook." Similarly, turing machine capacities analyze into other turing machine capacities. Since we do this sort of analysis without reference to an instantiating system, the analysis is evidently not an analysis of an instantiating system. The analyzing capacities are conceived as capacities of the whole system. Thus functional analysis puts very indirect constraints on componential analysis. My capacity to multiply 27 times 32 analyzes into the capacity to multiply 2 times 7, to add 5 and 1, etc. These capacities are not (so far as is known) capacities of my components: indeed, this analysis seems to put no constraints at all on my componential analysis.

The explanatory interest of functional analysis is roughly proportional to (i) the extent to which the analyzing capacities are less sophisticated than the analyzed capacities, (ii) the extent to which the analyzing capacities are different in kind from the analyzed capacities, and (iii) the relative sophistication of the program appealed to—i.e., the relative complexity of the organization of component parts/processes that is attributed to the system. (iii) is correlative with (i) and (ii): the greater the gap in sophistication and kind between analyzing capacities and the analyzed capacity, the more sophisticated the program must be to close the gap.[3]

It is precisely the width of these gaps which, for instance, makes software technology so interesting in its application to psychology. Software technology supplies us with extremely powerful techniques for constructing diverse analyses of very sophisticated tasks into very unsophisticated tasks. This allows us to see how, in principle, a mechanism such as the brain, consisting of physiologically unsophisticated components (relatively speaking), can acquire very sophisticated capacities. It is the prospect of promoting such capacities as the ability to store ones and zeros, into the capacity to solve logic problems and to recognize patterns, that makes the analytical strategy so appealing in cognitive psychology.

As the program absorbs more and more of the explanatory burden, the physical facts underlying the analyzing capacities become less and less special to the analyzed system. This is why it is plausible to suppose that the capacity of a person and of a machine to solve a certain problem might have substantially the same explanation, although it is not plausible to suppose that the capacities of a synthesizer and of a bell to make similar sounds have substantially similar explanations. There is no work to be done by a sophisticated hypothesis about the organization of various capacities in the case of the bell. Conversely, the less weight borne by the program, the less point to analysis. It must be admitted, I think, that there is no antecedently identifiable level of complexity above which functional analysis is useful and below which it is not. In the previous chapter, Archimedes' Property—a dispositional property defined by Archimedes' law—was explained by analyzing the systems that have it, but the disposition itself was not analyzed into subdispositions.[4]

Ultimately, of course, a complete property theory for a dispositional property must exhibit the details of the target property's instantiation in the system (or system type) that has it. *Analysis* of the disposition (or any other property) is only a first step; *instantiation* is the second.

Functional analysis of a capacity C of a system S must eventually terminate in dispositions whose instantiations are explicable via analysis of S. Failing this, we have no reason to suppose we have analyzed C as it is instantiated in S. If S and/or its components do not have the analyzing capacities, then the analysis cannot help us to explain the instantiation of C in S. This point is easy to lose sight of in practice because functional analysis is often difficult. Having, finally, arrived at an analysis of C, we are under pressure to suppose the analyzing capacities must be instantiated in S somehow.

Analysis of capacities can take a number of significantly different forms, and the relation between functional organization and physical structure turns out—once we have abandoned an uninformatively high level of abstraction—to be different for different forms. Let us begin with two large distinctions that cut across each other.

Morphological versus systematic analysis. John Haugeland (1978, p. 216) distinguishes between morphological and systematic analyses. In a systematic analysis, such as a schematic diagram, a recipe, or a computer program, the explanatory force of the analysis derives largely from a specification of how the analyzing functions interact, a manifestation of one precipitating manifestation of another in the characteristically systematic way that is naturally specified in a flow-chart or program. Morphological analyses, on the other hand, appeal to analyzing functions that do not interact in theoretically significant ways. Haugeland's neat illustration is an analysis of the capacity of a fiber optics bundle to transmit images.

Imagine explaining to someone how a fiber optics bundle can take any image which is projected on one end and transmit it

to the other end. I think most people would come to understand the phenomenon, given the following points. (If I am
right, then readers unfamiliar with fiber optics should still be
able to follow the example.) (i) the bundles are composed of
many long thin fibers, which are closely packed side by side,
and arranged in such a way that each one remains in the same
position relative to the others along the whole length of the
bundle; (ii) each fiber is a leak-proof conduit for light—that is,
whatever light goes in one end of a fiber comes out the other
end of the same fiber; (iii) a projected image can be regarded
as an array of closely packed dots of light, differing in brightness and color; and (iv) since each end of each fiber is like a
dot, projecting an image on one end of the bundle will make
the other end light up with dots of the same brightness and
color in the same relative positions—thus preserving the image.
[Haugeland, 1978, p. 216]

Of course, organization is not irrelevant in a case like this: the
fibers must maintain the same positions relative to each other, for
instance. But the manifestation of one capacity is not the precipitating condition for another; each fiber does its stuff regardless of
what the others are doing.

Interpretive versus descriptive analysis. Some analyses specify
analyzing functions in a vocabulary that yields symbolic interpretation rather than description of the relevant inputs and outputs.
Suppose we are analyzing the capacities of a system of relays, and
suppose our analysis is specified in program form. We might write
a program consisting of such instructions as 'CLOSE RELAYS A
THROUGH D,' or we might write a program consisting of such
instructions as 'BRING DOWN THE NEXT SIGNIFICANT
DIGIT.' Suppose further that in this case closing relays A through
D is (instantiates) bringing down the next significant digit. Then
there is an obvious sense in which 'CLOSE RELAYS A THROUGH
D' describes what is to happen, while 'BRING DOWN THE NEXT
SIGNIFICANT DIGIT' interprets that happening. The first sort
of instruction is appropriate to an analysis of, e.g., the capacity
to control an array of LED's, whereas the second sort of instruction is appropriate to an analysis of the capacity to do long division.

The morphological/systematic distinction and the interpretive/descriptive distinction together yield a four-way classification of functional analyses. The significance of this classification lies in the fact that the constraints on instantiation are different in each of the four cases. Morphological analysis neglects interactions (if any) between subcapacities which may therefore be instantiated in physically independent structures. In systematic analyses, however, interaction looms large, hence the major burden of the instantiation step is to enable explanation of the interactions.

	Descriptive	Interpretive
Morphological	Image transmission by a fiber optics bundle	Number representation in an abacus
Systematic	Production of an automobile by an assembly line	Arithmetical computation in a calculator

Intuitively, what this means is that the organization of the system—the interdependencies among the analyzing functions—must be rendered explicable by the details of the instantiation: we have to see how the *organization* is instantiated. If, for example, bringing down the next significant digit must follow subtracting the current subproduct, then the instantiation should ultimately exhibit the latter as an effect of the former. Thus unlike the capacities appealed to in a morphological analysis, the capacities appealed to in a systematic analysis cannot be instantiated in causally independent structures.

Any functional analysis can be expressed in program of flowchart form, the elementary instructions specifying the analyzing capacities and the input-output properties of the whole program specifying the analyzed capacity. Thus rather than say that an analysis is instantiated in a system, we can say, equivalently, that the system executes[5] the (or a) program expressing that analysis. Putting matters in this way captures nicely the point about instantiating organization, for S cannot execute P unless S is so structured as to ensure the sequencing of transactions as specified in P.[6] From this perspective we can see that when we show how an analysis is instantiated in a system S, what we come to understand is how S is able to execute the program specifying the analysis.

II.1. INTERPRETIVE ANALYSIS

Interpretive analysis is the proper strategy for explaining a sophisticated capacity whose inputs (precipitating conditions) and outputs (manifestations) are specified via their semantic interpretations. The capacity to add, for example, is the capacity to produce as output the correct sum of the inputs. The outputs must be interpretable as numerals representing the sum of the numbers represented by the numerals interpreting the inputs. Two inputs (outputs) count as the same—i.e., as tokens of the same type—just in case they have the same interpretation. Capacities specified in this way I call information-processing capacities.

There are a lot of fancy definitions of information processing floating around, but for present purposes something very plain will do. As I use the term, an *information processor* is simply a symbol manipulator. *Symbols* are distinguished from other things by the possibility or actuality of systematic semantic interpretation. To alter symbols is therefore to move from one meaning to another, and that is why symbol manipulation is information processing. To manipulate symbols is simply to alter them systematically— i.e., according to some antecedently specifiable plan, such as a program or flow-chart.

An information processor can be thought of as the program specifying the manipulations or as some system that executes such a program. 'Turing Machine' is ambiguous in just this way, and the same ambiguity infects 'information-processing capacity,' for we may think of such capacities as belonging to the program or to a device that executes it. This is confusing, and we could simplify matters by insisting that it is the device that has the capacity and not the program. The program can't really do anything; programs for doing housework don't (alas) do housework, nor do adding programs add. There is much merit to cleaving to this usage, for it makes it clear that programs aren't causes but abstract objects or play-by-play accounts. Unfortunately, common practice has it otherwise. If we have an information-processing capacity instantiated as a system of other information-processing capacities, a possibility I will take up shortly, it is natural to say that the instantiating system has the instantiated capacity in virtue of executing the program specifying the instantiating system, and this attributes capacities to programs. Still, we could just as well say that the device exercises the instantiated capacity by executing the program specifying the instantiating system. It is relatively harmless in a practical programming context to talk about what a program or compiler can and can't do, but this sort of talk is seriously misleading if the program in question is supposed to specify a function-analytical explanation of the capacity of some specified system.

Anyone who has ever written a computer program has engaged in interpretive analysis of an information-processing capacity, for the point of a programming problem is simply to analyze a complex symbol-manipulating capacity into an organized sequence of simpler symbol-manipulating capacities—viz., those specified by the elementary instructions of the programming language. Indeed, any problem of interpretive analysis can be thought of as a symbolic programming problem, since every functional analysis can be expressed in program or flow-chart form, and interpretive analysis specifies its capacities as symbolic transformations.

A functional analysis is complete when the program specifying it is explicable via instantiation—i.e., when we can show how the program is executed by the system whose capacities are being explained. This presents special problems when the program specifies an interpretive analysis. The concept of program execution seems a simple matter: a device—be it brain or computer—executes the program if it does what each instruction says to do, and it does these things in the order specified. So program execution seems to come down to instruction execution, and to execute an instruction is just to do what the instruction says to do.

The problem with this line of thought is that, depending on what sort of instruction is under consideration, it may be far from clear what counts as doing what the instruction says to do. It is perhaps clear enough whether some device is, say, closing the relays labeled 'A' through 'D,' hence clear enough whether it is executing the descriptive instruction 'CLOSE RELAYS A THROUGH D.' But how about 'CARRY ALL BUT THE LEAST

SIGNIFICANT DIGIT'? If our program consists of instructions like this, what sense can we make of the claim that a bunch of relays or flip-flops or neurons does what the program says to do? Perhaps we can explain the electrochemical capacities of neurons, but this will not help if the capacities our analysis appeals to are capacities to manipulate symbols. It is evident that there is no set of physical features a thing must have to have a capacity to perform a given symbolic operation: all adding machines add, but they are physically as disparate as wind-up alarm clocks and transistor radios. Indeed, it is hard to see how the physical facts could bear at all on whether a device executes a program of information processes, for such programs say nothing whatever about physical make-up, hence say nothing that could conflict or agree with a statement specifying physical make-up. Early researchers were quite clear about this matter. For instance, Newell, Shaw and Simon, reporting on the Logic Theorist (1958), stressed that the theory they were proposing was entirely neutral with respect to the physical properties a thing must have for their theory to be true of it. This seems to flout the requirement that the instantiation of elementary capacities be explained via componential analysis: no matter how elementary a symbolic transaction is, specifying a capacity to perform it is not specifying a physical disposition, and this makes it difficult to see how physical analysis could ever get a grip on the atomic capacities featured in an information-processing program.

Actually, of course, things aren't so bad as I have been pretending they are. If a smear of ink can be a numeral—i.e., represent a number, why not a closed relay or a neural connection? This is fair enough, and helpful up to a point. Evidently, in the right circumstances, an execution of the instruction to close relays A through D could count as execution of the instruction to carry all but the least significant digit. But under what circumstances? Well, very roughly and intuitively, closing relays A through D must stand to other transactions in the device as the instruction to carry all but the least significant digit stands to the other instructions in the program. There must be, in some sense yet to be explained, an "isomorphism of structure" between the information-processing program and some program couched in descriptive terms known to be executed by the target system. Even this very crude formulation is enough to make it clear that the concept of execution for information-processing programs is a tricky affair. The problem is that, given any physical transaction you like and any symbolic operation you like, there will generally be some set of conditions—some context—in which that physical transaction would count as a performance of that symbolic operation. This follows more or less obviously from the reflection that the symbols—neurons or whatever—are, from our point of view, in code. In a cipher any numeral can, taken independently of the others, be assigned any significance whatever. It is only a definite context which places any constraint on the significance to be assigned to an individual numeral, the requirement being that when each numeral is assigned a meaning by a determinate rule, a coherent message should result. We cannot get at program execution one instruction at a time for reasons exactly analogous to those preventing us from getting a cipher significance one numeral at a time.

Actually, ciphers are easier than nervous systems in two respects. First, although there are indefinitely many different ways to make sense of a cipher if there are any, what we are after is the intended message; hence there is a nearly unique right answer among the infinity of workable solutions. And we generally can tell, given the context of the production of the message, whether a given solution is likely to be the right one or not. But when we are attempting to treat transactions in the nervous system as symbolic operations, there is no "intended interpretation": we are seeking (among an infinity of possible selections) an interpretation that will be theoretically fruitful, and, as is the case with science generally, there is no way to tell in advance whether a given way of describing matters will prove a help or a hindrance. The fact that workable solutions are not unique and that the first one we hit on is not the only one (and may not be a very good one) is often forgotten simply because it is so difficult to come up with any workable solution at all. But there is no reason to suppose that the criterion of explanatory usefulness selects a unique solution as the correct solution.

The second respect in which ciphers are easier is more serious: we know how to individuate numerals in standard notation, and we know that numerals are the significant units in a cipher.[7] In

short, we know what to assign significance *to*. But we do not
know this about natural systems. This introduces the possibility
of a truly radical indeterminacy into the problem: perhaps equally
workable solutions can be based on incommensurable ways of
individuating the physical parts and transactions to be treated. I
once purchased a plastic model of a computer circuit consisting,
according to the directions, of three flip-flops whose interconnections could be varied in all the standard ways. By ignoring this
interpretation in favor of another with a different domain, it is
possible to view the device as consisting of six units, each capable
of assuming eight states, whose interconnections can be varied in a
variety of nonstandard ways. Had the thing grown out of the
ground in my garden, or been intended as a paperweight, there
would evidently be no point in asking which interpretation is right.
The only question would be, which is more useful for the purpose
at hand—for instance, for explaining the behavior of some user or
the capacities of some larger containing system. This is precisely
our situation with respect to brains and other natural systems.

It evidently makes sense, though complicated sense we now
see, to treat systems of flip-flops or relays as systems of symbols
whose values are determined by their states. And this allows us to
make sense of the claim that such systems execute information-
processing programs, for when we have a rule that tells us which
part to treat as which symbol, and which state to treat as which
value, what we have is a way, though not a unique way, of translating an information-processing program into one specifying
physically described dispositions. Given that *that* makes sense, an
analogous claim about organic systems makes sense as well. The
constraint requiring that we exhibit the details of instantiation for
each analyzing capacity now applies (though may not be satisfied)
in a straightforward way, for when I have provided the translation,
I have specified the primitive capacities, and hence the instantiation laws, in a language appropriate to the derivation of causal
connections from standard nomic attributions.

Revealing an instantiation of an interpretive analysis requires
de-interpretation, but instantiations need not, in the first instance,
be specified descriptively. An information-processing capacity may
be explained by showing how it is instantiated in a system the
analysis/properties of which are specified in information-processing

terms distinct from those featured in the specification of the instantiated information-processing capacity. This can produce a considerable explanatory gain. For example, we may explain a capacity to judge the validity of argument forms on the assumption that the capacity is exercised by exercising the capacity to construct truth-trees. The gain derives from the fact that the capacity to construct truth-trees is analyzable into elementary symbol-crunching capacities that are not even prima facie inferential. This is the central idea underlying computer software design: analyze a capacity into subcapacities that have known instantiations in already existing software—i.e., in information-processing capacities whose descriptive instantiations have already been accomplished. I call instantiations specified in information-processing terms information-processing instantiations, to distinguish them from descriptively specified instantiations.[8] I will sometimes call descriptively specified instantiations physical instantiations for brevity, but this should not be taken to imply that such instantiations are specified in the language of physics.

Analysis, descriptive instantiation, and information-processing instantiation can be used in combination to produce a truly complex explanatory picture. This is the sort of picture we must construct in order to understand the capacities of a digital computer programmed to solve cognitive problems. A problem solver is a system with an information-processing capacity analyzed as a system of information-processing capacities each of which is typically instantiated as a list processor. Each list processor is in turn analyzed as a system of simpler list processors; elementary list processors are instantiated as number crunchers, and so on, until we arrive at electronics.[9]

If the instantiated information-processing analysis is systematic, as it usually is, then, of course, the instantiation must explain the significant interactions. Hence, in this sort of case, we do well to put the question in terms of program execution. What we need to show is how the system executes the program specifying the analysis. If the analyzing information-processing capacities are explained via information-processing instantiation, then we must use an information-processing characterization of S to explain how S executes a program specified in different information-processing terms. For instance, suppose C and C′ are information-processing capacities specified by successive instructions I_c and $I_{c'}$ in a program P, and suppose C and C' have information-processing instantiations iC and iC'. Then, since execution of $I_{c'}$ follows execution of I_c, we must explain why exercise of C precipitates exercise of C' (in the relevant context). After instantiation, the question becomes, why does exercise of iC precipitate exercise of iC'? Since iC and iC' are themselves information-processing capacities, however, this shift in question produces no explanatory progress in itself. It is a transition law that wants explaining here, and that requires the language of causal interaction, a language that is evidently distinct from the language of information-processing capacities. Thus, though individual information-processing capacities can fruitfully be explained by an information-processing instantiation, the interactions of a system of such capacities cannot. To explain how a system executes an information-processing program, therefore, requires a descriptively specified instantiation. It should be emphasized, however, that intervening information-processing instantiations may be an essential preliminary step to physical instantiation. The dimension shift effected by information-processing instantiation allows the theorist to trade an unanalyzable information-processing capacity for an analyzable one. The advantage is easily seen in the case of computers: any capacity that has been instantiated in a system of binary number crunchers has been instantiated in a system of information-processing capacities that have known descriptively specified instantiations.

II.2. THE EXPLANATORY ROLE OF INTERPRETATION

There is nothing irredeemably mysterious, then, about saying that natural systems execute information-processing programs—i.e., that they instantiate interpretive functional analyses. But given the problems just rehearsed—given the fact that there is no unique right answer to the question "Which programs does this system execute?"—it is not obvious why anyone would *want* to say such things. What explanatory value could such an analysis possibly have?

The explanatory role of interpretative analysis varies greatly depending on the type of information-processing capacity analyzed;

hence there is not a great deal that can be said without distinguishing cases. Therefore, the present section is little more than a preparation for the material in the next chapter.

Unlike the states of a digital computer, the states of natural systems do not have standard or intended interpretations. They are *assigned* semantic significance in order to explain the system's capacities. In a sense, this is true of computers as well. If some future interstellar archaeologist were to discover a computing device of an advanced but extinct population, questions about what the device could do would have to be distinguished from questions about what it was intended to do. Having discovered something it could do, it would be perfectly in order to construct an interpretive functional analysis to explain *how* it could do it, without regard to whether it was *designed* to do it. Were we to discover that the device could fly, we would be obliged to explain *how,* whether or not anyone ever intended it to fly. And in the process we would doubtless be obliged to attribute functions to various components without regard to whether those components were intended to have those (or any other) functions. We would be in an exactly similar situation were we to discover that the device could calculate, except that the functions in question would be information-processing capacities—i.e., capacities defined via semantic interpretations assigned to inputs and outputs. Interpretive functional analysis is therefore not like translating a foreign language or code. The poems of Baudelaire have a meaning (in French), and the job of a translator is to render them (in English). The fact that good translations are not unique—that there may not be a *best* translation—should not be allowed to obscure the difference between translating French and, e.g., "translating the DNA code." A translator of Baudelaire does not *assign* interpretations, irrespective of the conventions of French (hence irrespective of the intentions of French speakers), in order to explain the capacities of a poem or some containing system. A translator struggles to discover what the French means; a scientist struggles to discover an assignment of meanings to DNA configurations that will make the functioning of DNA intelligible.

Whether or not a device was designed to add, it may be an adder—i.e., be capable of adding—in virtue of the fact that it is possible to interpret outputs as numerals representing sums of numbers represented by numerals interpreting inputs. What makes a device an adder is simply the possibility of such an interpretation. When we discover that such an interpretation is possible for a device d, we have discovered that d has a certain information-processing capacity. To explain this capacity we need to find some way of interpreting the causal sequences connecting inputs and outputs as steps in an addition algorithm.[10] The interpretive strategy is motivated by the need to see the causal sequences as calculations, for only thus can we come to understand why it is that outputs are always interpretable as numerals representing sums of the numbers represented by the numerals interpreting the inputs.

Not all information-processing capacities require explanation via interpretive analysis. An AND gate, for instance, is a device with an information-processing capacity that is not subject to analysis into other similar capacities (unless it is built of OR gates and inverters, or something equally perverse). The interpretation of a bit of diode circuitry as an AND gate is justified by its possibility: there is a systematic way of mapping potential differences (or dc edges) onto truth values such that output voltages (edges) are assigned the value TRUE if and only if all input voltages (edges) are assigned the value TRUE. This makes the circuit an AND gate. (The same sort of reasoning will make it a lot of other things as well, of course.) But such an interpretation has no explanatory role except as a move in an analysis designed to explain the information-processing capacities of some larger containing system. To explain the truth-functional capacity of a (normal) AND gate does not require, hence does not justify, any further interpretation; what is required is physical instantiation. But explanation of the information-processing capacities of an electronic calculator incorporating such a circuit does require interpretation of internal causal sequences, and therefore confers explanatory value on the truth-functional interpretation of the AND gate circuitry.

When an information-processing capacity is exercised, a symbol gets transformed. Often, though not always, to understand how the transformation is effected, we need to see the causal sequences leading from inputs to outputs as *computations*—i.e., as stages in step-by-step transformations of the symbols interpreting inputs into the symbols interpreting outputs. This is the explanatory value of interpretation: we understand a computational capacity when we see state transitions as computations. [11]

Once we are tolerably clear about the explanatory role of interpretive functional analysis, we can see why the radical non-uniqueness of such analyses is no embarrassment. Any way of interpreting the transactions causally mediating the input-output connection as steps in a program for doing ϕ will, provided it is systematic and not ad hoc, make the capacity to ϕ intelligible. Alternative interpretations, provided they are possible, are not competitors; hence the availability of one in no way undermines the explanatory force of another. To speak of the data or facts as somehow *underdetermining* interpretation is therefore a misunderstanding, for the possibility at issue is the quite different one of the data or facts completely determining several different interpretations, each of which does the explanatory job to be done. Two distinct interpretive functional analyses, therefore, may not only be equally supported, but equally true—i.e., both true—and equally explanatory. Surely there is no need to choose between equally explanatory truths.

The source of confusion here, once again, is a failure to sufficiently distinguish analysis and subsumption. A transition theory explains changes in a system as effects of causes. Barring cases of overdetermination, alternate stories about the cause of a given effect cannot all be true. If, mesmerized by the idea that all scientific explanation is causal subsumption, we suppose that an interpretive functional analysis must be providing causes of effects (exercises of the analyzed capacity, presumably), then, of course, the non-uniqueness of true and equally explanatory analyses is acutely embarrassing. The proper therapy is not to insist that only one such analysis could really be instantiated in a given system, or to argue that data always underdetermines theory, or that considerations of "simplicity," entrenchment of terms, or prominence of advocates will narrow the field; the proper therapy is an appreciation of the differences between subsumptive and analytical explanation. To take one well-known example: if the capacity to speak and understand a natural language is an information-processing capacity and if a grammar of a language is an interpretive functional analysis of that capacity, then the non-uniqueness of grammars is, in itself, not a difficulty, hence requires no solution. Predictively adequate grammars that are not instantiated are, of course, not explanations of linguistic capacities. But nothing about the logic of interpretive analysis requires that a unique grammar be instantiated in order to satisfy the constraints on good explanation. Talk of "acquiring a grammar" can be misleading in this connection (though it needn't be): what is acquired is a structure that is interpretable as a grammar—i.e., an instantiation. If the structure acquired is interpretable as one grammar, it may be interpretable as another one too. This is no embarrassment so long as we keep in focus the fact that the point of interpretation is to explain how acquiring the structure in question could be acquiring the capacity a grammar analyzes—viz., the capacity to understand a language. To explain how acquiring a certain structure could be acquiring a language, we need to show that the structure is interpretable as an instantiation of *some* grammar of the language. Substituting 'exactly one' for 'some' evidently adds nothing to this explanation. In actual practice, of course, we don't identify the structure first, then provide an interpretation, but the reverse: our best shot at a grammar is posited as our best shot at an indirect specification[12] of the structure it is supposed to interpret.

II.3. REPRESENTATION AND INTERNAL MANUALS

Exchanging talk of instantiation for program execution, while helpful in making clear what instantiation of a systematic analysis must accomplish, is potentially misleading when it comes to the explanatory role of interpretive analyses. There is little temptation to suppose that systems do what they do—manifest the capacities they do—because their capacities are subject to a certain interpretive functional analysis. But there *is* a temptation, often not resisted, to suppose that systems do what they do because they are programmed to do it, hence to treat programs as causes of behavior rather than as interpretive analyses of the capacity to produce it. This temptation is encouraged by an analogy: just as we can explain the capacity of someone innocent of electronics to build a stereo receiver by reference to the program of instructions that comes with the kit, so, it seems, we can explain the capacity to learn a natural language by reference to the program of instructions that comes with the human nervous system. Such examples can be misleading in that the manual provided with the kit is a complex external stimulus that directs behavior in addition to merely analyzing the capacity to produce it. Organisms, however, do not exercise their psychologically interesting capacities by consciously following external programs of instructions. This obvious fact makes it tempting to keep the analogy intact by supposing that the program is *there* but internally represented, directing behavior much as a manual would. This internal manual model is clearly at work in the following well-known passage.

> Here is the way we tie our shoes:
>
> There is a little man who lives in one's head. The little man keeps a library. When one acts upon the intention to tie one's shoes, the little man fetches down a volume entitled *Tying One's Shoes.* The volume says such things as: "Take the left free end of the shoelace in the left hand. Cross the left free end of the shoelace over the right free end of the shoelace . . . etc."
>
> When the little man reads the instruction 'take the left free end of the shoelace in the left hand,' he pushes a button on a control panel. The button is marked 'take the left free end of a shoelace in the left hand.' When depressed, it activates a series of wheels, cogs, levers, and hydraulic mechanisms. As a causal consequence of the functioning of these mechanisms, one's left hand comes to seize the appropriate end of the shoelace. Similarly, *mutatis mutandis,* for the rest of the instructions.
>
> The instructions end with the word 'end'. When the little man reads the word 'end', he returns the book of instructions to the library.
>
> That is the way we tie our shoes. [Fodor, 1968, p. 627]

Here, the shoe-tying program—or, rather, reading it—is thought of primarily as a cause of shoe-tying behavior and only incidentally and inessentially as an analysis of the capacity to tie one's shoes. The internal manual model thus suggests a very different explanatory role for the programs than the one I have just sketched.

Central to the internal manual model is the idea that programs are represented in the systems that execute them.[13] We do well to begin, then, by examining the connection between representing a program and executing it. Evidently, a program may be represented in a system that does not execute it, a pencil and paper token of the program being an example. And a system that does execute a program may represent it in virtue of features irrelevant to execution—e.g., in virtue of each instruction being printed on the component that instantiates the capacity that instruction specifies (an arrangement that would facilitate repairs). We need to focus on cases in which representation is related to execution.

One fairly straightforward relation is this one:

(1) If S physically instantiates P, then S represents P.

To see that physical instantiation is sufficient for representation, notice that if S physically instantiates P, then S physically instantiates the capacities specified by the elementary instructions of P. If S physically instantiates those capacities, there are relatively permanent causal-structural features of S that ultimately account for each of those capacities.[14] Hence, we may simply draft those features as the required representations, each instruction being represented by whatever features it interprets. Representation, understood in this way, is the inverse of interpretation: once interpretive assignments have been made, we may think of the features interpreted as encodings of the instructions interpreting them.

Proposition (1) does not give us the sort of connection between execution and representation envisioned by the internal manual model. Let us call the sort of representation given by (1) E-representation ('E' for 'execute'). When S executes P, events take the course they do because S is structured in a certain way, but S is not structured in that way because P is E-represented in S, for to say that P is E-represented in S is just another way of saying that S has the structure in question.[15] Since 'P is E-represented in S' is equivalent to 'P is physically instantiated in S', an E-represented program cannot be thought of as an internal manual that guides S through the steps in the causal sequence leading to ouput. It is simply an indirect (i.e., interpretive) *specification* of that causal sequence.

The situation is even less congenial to the internal manual model if we assume that P is instantiated in S as an information-processing system rather than physically instantiated in S. If S executes P but does not physically instantiate P, then there is a capacity C specified by an elementary instruction I of P that has an information-processing instantiation in S. It is tempting to suppose that representation of I reduces to representation of the program P(I) that is the information-processing instantiation of I, but this temptation is to be resisted. I and P(I) are input-output isomorphic, but are not semantically equivalent (or even related in the typical case), hence not alternate representations of the same thing. If S physically instantiates P(I), then S E-represents P(I), but the features representing P(I) do not (except by wild coincidence) represent I. An example should make this clear. Suppose S physically instantiates P(I), a program that constructs truth-trees for inference schemata in first-order form. Then P(I) is an information-processing instantiation of the capacity specified by the instruction I: DETERMINE WHETHER X IS A VALID INFERENCE SCHEMA IN FIRST-ORDER FORM. Evidently, nothing in S need represent I. Indeed, the point of specifying the instantiation is to explain how S can execute I without trafficking in truth-values or making inferences comparable to the ones it is supposed to test. Hence, to treat the features instantiating P(I) as a representation of I would be to undo the very change of representative content that motivates the instantiation in the first place.

It seems we must admit that a program may be executed by S even though S does not represent it: execution of P by S guarantees representation of P in S iff P in physically instantiated in S (I missed this in Cummins, 1977, where I held that execution is always sufficient for instantiation.) A cook may therefore execute a recipe that is not represented in the cook or anywhere else, and this need not undermine the explanatory point of appealing to such a recipe. While such a recipe, if discovered, would constitute a function-analytical explanation of the cook's capacity to cook, it obviously could not be appealed to as the cause of the cook doing the right things in the right order, for the cook would have no causal interaction with any representation of the recipe.

The internal manual model, therefore, cannot be a correct picture of the explanatory role of programs that are instantiated as information-processing systems. This is a significant point, since source programs run on general purpose computers have information-processing instantiations. Misunderstanding of the relation between programming languages and machine languages has obscured this point. When a program written in a programming language PL is run on a computer, the program is compiled. What the compiler effects is a "translation" of PL source instructions into a machine language ML, each instruction I in the source program corresponding to a more or less elaborate routine ML(I) in ML.[16] The instructions of ML(I) are direct interpretations of physical processes in the machine—that's why it is called machine language. Since ML(I) is E-represented in the machine, and I is "equivalent" to ML(I), it is tempting to suppose that I is represented in the machine as well, by whatever represents ML(I). But this line of thought confuses two ways in which programs (including single instructions) can be equivalent. I and ML(I) are input-output isomorphic, but they are not representationally equivalent: they don't have the same semantic properties at all. To suppose they do is to miss the whole point of compilation (information-processing instantiation). ML traffics in binary numbers or truth-functions (typically), whereas PL traffics in arrays, records, square roots, lists, or whatever. Compilation, in short, *is not really translation.* Realizing this, we can see that a general purpose computer executing a PL program typically represents no PL at all.[17] Anyone who thinks human cognitive capacities are explained by programs that stand to "brain language" as PL programs stand to ML programs will have to abandon the internal manual model of explanation by program. Explanation by appeal to a program having an information-processing instantiation, therefore, is not a species of causal subsumption, and research strategies that are in the business of generating such explanations are not in the business of discovering causal laws.

Let us pause to consolidate. Programs having information-processing instantiations are not represented by the systems that execute them (except coincidentally or inessentially). Physically instantiated programs are represented by the systems that execute them, but not in the way required by the internal manual model. If the internal manual model applies at all, therefore, it must apply to programs that are instantiated neither physically nor in an information-processing system.

What the internal manual model requires is a distinction between a program merely being represented *by* a device (E-representation), and a program being represented *for* a device. Defenders of the model typically suppose that an internally represented program constitutes a kind of knowledge—a manual of information available to the system. The program is supposed to stand to the system that executes it much as the printed recipe stands to the cook who follows it, the only difference being that the program is internalized. The information is there for use by the system in much the same way, but "there" is inside. This is what allows one to retain the idea that the system does what it does because it is instructed to do it. The passage from Fodor above brings this out because the manual and the person who follows it are explicitly duplicated inside.

According to this view of the matter, we do whatever we do when tying our shoes because the shoe-tying program—call it ST—so instructs. Let us alter the story slightly but inessentially: rather than read a volume and push buttons, the little man feeds a deck of cards into a reader. Again, imagine the cards replaced by circuit boards: the little man simply closes an appropriately labeled switch that incorporates the relevant board into the mechanism as a whole. Once the switch is closed, the system as a whole E-represents a program having ST as a subroutine. The little man executes the instruction CALL ST when he closes the switch. But now it is clear that the little man is eliminable by supposing that whatever caused him to close the switch simply causes the switch to close. The little man is no loss, of course: the point, ultimately, is to analyze little men and women away. But with the little man goes any hint that anything is being instructed to do anything: the shoelace is not taken by the hand because it or anything else is instructed to do so. And since our latest version of the story is a harmless variation of the original, the suggestion of an internal manual in the original must have been entirely spurious. And it is obvious what the spurious feature is. "When the little man reads the instruction 'take the left free end of the shoelace in the left hand,' he pushes a button on the control panel." He pushes the button because ST so instructs,

and the left hand takes the left free end of the shoelace because
the button is pushed; hence, the left hand takes the shoelace because ST so instructs. But what is essential is just that the right
buttons get pushed in the right order, and that will happen only if
ST is E-represented. If that is why things happen as they do, then
it is false that the left hand takes the shoelace in obedience to an
instruction in ST. Instead, it is as if writing in the manual caused it
to change shape in such a way that (i) when you write 'do so-and-
so' in the book, the book acquires a shape S, and (ii) when things
having shape S are jammed into the mechanism, the system does
so-and-so. (For 'book', read 'punch card'; for 'write' read 'punch
holes'.) This would be an efficient and convenient way of producing the right shapes (E-representations), or of keeping track of the
functional properties of the available shapes. It would not be a
way of providing the system with something to read and obey.[18] A
system that acquires the capacity to tie its shoes acquires an E-
representation of a shoe-tying program. But such a system need
not understand the program, or know what is in it, in any sense at
all. It just needs to be restructured in a way which we, as theorists,
can interpret as an E-representation of a shoe-tying program.

It will seem to many that I am straining at a gnat. Surely advocates of the internal manual model do not mean to duplicate
internally the capacity to read, understand, and comply with a
set of instructions. Saying that the little man reads the book and
pushes a button on a control panel is just a dramatic way of saying
that some such story as the one about circuit boards or punch
cards must be true, a way of saying this that is useful precisely
because it abstracts from *which* such story is true in a particular
case. If there really is a book, and it is its shape that counts, then
reading the book is instantiated as reacting to its shape. If it is
punch cards, then reading the book is instantiated as reacting to
punch patterns. And so on.

If this is what advocates of the internal manual model have in
mind, I have nothing to object.[19] But on this understanding, the
spirit of the model has been abandoned, and we are no longer
talking about a species of causal subsumption, for we are no
longer supposing that an internal representation of the program,
or reading it, causes events to take the course specified in the
program. We cannot hold that reading the book is instantiated as

reacting to its shape and that the system reacts to shape in the way it does because of what it reads.

The point can be put another way. The function of the little man in Fodor's story is to mediate between the representation of ST on the one hand and the system that executes the instructions of ST on the other. In the story, the system has access to ST only through the little man who reads it. When we mechanize that access—when we actually specify some instantiation—it becomes clear that what we do is get ST E-represented in S. The appearance of a distinction between E-representation and the sort of representation presupposed by the internal manual model is therefore an artifact of an undischarged homunculus. When we instantiate the READ ST function, in other words, we incorporate the representation of ST into the causal structure in just the way that the program that calls ST is already supposed to be incorporated into the mechanism. The result is that the relation of the system to ST is no longer analogous to the relation of the cook to the recipe he or she reads, and therefore appeal to ST cannot explain shoe tying in the way appeal to a recipe explains cake baking.

CHAPTER THREE
Understanding Cognitive Capacities

Humans differ most dramatically from other fauna in their cognitive capacities. Indeed, this is about all humans can boast of: we are notably inferior to other animals in our noncognitive endowments. Thus it should come as no surprise that a distinctively human psychology should be a psychology of the cognitive. The wonder is rather that cognitive psychology was so late to arrive on the scientific scene, being now less than thirty years old. Of course, rationalistic "philosophical psychology" has been with us forever, but that wasn't science, and, in my view, cognitive psychologists would do well not to follow Chomsky in touting this heritage (if such it is) so loudly.

The late arrival of cognitive psychology is rather easily accounted for, I think, by the following fact. Until quite recently, no one had the slightest idea what it would be *like* to scientifically explain a cognitive capacity. In part, no doubt, this was because everyone was mesmerized by the idea that scientific explanation is subsumption under causal law, and cognitive capacities could not possibly be explained that way. Another important factor was that until recently no one had any serious idea– i.e., no scientifically workable idea—how to *describe* cognitive capacities; hence no one had any serious idea what the explanandum was. An obvious example of this is the capacity to learn language: before Chomsky, no one knew how to describe what was learned with the kind of detail and precision that makes explanatory theory a serious possibility.

There are other fascinating reasons why no one knew until fairly recently what a scientific explanation of a cognitive capacity would be like. Some of these will be touched on in Chapter III. Meanwhile, I want to consider what such an explanation *would* be like.

My strategy will be to sneak up on the genuinely cognitive by stages. The real thing won't emerge for discussion until Section III.3.

III.1. INFERENTIALLY CHARACTERIZED CAPACITIES

A capacity is specified by giving a special law linking precipitating conditions to manifestations—i.e., by specifying "input-output" conditions. What makes a capacity cognitive is that the outputs are cognitions. Thus a natural way—perhaps the only way—to specify a particular cognitive capacity is to specify particular epistemological conditions on the relation outputs bear to inputs. Playing on etymology a little (but only a *little*), we can say that what makes outputs cognitions, or at least candidate cognitions, is that they are cogent—epistemologically appropriate—relative to inputs (cf. Haugeland, 1978).

Since only truth-value bearers can be epistemologically related, the inputs and outputs must be interpretable as tokens of sentence types: a cognitive capacity is an information processing capacity in the sense of Section II.3, and a system instantiating a cognitive capacity is a sentence transformer. Furthermore, to say one proposition is cogent relative to some others is just to say that it is validly or reasonably inferable from those others. Thus for a capacity to be cognitive, precipitating conditions (inputs) and manifestations (outputs) must be interpretable as sentence tokens, and outputs must (typically) be inferable from inputs in a characteristic way—i.e., in a way characteristic of the particular capacity in question. We may sum this up by saying that cognitive capacities are *inferentially characterizable capacities* (ICC's hereafter):[1] the transition law specifying a cognitive capacity is a rule of inference.[2] It is in cases of this sort that it is appropriate to think of outputs as cognitions, but certainly not in all cases of this sort. Cognition is a propositional attitude, and certainly the exercise of an ICC needn't be a propositional attitude. Chess-playing machines evidently have ICC's, but it is (or ought to be) less than evident that they are literally intentionally characterizable; hence it ought to be less than evident that they have propositional attitudes (but cf. Dennett, 1978, ch. 1). In this section, however, I want to leave intentionality aside and discuss ICC's. I shall need some term for the outputs of an ICC, so I shall call them *cognitions, postponing until the next section the relationship, if any, between cognition and *cognition.

A capacity that is not inferentially characterizable, hence not explicitly *cognitive, might nevertheless be implicitly *cognitive in virtue of being instantiated in a system the component capacities of which are explicitly *cognitive (ICC's). It is precisely this possibility that gives *cognitive analysis some serious hope of being a fairly *general* approach to psychological theorizing. If the capacity to respond differentially to variations in (visual) depth is *cognitive, it is so implicitly: *cognitive because it is a capacity that is instantiated in a *cognitive system. Although implicitly *cognitive capacities are of great importance to the general implementation of the cognitivist program, the notion of an explicitly *cognitive capacity is evidently the fundamental one, and I shall concentrate my attention on it.

To explain an inferentially characterized capacity is to explain the capacity to conform to the characteristic inferential pattern. More precisely, to explain an inferentially characterized capacity is to explain how it happens that the output is characteristically interpretable as a sentence that is inferable in a specified way from the sentence interpreting the input that precipitated it. What would make us understand this sort of fact? That is, what would make us understand how a system is able to conform to a characteristic inference pattern? It seems to me that (at least) the following two things are required:

(a) First, we must understand what makes the output right or cogent relative to the input (i.e., *we* must be able to infer outputs from inputs). If we don't understand this, we have no reason to speak of an ICC in the first place, for we don't know whether the (or any) characteristic epistemological conditions are typically satisfied or not. In short, we will have no inferential characterization. Someone who cannot evaluate chess moves cannot tell a chess player from someone who simply avoids illegal moves.[3] (b) Second, we must see that the system is so structured as to (characteristically) exploit in producing an output whatever it is that makes that output cogent relative to current input. Anything less than this will leave us mystified as to how the system "gets it right."

It should be clear that (a) isn't really a condition on explaining an ICC, but rather a reminder that we must have an inferential characterization of the capacity—at least a crude one—in order to have a *cognitive explanandum to theorize about. This point is not as trivial as it seems: recognition is standardly regarded as exercise of a *cognitive capacity, but there is certainly no widely accepted inferential characterization, or even widespread realization that one is required to justify calling it a *cognitive* capacity.[4]

Though it appears innocent enough, (b) is the substantial requirement, for it says that the instantiation of an ICC in S must demystify the epistemological successes which are the exercises of the ICC in S, and ultimately this means that drawing the right conclusion must be (interpret) a physical transition characteristic of physical systems like S.

Though vague and highly abstract, (a) and (b) together make it clear that the appropriate explanatory strategy for an ICC is interpretive analysis. Hence, there are two tactics to pursue: we may begin by analyzing an ICC into sub-ICC's—functional analysis—or we may proceed immediately to componential analysis.

Inferential Analysis

An ICC is a *cognitive capacity in the most minimal possible sense. A device with an ICC certainly needn't be intelligent. Indeed, if its ICC's are explicable by instantiation, it cannot be characterized as intelligent or rational at the dimension on which it is inferentially characterized. It is simply a proposition transformer whose transformations mirror an inferential connection. It doesn't arrive at its output by "figuring it out," for if the ICC in question is explicable via instantiation, any "figuring out" it does is on another dimension, hence about something else, and not about "it."[5]

We get a somewhat less anemic case of *cognition when we

consider an ICC that is susceptible of *inferential analysis.* In
a case of this sort we can answer the question "How does it
get the right conclusion?" without changing the subject—viz.,
by exhibiting the subinferences appealed to in the analysis. But
this can nevertheless be pretty unexciting stuff. We could build
an AND-gate by connecting inverters and OR-gates, and the result

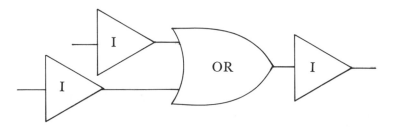

would be a device whose capacity to conjoin is inferentially analyzable. There is an easy to grasp (but hard to explain) sense in
which this sort of device "figures out" whether the conjunction of
the inputs is true by determining whether the disjunction of their
denials is true. But scare quotes on 'figures out' are very much in
order, and it is instructive to consider what we could add to change
that fact.

It seems clear to me—though I don't see how to argue the
point—that what makes the scare quotes mandatory is the manifest absence of intelligence. To *really* figure something out, a
system must exhibit at least minimal intelligence. I certainly have
no philosophical analysis of intelligence to offer, let alone a psychological analysis. But I think we can learn something worth
knowing by considering the implications of some rather simple-
minded necessary conditions.[6]

I've already mentioned one necessary condition: the ICC in
question must be inferentially analyzable. If it is not, then, though
we may marvel at the nifty way our device gets the job done, any
intelligence exhibited is exercised on some other dimension, or
perhaps by the designer (if it is an artifact) who thought up this
particular instantiation. The device is not intelligent on the dimension in which the object capacity is inferentially characterized. By
analogy with our distinction between explicitly and implicitly
*cognitive capacities, we could say that the object capacity only

implicitly features intelligence, hence is only implicitly *cognitive in any very interesting sense.

A further necessary condition is this: exercise of an ICC is intelligent only if output-production involves "informed choice." If the process leading to output can be adequately flow-charted without branches, or if the branching is totally insensitive (or only perversely sensitive) to factors bearing on the correctness of the output, then the output is not intelligently produced. I think this fairly captures the most glaring lack in the baroque AND-gate. Though its most notable capacity is inferentially analyzable, a proper analysis would reveal no choice points. Appearances to the contrary, what each component does is not dependent in the requisite sense on what other components do, for the operation of each component is not conditional on which input it gets. An inverter, for instance, doesn't determine the interpretation of current input, then construct an ouput that has the complementary interpretation; it simply inverts current input willy-nilly. There are no choices made at all, let alone informed choices.[7]

I'm not at all sure how to characterize informed choices, but I am sure that the baroque AND-gate doesn't make any, and I'm sure that that is why it seems so stupid. It *cognizes if you like, but it isn't intelligent *cognition because it doesn't *cogitate: there can be no intelligent *cognition without *cogitation, and hence no interesting *cognition—no *cognition seriously worth the name— with *cogitation.

This point, if it is right, has an important implication: interesting *cognitive capacities are not explicable via instantiation. If S's capacity to play chess resisted inferential analysis, then we should have to admit that its abilities are mysterious, or that it isn't the chess playing that is intelligent, but something else, viz., some inferentially analyzable capacity featured in the explanation of the instantiating information-processing system. And if the available instantiations were not inferentially analyzable, then even this alternative to mystery would be unavailable.[8]

*Cognition and *Cogitation

The idea that only *cogitation could explain *cognition—interesting *cognition—is unblushing rationalism, and it is not likely to seem inevitable simply on the basis of the fact that baroque

AND-gates don't make informed choices. We require some positive argument for the claim that intelligent *cognizers must be explained as *cogitators. Here is a first pass at such an argument.

The "what else?" argument. To explain a *cognitive capacity is to explain the capacity to satisfy the defining epistemic conditions. To specify such conditions, we describe some inferential pattern adherence to which gives the desired input-output relation. Since it is adherence to this or some comparable pattern of inference that makes a given output "right," what could explain the capacity to get the right output other than an inferential analysis of that capacity? To understand the capacity to get the "right" output, we must see that the system is so structured as to exploit whatever it is that makes an output right, and what makes a given output right is that it is derivable via the characterizing inferential pattern.

I call this a "what else?" argument because it assumes without argument that only inferential analysis could explain a capacity to adhere to an inferential pattern. This assumption is false, as we have seen, for some unanalyzed ICC's can be explained simply by exhibiting their instantiations. Nevertheless, I think the argument is on the right track, for it is only in rather special cases that exhibiting the instantiation of an unanalyzed ICC *could* exhibit a system's structure in a way that would reveal how it exploits whatever makes outputs right.[9] Roughly, the instantiation strategy will be a bad explanatory strategy whenever the capacity to be explained is characterizable only by specifying a rationale—i.e., an inferential analysis involving interlocking informed choices. My claim is that such a capacity is explained only on the hypothesis that the system executes the rationale. What else could explain it? Let us break with the best tradition of "what-else?" arguments and explore the alternatives.

Fortunately, there are only two alternatives to explore. First, it might happen that the device with the capacity in question doesn't execute the characterizing rationale but some other rationale. Since the class of rationale's input-output equivalent to a given one is infinite, this constitutes a serious practical problem—which rationale is executed?—but leaves my thesis intact.

If the device does not execute the characterizing rationale or any input-output equivalent rationale, then the capacity must be explicable via instantiation (if it is explicable at all). So let's imagine that we have a device with a capacity C that we can only characterize via some rationale, and let us consider the hypothesis that C is instantiated as I, a symbol cruncher perhaps, or a physically specified system. This hypothesis commits us to the claim that C and I are isomorphic.[10] What would justify such a commitment?

Well, we could have inductive evidence: perhaps a computer programmed to have I simulates a device exercising C rather well. If we believe C and I are isomorphic on this basis, then we believe that the simulation is not coincidence: there must be something that guarantees it. What could this be? I is characterized via some program of symbol crunchers or physical state changers. If we could translate that program into R—the rationale characterizing C—the successful simulation would be explained, but only because we have discovered that R is executed after all: I is R in disguise.[11]

Would anything short of exposing such a disguise do the trick? I can't see how: we must see that our device is so structured as to exploit whatever it is that makes outputs right. What makes them right is just that they are what emerge if a certain rationale is adhered to. Cashing the technical term, what makes outputs right is that they are what emerge when, among other things, certain interdependent informed choices are made in certain ways. By hypothesis, I exhibits nothing of the kind, at least not the ones relevant to the cogency (or lack thereof) of outputs of a system with C. C cannot be instantiated as I.

A fairly natural reply goes like this: if a computer running the I-program simulates things exercising C, and the simulation is a good one—not restricted to a few artificial situations—then we have good grounds for supposing that anything that executes the I-program has C, and we have these grounds whatever we think about why the simulation works. If we can't translate the I-program into a rationale, then it is the thesis about explanation that must go, not the generalization correlating I and C.

Of course, really successful simulation constrains us to accept the isomorphism of C and I. But it also provides us with a new characterization of C—namely I—that represents exercise of C as unintelligent *cognition (at best), and explanation of that sort of capacity is beside the present point. Thus the claim that C is instantiated as I (where I is not R or some equivalent rationale in disguise) reduces to the claim that C is characterizable without appeal to a rationale, contrary to what we are assuming.

Discoveries of this "debunking" sort are possible. Consider Schwartz's density computer. Given a sphere, the device determines whether its density is greater or less than one. A natural way to specify the capacity in detail is this: given the mass and circumference of a sphere—perhaps by measurement—the device gives the output "The density of s is greater than one," iff the density of the sphere is greater than one. If we specify the capacity this way, the natural way to explain it is: the device computes $(8m \ \pi^2)/c^3$ and compares the result with one. Indeed, this is so natural it may seem inevitable. However, the device will be well simulated by a system that simply puts the sphere in a bucket of water and outputs, "The density of s is greater than one," just in case the sphere sinks. Faced with this fact, we must ask whether we were too stingy in our characterization of inputs. We were simply assuming that all our device has to work with is mass and circumference. But, as the simulation shows, if it is given the sphere itself, this assumption is unjustified. In this case, the simulation allows us to see that the target capacity may not be as sophisticated as we thought, for it gives us a nonrationale characterization. Indeed, it turns out to be a different capacity than we thought, for the inputs aren't what we thought they were. Or rather: our characterization of input was so loose that what we unwittingly characterized was a family of ICC's, some much more sophisticated than others in their inferential structure.

Sometimes we know enough about the system we are dealing with to rule out this sort of thing, but we don't know enough to be sure of our input characterizations. Few have seriously disagreed with Berkeley's claim that depth is not immediately perceived by sight,[12] and while a lot of controversy surrounds the problem of characterizing the capacity to learn a language, it seems clear that the inputs are on the poor side: learning a language is certainly much more like calculating densities than it is like measuring them. Still, it must be admitted that it is not clear which capacities must be rationale-characterized, let alone which rationale characterizes them. My point is simply that if rationale-characterization is the only characterization available, then explanation by *cogitation (i.e., "serious" inferential analysis) is the only appropriate explanatory strategy. If another characterization is possible, then so are other explanations, but they will not be explanations of intelligent *cognition; they will be "debunkings," explaining away the appearance of intelligent cognition.[13]

To rationale-characterize a capacity C is to analyze C into ICC's some of which are *branching* ICC's—i.e., capacities to make informed choices. (I will need a term for ICC's that are characterizable only by specifying a rationale. For want of a better term, I will call them *discursive capacities.* "In *philosophy,* going from premises to conclusions in a series of logical steps . . . ," *Webster's New World Dictionary.*) Now, although a capacity that is only rationale-characterizable—i.e., a discursive capacity—is not explicable via instantiation, a branching ICC that is not itself a discursive capacity is explicable (sometimes) without analysis. So it might seem that a program of branching ICC's—a discursive capacity in fact—could be explained via instantiation by something akin to composition of functions. Let C be a discursive capacity analyzable into ICC's $b_1, \ldots, b_n$, and let $i_1, \ldots, i_n$ physically instantiate $b_1, \ldots, b_n$, respectively in S. Equivalently: S executes a program R specifying C; the elementary instructions of R specify b_1, $\ldots, b_n$; I is a noninterpretive (descriptive) program executed by C, whose elementary instructions specify $i_1, \ldots, i_n$ such that, in S, execution of R is instantiated as execution of I (i.e., as organized exercise of the i_i). Now why doesn't the fact that S executes I explain S's capacity C?

First, this scenario does not tell against the claim that C is inexplicable without analysis of C, for I enforces an analysis of C: I is specified as a de-interpretation of R, and R inferentially analyzes C. But it might seem that, equipped with I, we could dispense with R, hence with *inferential* analysis of C. And if we could do that, we could explain a *cognitive capacity in S without exhibiting *cogitation in S, since I does not specify a rationale.

The trouble with this idea is that it fails to satisfy condition (b): it is precisely the fact that R is an interpretation of I that allows us to understand how S "gets it right." With the help of electronics, or neurophysiology, or chemistry (depending on S), we can understand S's capacity to execute I. From this much, plus the IN-OUT isomorphism (within idealization) of I and R, we can *deduce* that S has C. But to understand why having the capacity to execute I amounts to having C, we need to see that R is an interpretation of I. Lacking this, it will remain a mystery how S manages, by executing I, to satisfy the epistemological conditions specified by R.

This point is trivial, or ought to be. And it would be, I think, but for the doctrine that causal subsumption is explanation. Accepting this doctrine makes it (almost) inevitable that the issue will be formulated thus: can the laws of physics (or whatever) subsume the events that are exercises of C in S? Well, of course: every exercise of C is some physical event or other. But so what? That sort of subsumption—indeed *any* sort of subsumption—of an exercise of C is evidently irrelevant to an understanding of why execution of I guarantees (within idealization) satisfaction of the epistemological constraints specified by R and definitive of C—irrelevant, in short, to explaining C (in S). The most insidious feature of the D–N model of explanation is that it blinds people to the sorts of scientific questions that cannot be resolved by causal subsumption. Explanation of state transitions in S just won't resolve the perplexities generated by S's possession of a discursive capacity, or any other sort of information-processing capacity. A record of the physically specified state transitions of an adder, together with the relevant subsumptions, would leave us baffled as to how the thing adds, even if the record included only the transitions and features that are interpretable as executions of the instructions of an addition algorithm. In reality, the record would not be so conveniently selective if it were constructed without regard to its interpretability: from the point of view of physics—property-physics as well as transition-physics—a de-interpretation of the algorithm represents a completely arbitrary selection of characteristics and events. This is why *strictly* "bottom up" strategies in *cognitive psychology—i.e., strategies that proceed with neurophysiology unconstrained and uninformed by *cognitive interpretability—have no serious chance of generating instantiations of *cognitive capacities. To recommend such a strategy invariably amounts to changing the subject.

Constraints on Interpretation

Given the foregoing account of the explanation of *cognitive capacities, the following three highly plausible constraints on interpretation of physically characterized transactions appear embarrassingly unmotivated.

(a) Interpretation shall respect cell boundaries.

Suppose we find that we can interpret causal chains from input to output as *cognitions, but that these interpretations ignore cell boundaries? This is evidently as possible as it is unwelcome.

(b) An account of a system's *cognitive capacities shall not utilize interpretations that effect incommensurable parsings of the system's physical components.

Suppose, as in (a), that we find *cogitations to explain c-1, and *cogitations to explain c-2, but this requires carving up the organism's physical structures in incommensurable ways—as if we cut two unrelated jig-saw puzzles out of the same board. This certainly can happen with electronic circuits—why not brains?

(c) Interpretations must, at a fundamental level, be invariant over time.

Violation of (c) yields a really baroque nightmare. Imagine a class of adders all of which execute the same program but—being physically disparate—execute it under different interpretations. No problem. Now imagine that one of these undergoes internally generated change—a kind of decay—so as to serially assume the physical structures of the other adders in the set. Finally, imagine that this process is continuous so that at any instant the device executes the program under some interpretation, but different interpretations are required at successive instants. Again, this is plainly possible—at least logically—and it wouldn't detract one whit from our ability to explain the device's capacity to add. But surely we want to rule this out.

I think the motivation for all three constraints is the same, and applies only to biological systems: *cognitive capacities are either inherited or acquired, i.e., acquired genetically or (roughly) perceptually. Begin with (a). *Cognitive capacities genetically acquired—i.e., acquired by replication of structure—demand the availability of an interpretation that takes for its domain the sorts of physical structures genes determine.[14] Capacities acquired via perceptual feedback and the like demand an interpretation that interprets the sorts of structures that can be altered by perceptual input, and these had better be of a piece with those dictated by genes, else there is no guarantee that offspring will be able to acquire the capacities in question.[15]

Next, consider (b). The motivation for (b) follows trivially from the discussion of (a). Evidently, two capacities genetically acquired must admit of commensurable interpretations, for they must both ultimately boil down to gene-dictated structures. And since non-genetically acquired capacities must admit of interpretations commensurable with genetically determined structures as well (see (a)), all normally acquired capacities must admit of interpretations commensurable with genetically determined structures.

Finally, consider (c). The imagined violation of (c) is, I suppose, metaphysically and logically possible, but we could never have any good reason to suppose such a thing actually occurred. The imagined "decay" must be lawlike, to guarantee the possibility of the successive interpretations. This law itself specifies an information-processing capacity. Call this capacity D. Now either there is a program P–D execution of which explains D and provides a time invariant interpretation of the system, or there is not. If there is, then (c) is not violated. If there is not, then we will have no reason to suppose the system actually has D. We could, perhaps, discover that S executes the addition algorithm at t under interpretation I–t for several times t, but lacking P–D, we can only view this as coincidence: There will be no way of projecting the next required interpretation. Conversely, only a program like P–D, known to be executed by the system, would allow such projections. Hence, we will be able to dismiss coincidence iff (c) is not violated.

Acquisition is here presumed to be itself either genetically or (roughly) *cognitively determined. What of a *cognitive capacity that is randomly generated, or generated by a process that is independent of biological economy—e.g., a blow on the head, radiation, etc.? These, of course, need not admit of interpretations with domains populated by items subject to biological replication. But neither will they, for that very reason, be characteristic of the organism-type. They will be radically uninheritable in the sense that (i) they cannot be directly passed on, and (ii) the capacity to acquire them cannot be passed on either (i.e., no capacity to acquire them can be passed on, since they are characterized by the fact that their acquisition is not the result of executing a genetically determined or learned program).

Thus systematically acquirable capacities must respect (a), (b), and (c). How much of our *cognitive endowment at a given moment is unsystematically acquired is an empirical issue. Disease, injury, and a certain amount of random variation are bound to have some influence, but it is wildly improbable (though not impossible) that such factors produce, rather than limit or impair, our information-processing capacities.

III.2. KNOWLEDGE AND THE FLOW OF INFORMATION

In a recent pioneering and lucid work, Fred Dretske (1981) elaborates an approach to the problem of semantic interpretation that is entirely different from the one I have been urging. A full exposition and discussion of Dretske's approach here would simply make this book too long and take us too far afield. It would also be premature: it will be some time before the full implications of Dretske's ideas become apparent. Still, I would be seriously remiss if I did not make some attempt to relate Dretske's treatment of semantic interpretation to the present work.

The fundamental idea behind Dretske's theory is that semantic content—the proper propositional interpretation—of a state of a system is fixed by the flow of information into the system that causes the system to be in that state. In order to make this idea workable, two essential preliminary tasks must be undertaken. First, it must be shown that standard Information Theory[16] can be altered or extended so as to underwrite attributions of specific propositional contents to states of a system. As is, standard Information Theory makes no provision for claims about *what* information a state or event carries; it only makes provision for claims about *how much* information is carried. Thus Dretske's first major contribution in *Knowledge and the Flow of Information* is to show how the concepts of Information Theory can be used to explicate the idea of a state having a specific propositional content. Second, it must be shown how a state having informational content of propositional form can have that informational content exclusively as its semantic content.[17] This, to my mind, is Dretske's second major innovation. In the following pages I will briefly review Dretske's route from Information Theory to semantic content, but the reader is urged to study the original.

Extending Information Theory: Essential Background

Information Theory, as Dretske emphasizes, concerns itself solely with quantities of information—typically average quantities over time or trials—and not with content. The theory allows us to say how much information is associated with a given event, but not what information is carried by that event. The immediate goal of Information Theory is to characterize the flow of information between a *source* and a *receiver*. The fundamental idea is extremely simple: we compare the amount of information available at the source with the amount of information from the source available at the receiver.

The amount of information at the source associated with a given event (or state of affairs) is measured as a function of the probability of that event relative to the other possibilities—i.e., relative to the other possible events at the source. If there are n possible events at the source, $s_1, s_2, \ldots s_n$, the amount of information associated with the occurrence of s_i is a function of the probability of the occurrence of s_i:

(1) $I(s_i) = -\log_e p(s_i)$,

where $p(s_i)$ is the probability that s_i occurs, and $I(s_i)$ is the information associated with the occurrence of s_i. The reciprocal logarithmic function is chosen to give a measure of $I(s_i)$ in bits. Intuitively, the idea is that the amount of information associated with the occurrence of s_i depends on how unlikely that occurrence happens to be. If $p(s_i) = 1$, then $I(s_i) = 0$: s_i was bound to occur anyway, so the fact of its actual occurrence is no news—generates no new information beyond what was available before the occurrence of s_i. On the other hand, if $p(s_i)$ is close to zero, then the occurrence of s_i is a "surprise" (hence, $I(s_i)$ is called the surprisal of s_i); its occurrence could tell us something we were not more or less expecting in any case.

This intuitive explanation of (1) already makes implicit reference to an assumed receiver that might be or fail to be "surprised" by the occurrence of s_i given antecedent "expectations." While helpful, this needs to be taken with a grain of salt: the receiver need not be a cognitive agent in any sense, however loose. All that is required is that we be able to devise a measure of how much of the information generated at the source by the occurrence of s_i arrives at the receiver from the source. This we may do by distinguishing a range of possible events at the receiver, $r_1, r_2, \ldots r_m$, and considering the conditional probability, $p(s_i/r_j)$, that a given event, s_i, occurs at the source given that some event r_j occurs at the receiver. We can get an intuitive grasp on this idea by supposing that $p(s_3/r_1) = 1$. In this case, the occurrence of r_1 at the receiver is a perfect indicator of the occurrence of s_3 at the source. (Of course, s_3 might occur even though r_1 does not, but if r_1 occurs, then s_3 must have occurred at the source.) In this situation, occurrence of s_3 at the source is a "sure thing" given occurrence of r_1 at the receiver, so all the information $I(s_3)$ associated with the occurrence of s_3 at the source "arrives at" the receiver. The mathematical expression for the amount of information transmitted from source to receiver is a generalization of this idea—viz., that the amount of information transmitted is a function of how much of the information $I(r_j)$ associated with the occurrence of r_j at the receiver is due to (or can be accounted for in terms of)[18] the information $I(s_i)$ associated with the occurrence of s_i at the source. Following Dretske, I will call this quantity '$I_{s_i}(r_j)$'. Since the occurrence of r_j may show only a partial dependence on the occurrence of s_i (either because $p(s_i/r_j)$ is less than one, or because $p(\bar{s}_i/r_j)$ is greater than zero), $I_{s_i}(r_j)$ can be less than (but not greater than) $I(s_i)$. $I_{s_i}(r_j)$ is a measure of the amount of dependency between s_i and r_j, and this dependency may be less than perfect.

The amount of information associated with the occurrence of r_j that is not due to events at the source is called the noise; the amount of information available at the source that is not available at the receiver is called the equivocation. Thus

(2) $I_{s_i}(r_j) = I(r_j) - \text{noise} = I(s_i) - \text{equivocation}.$

To get an expression for $I_{s_i}(r_j)$, therefore, we need to develop one for noise and/or equivocation. This can be passed over here, however, because it is inessential to what follows.

Extending Information Theory: From Quantity to Content

In the preceding pages, I have, following Dretske, already given a nonstandard interpretation to the formulas (1) and (2) by treating them as giving expressions for the amount of information associated with particular events (including transmissions). Standard applications are concerned only with average information—i.e., only with the average amount associated with repeated occurrences of the events in question. But if we are to use the resources of Information Theory to explicate the notion of informational content, we must focus on particular events. This is simply because it makes sense to average the *amount* of information in two distinct messages, but not the *contents* of those messages.

In order to introduce the notion of informational content, we must drop our simple talk of events occurring at a source and speak instead of a source having or acquiring properties. Thus instead of $I(s_i)$, we will speak of $I(Fs)$, the information associated with the source having the property F. (We may think of the event s_i occurring, or the state of affairs s_i holding just in case the source s acquires, or has, the property F.) We may now ask of a signal r—i.e., some event at the receiver—whether it carries the information that s is F. Evidently, r cannot carry the information that s is F if $I_{Fs}(r)$ is less than $I(Fs)$, and since we can never have $I_{Fs}(r)$ greater than $I(Fs)$, it follows that r can carry the information that s is F only if $I_{Fs}(r) = I(Fs)$. Given this result, it follows further that r can carry the information that s is F only if $p(Fs/r) = 1$, for, if $p(Fs/r)$ is less than one, $I_{Fs}(r)$ will be less than $I(Fs)$.[19] Hence, Dretske is led to define informational content as follows: a signal r carries the information that s is F (i.e., has the informational content that s is F) iff $p(Fs/r) = 1$.[20]

Since statements of conditional probability are understood by Dretske to be expressions of objective fact—to hold or fail to hold whatever anyone, including the receiver, might believe about the matter—Dretske takes this definition to constitute a nonpsychological and nonepistemological explication of the notion of informational content. I concur.

From Informational Content to Semantic Content

The definition of informational content just rehearsed provides no warrant for talk of *the* information carried by r. For suppose it is a natural law that all F's are G's. Then, if $p(Fs/r) = 1$, $p(Gs/r) = 1$, since the law guarantees that $p(Gs/Fs) = 1$. Hence, if r has the informational content that s is F, it also has the informational content that s is G. Neither of these is *the* informational content of r. Yet a sentence or propositional attitude can plainly have the "content" that s is copper without having the "content" that s conducts electricity. Dretske uses the term 'semantic content' to distinguish this sense of 'content' from informational content.

To understand Dretske's definition of *semantic content,* we need a preliminary concept, the concept of one informational content being *nested* in another. The information that t is G is *nested* in s's being F iff s's being F carries the information that t is G (p. 71). Evidently, we will have the information that t is G nested in s's being F exactly when $p(Gt/Fs) = 1$. Any signal that carries the information that s is F will also carry whatever information is nested in s's being F, since if $p(Fs/r)$ is one and $p(Gt/Fs)$ is one, then $p(Gt/r)$ is one as well.

Using the concept of nesting, we can pick out in a natural way a unique semantic content of an event or state of affairs r from among all the infinity of informational contents of r—viz., that informational content of r (if it exists) that is itself not nested in any other informational content of r: the *semantic content* of r is that s is F iff (i) r has the informational content that s is F, and (ii) s's being F is nested in no other informational content of r. (p. 185)[21] There are a number of reasons for thinking that the informational content of r thus singled out as its semantic content is indeed what we should antecedently identify as r's semantic content, but canvassing these would take us too far afield. Still, the following consideration suggests that Dretske is on the right track: We identify the content of a sentence (or belief) with the explicit information it "carries"; information that can be *inferred* given knowledge of the laws of nature and logic is excluded, and this corresponds exactly to the exclusion from r's semantic content of the information nested in it.

Semantic Content and Propositional Interpretation

Dretske's proposal concerning semantic content suggests the possibility that a state sigma of a system S could have the content that t is F even though propositional interpretation of sigma as a token of 't is F' is not part of any interpretive functional analysis of a capacity of S. And conversely, it seems possible that an

interpretive functional analysis of some capacity of S might underwrite propositional interpretation of sigma as a token of 't is F'
even though t's being F is not the semantic content—or even an
informational content—of sigma. The question arises, therefore,
how far Dretske's notion of semantic content and my notion of
propositional interpretation coincide on cases—i.e., license the
same proposition-state correlations. This is a difficult and largely
empirical question; at this point, no one knows what propositional
interpretations will be underwritten by cognitive science, nor
which semantic contents will turn out to be realized in the brain.
In the next few pages, therefore, I will restrict myself to investigating a reason for supposing that the two notions might well turn out
to coincide on cases. I will then conclude this section by suggest-
ing one respect in which my approach provides a more fundamental characterization, and another respect in which Dretske's
approach is the more fundamental.

One reason for supposing that the interpretive approach I have
developed might coincide with the informational approach of
Dretske is this: if the flow of information into and through a cognitive system is what we describe, in whatever terms, when we
describe the cognitive encounters of such a system with its environment, then an interpretive functional analysis of a system's
cognitive capacities is bound to assign propositional interpretations in such a way as to illuminate the inferential connections
instantiated in that flow of information. If semantic contents
matter, then a good interpretive functional analysis should find
them.

But what if semantic contents don't matter? Couldn't there be
states of the human organism that *have* semantic contents, but
that such states (or their possession of such contents) are epiphenomenal with respect to human cognitive economy? I think this *is*
possible; I see no reason in principle why, for example, a barely
noticeable rash in certain people could not have the semantic
content 'The level of ultra-violet radiation exceeds t here', where
t is some particular numerical value. It is tempting to object that
the imagined rash couldn't have this semantic content, but why
not? It certainly isn't obvious that such a rash must have some
other informational content not already nested in the one pro-
posed. The information-flow approach assumes that there can

be structures in the brain with comparable semantic contents; there is surely no a priori reason to think there couldn't be such structures in the skin, nor any empirical evidence that I am aware of either. What there is considerable empirical evidence for is the claim that such things as skin rashes play no prominent or standard cognitive role. Hence, functional analysis will not underwrite propositional interpretation of skin rashes.

This sort of consideration is not a criticism of the informational approach: perhaps skin rashes just *do* have semantic contents. The fact (if it is one) that such semantic contents are cognitively idle doesn't show that they don't exist. What *is* suggested, however, is that only those semantic contents that are also underwritten by functional analysis will be worth bothering about. This is the sense in which the interpretive approach to content is more fundamental than the informational approach. We ignore skin rashes in favor of retinal events because we are convinced that information flow in the retina is cognitively significant. But we are convinced of this, not because the retina has semantic contents and skin rashes do not, but because we know retinal capacities figure in the analysis of cognition, whereas the capacity for skin rashes does not. Explanatory goals and pressures select which informational paths are worth interpreting. If this statement is on the right track, then we must qualify the claim that the informational approach coincides on cases with the interpretive approach: they coincide (at most) on the cases that matter. So far as I can see, only the interpretive approach could tell us which ones matter.

Thus, there is a sense—an epistemological sense perhaps—in which the interpretive approach is more fundamental than the informational approach. But *ontologically,* it seems the informational approach is the more fundamental. Semantic contents, as Dretske explains them, are *there* (if there are any) whatever anyone might think, whereas propositional interpretation depends essentially on what we find explanatory. An alien species of cognitive agents could be expected to agree with us on semantic contents, yet find our interpretive functional analyses opaque and/or unhelpful.

The ontological priority of semantic contents to propositional interpretations suggests that interpretive functional analysis should not assign propositional interpretations where there are no

corresponding semantic contents. It might be claimed that we
should not assign a state the content that s if F if it has a different semantic content, or no semantic content at all. I think we
should resist this claim, however. Perhaps the situation will not (or
cannot) arise, but if it does (or could), it seems to me that explanatory exigency should carry the day: we should interpret where,
when, and how interpretation is feasible and produces clear explanatory gain. To do otherwise is to assume without argument or
evidence that important inferential connections must involve a
rather special kind of information transfer and no other. For all
we know, information, in the special sense given this term by
Dretske's extension of Information Theory may not be involved
in certain inferential and cognitive connections at all, let alone
involved in the very special way exclusive focus on semantic contents would dictate. I would (personally) be surprised if good
analysis typically did not underwrite interpretations coinciding
with semantic contents, but scientific advance often surprises me.
Hunches are often good guides to research because they are often
the only alternative to unguided research, but hunches are not
often good guides to the truth.

  The interpretive account of semantic content that I favor, however, evidently allows for semantic content in many cases in which
Dretske's account does not. Suppose I sit down at my typewriter
and type an arbitrary sentence in English: *Aristotle had flat feet,*
say. The result is a paradigm case of something with "semantic
content," a token of a linguistic type. We may think of the sub-
strate—the thing that has semantic content—as a state of the paper,
viz., having the sentence printed on it. Now this state—call it S_A—
may carry no information at all about what the sentence is about
(Aristotle, flat feet), since there need be no causal route however
remote from Aristotle's having flat feet (if he did) to the paper being in S_A. Or, if one is inclined to insist on *some* causal route, it
certainly will not be the case that the conditional probability that
Aristotle had flat feet, given S_A, is one. Indeed, I don't know
whether Aristotle had flat feet or not, nor, I suppose, does anyone
else. But this is no bar to identifying the semantic content of S_A.
S_A has its semantic content, not in virtue of the information it
carries, but in virtue of the fact that speakers of English are parties
to conventions governing its communicative use. (Bennett, 1973;
Cummins and Dietrich, 1982). In short, it has a conventional in-

terpretation. Moreover, it is that interpretation a theorist must assign to S_A in order to have any serious hope of explaining the communicative capacities of speakers of English.

If S_A has a semantic content on the information theoretic account, I suppose it is something like, "Cummins wants to illustrate a point about semantic content." At least the conditional probability that Cummins wants to illustrate a point about semantic content, given S_A, would be one, and the nesting relationships appear about right. With care, we could surely cook up a case in which the interpretive and informational contents differed in just the way my example suggests.

The representational states of computers, like S_A, typically owe their semantic contents to interpretation, not to informational content, and for the same reasons: entering 'Aristotle had flat feet' into a data base is just getting the device into a state interpretable as representing the proposition that Aristotle had flat feet, just as typing the sentence on paper is getting the paper into a state interpretable as representing the same proposition. In both cases, the informational content may be unrelated to the appropriate interpretation.

How about the representational states of brains? Well, suppose you read the sentence I typed, and believe it. I suppose, if the result is a representational state of you (or your brain), its semantic content will have to do with Aristotle, not me. You may not even know that I typed the sentence, yet the "semantic content" assigned to your state by the informational account will feature me, not Aristotle, even though you may not know that I typed the sentence. So it seems that interpretation-motivated content will diverge from information-motivated content in some cases involving communcation at least, and that the former, not the latter, will be cognitively relevant.

Still, the informational account seems right for normal cases of perception. It is hard to believe that an interpretive analysis of perceptual capacities could attribute contents much different from those licensed by Dretske's account without going seriously astray. But this may simply be a kind of coincidence based on the fact that perception issues in a kind of representation that *in an evolved system,* can't be seriously wrong very often. Whenever, as in perception by an evolved system, representation is largely accurate, and largely representation of causally local facts, the two accounts

will not diverge radically. But perception by an artifact or a
damaged natural system, and other forms of cognition (and *cognition) in evolved systems, may be pretty wildly "creative," and then
the interpretive and informational accounts can be expected to
diverge widely.

Dretske does argue (chapter 8, esp., pp. 208–9) that an informational account can accommodate false belief. Roughly, the idea is
that an internal response-type r that normally has the semantic
content that s is F may be "triggered" by situations (internal and/or
environmental) that are similar to situations in which s is F, but
which don't involve s being F; a kind of internal stimulus generalization. In such a case, r will still have its usual functional role in
the cognitive (or *cognitive) economy of the system, which will
thus behave as if it had the information that s is F.

Perhaps this account can be made to work, but as it stands it
seems quite inadequate to deal with a wide variety of communicative cases involving fixation of belief on the basis of Grician
mechanisms. My telling you that s is F isn't similar in any nonquestion-begging sense to situations in which s is F. In addition,
there is a technical problem with the account. If the sort of stimulus generalization required by the account is possible, then we
have equivocation, and hence r could *never* have had the semantic
content in question. To avoid this difficulty, Dretske must assume
that stimulus generalization vis a vis r occurs only after r is well entrenched in the organism's cognitive economy. This seems wildly
ad hoc, and in any case, it is an empirical conjecture which is both
crucial to Dretske's account of false belief, and entirely unsup-
ported by any evidence or independent theoretical considerations.

III.3. INTENTIONALITY AND COGNITION

In section III.1 I talked freely of inferences and ration-
ales, and "figuring things out," but I was careful not to call
any of this cognition. *Cognition isn't cognition, I said, because
cognition is a propositional attitude, and exercise of a discursive capacity need be no such thing. (This isn't quite right: I think mere
exercise of a discursive capacity might be or entail a kind of belief,
but not the sort of belief that involves intentionality. I will return
to this point shortly.) But full-blooded cognitive characterization

is, at least often and paradigmatically, intentional characterization, and that is why I've cautiously been discussing only *cognition: intentional characterization is absent in the previous sections.

But perhaps the absence of intentional characterization from section III.1 isn't very conspicuous. After all, haven't I been attributing inferences to systems, and isn't 'S inferred that P' an intentional characterization of S? But I haven't been *attributing* inferences; I've been indulging in inferential interpretation. Inferential interpretation is not tantamount to intentional characterization. To suppose otherwise is to confuse (i) with (ii):

(i) S inferred that P

(ii) S has a capacity C manifestations of which are interpretable as conclusions, and P interprets an exercise of C.

I suppose (i) entails:

(iii) S believed that P,

but it is obvious that (ii) entails no such thing. Hence, to attribute discursive capacities to a system S is not equivalent to treating S as an intentional system.[22] As the difference between (i) and (ii) illustrates, the idiom of inferential attribution is less cumbersome than that of inferential interpretation. Substitution of (i) for (ii) is therefore practically inevitable. It is also harmless, provided we keep track of what we're doing. But the mere convenience of (i) does not justify taking it literally when (ii) will do, if only because (ii) is much easier to explicate than (i). Substituting (i) for (ii) can make it seem that conditions sufficient for inferential interpretation are sufficient for intentional characterization.[23] As a result, even "innocent" substitution of (i) for (ii) can create the appearance of a violation of the fundamental requirement that analyzed capacities should not reappear in the analysis. For instance, we might want to hold that intentionally characterized capacities are instantiated as systems of discursive capacities. If we refer to an exercise of a discursive capacity in the manner of (i) rather than (ii), we seriously misrepresent our claim, making it seem much more trivial than it really is: it makes all the difference between the strong claim that intentional capacities can be computationally instantiated and the nearly trivial claim that intentional capacities can be instantiated in an intentional system.

Inferential interpretation *is* semantic interpretation, of course: To treat C as the result of an exercise of an ICC in S is to interpret

C as a sentence-token. Here, C represents whatever it does *to us as theorists;* it has a meaning *for us; we* understand it, but the system needn't understand it: C needn't be understood by S; hence, C needn't represent anything for S. (Think of a slotted cog wheel in a mechanical calculator: *we* must see its having a certain position as a representation of a number in order to understand how the machine calculates, but the machine needn't see this to calculate.) In contrast, intentional characterization, such as attribution of propositional attitudes, involves representation *to* and *for* the system that has them. If I believe the Eiffel Tower is taller than I am, then I represent (to myself) the Eiffel Tower as taller than I.

The distinction between *semantic interpretation*—e.g., a propositional interpretation underwritten by an interpretive functional analysis—and *intentional characterization* is crucial to what follows, and this is something of an embarrassment: whereas semantic interpretation has already been explicated, I cannot explicate intentional characterization at this point except (i) negatively: attributing representations to a system, in the sense in which this means supposing that the system "understands" the representations attributed, clearly involves more than merely characterizing the states of a system via assigned representational contents; (ii) vaguely: the representations in question are representations for (or to) the system that has them, and not merely for (or to) a user or theorist; (iii) ostensively: when you say of someone, including yourself, "S is thinking that the bus will be late, and deciding whether to wait or take a taxi," you are doing more than merely characterizing the states of S via the representational content you must assign them to understand S's *cognitive capacities.

The wrong impression could be given by (iii): I don't mean to suggest that every attribution of a propositional attitude is a case of intentional characterization. In fact, I will argue shortly that many attributions of propositional attitudes do not involve intentionality at all, although the sentences that do the attributing are intensional.[24] And, of course, it must be kept in mind that I am stealing a word, 'intentional', to make a phrase, 'intentional characterization', that I do not intend to use in any familiar way. In particular, I am not assuming that an intentional characterization is just any characterization one makes with an intensional sentence. Though what I am calling intentional characterizations are often made by using an intensional sentence, I don't think this has any serious philosophical significance at all. As I use the term, to characterize a system intentionally is to do two things: it is to interpret the system, and it is to assume that the system stands in some rather special relation to the states interpreted in virtue of their contents, a relation I have indicated by saying that the system must, in some sense, "understand" the states in question. Whatever it is in virtue of which a system merits intentional characterization, I cannot believe it has anything important to do with the intensionality of the sentences typically used to do the characterizing. (cf. Searle, 1979.)

This initial sketch of the distinction between semantic interpretation (or propositional interpretation, as I shall often say instead, since that's usually what it is), and intentional characterization leaves a lot to be desired. Still, I think the distinction locates a critical issue about intentionality, or what some philosophers have called intentionality: could any sort of propositional interpretation, however justified, ever license literal intentional characterization? This is plainly what Searle is after in a recent widely debated article (Searle, 1980), and it is pretty obviously one of the main questions for functionalist accounts of the mind-body problem. Moreover, this way of raising the question of intentionality leaves open the role of subjectivity, rather than just putting it to one side, for it leaves open the possibility that intentional characterization, unlike propositional interpretation, presupposes a subjective point of view in the sense brought out by Nagel (1974): perhaps a representation cannot be a representation for or to a system that has no subjective point of view. There may be more to explicating intentionality than explicating what I am calling intentional characterization and its relation to propositional interpretation, but this is surely a large part of what is needed.

III.4. NARROWING THE PROBLEM

There is a familiar distinction of common sense and philosophy between beliefs that one has but is not currently aware of—"dormant beliefs" if you will—and beliefs that are "currently present to consciousness." A paradigmatic conscious belief is one you are now thinking about or aware of in some sense—e.g., your belief that you are now reading, or that what you are reading is in English and not printed in red ink. If you are making plans as you read, the beliefs involved in your planning probably count as conscious. For example, if you are planning to put on some coffee to help you stay awake, then your plan probably involves the belief that there is coffee in the kitchen.

Paradigmatic "dormant" beliefs are those you have but have never actually thought of—e.g., that crocodiles do not wear silk pajamas. But the set also includes beliefs you are not *now* thinking of but have thought of. Thus "dormant" belief, like conscious belief, is relative to time and subject. "Dormant" beliefs are supposed to be dispositional because having one is supposed to be a matter of having a disposition to have a conscious belief. Of course, one might have beliefs that are currently active in controlling one's behavior without being aware of them, or even being able to be aware of them. These would be neither dormant nor conscious. Hence, reflective common sense can be brought to embrace a pair of distinctions, that between conscious and unconscious belief and that between "dormant" and "active" belief. But while we can have active beliefs that are not conscious, it does not seem that we can have conscious beliefs that are not active. A conscious belief might be dormant with respect to overt behavior, but it seems it couldn't be psychologically dormant, for if it is conscious, it is presumably affecting the course and content of consciousness.

However this may be, it seems that an account of propositional attitudes, hence of intentionality, must take account of the facts underlying this pair of rough but familiar distinctions. The line I am going to take is close to this familiar common-sense line, but rather different in some respects. To get at it, we need a preliminary notion, the notion of an UNDERSTANDER. I use upper-case letters to emphasize that I am thinking of 'UNDERSTANDER' as a label for a box in a flow chart and not, except coincidentally, as a term for people who understand what they hear or read. I said above that intentional characterization involves the assumption that the system characterized "understands" its representational states, this being another way of getting at the idea that representation in an intentionally characterizable system—i.e., an intentional system—is representation *for* or *to* that system. I propose to call whatever does the "understanding" presupposed by intentional characterization the UNDERSTANDER. This might be the whole system (e.g., a person) or a part of it. It doesn't matter for now how the UNDERSTANDER is instantiated, the only crucial point being that we must suppose that UNDERSTANDING is instantiated somehow in any system that merits intentional characterization.

Now what does an UNDERSTANDER UNDERSTAND? By definition, a system's UNDERSTANDER must be capable of UNDERSTANDING (though perhaps not perfectly) the content of any intentional characterization that could be true of that system. So, if you could come to believe that the sky is falling, then (assuming that this is an intentional state of you) your UNDER-STANDER (which may be you for all I know) must be able to UNDERSTAND some relevant representation to the effect that the sky is falling. (This might be a sentence in the "Language of Thought," or a sentence in English, or an image (?), or something else—it won't matter for now.)

Now, of course, the UNDERSTANDER cannot, at any given time, be *actually* understanding more than a few propositional attitude contents. Call the propositional attitudes whose contents are under the purview of S's UNDERSTANDER at t S's *explicit* propositional attitudes at t. All S's other propositional attitudes at t are its *implicit* propositional attitudes at t. My contention is that an implicit propositional attitude isn't *actually* an intentional state at all, but only *potentially* so. The underlying idea is simple: since implicit propositional attitudes aren't being UNDERSTOOD, and might never be, attribution of an implicit propositional attitude isn't intentional characterization but only propositional interpretation.

Before pursuing this idea, it is worth clearing up a possible misunderstanding. Many theorists have seen the need for a distinction between *core* beliefs and derived or generated beliefs (e.g., Dennet, Field, Fodor, Lycan). A core belief is one whose content is explicitly stored—i.e., instantiated as a structure interpretable as a sentence giving the content of the belief. One's beliefs are then conceived as one's core beliefs plus their obvious consequences, or plus the consequences the system can generate from the core beliefs. I have no quarrel with this distinction, but it is important to realize that S's core beliefs may not coincide with S's explicit beliefs. For all I know, the implicit/explicit distinction and the core/

derived distinction cut across one another. Of course, the UNDER-STANDER, to do its stuff, must have a token representation to understand, so explicit representation is a necessary condition of being an explicit belief. But this needn't qualify an explicit belief as a core belief. Presumably, when a derived belief is derived from the core beliefs, part of what happens is that a representation is derived (and UNDERSTOOD), so the existence of an explicit representation is not sufficient for being a core belief. To be a core belief requires being one of the explicitly represented beliefs that the generator uses as premises. Evidently, a belief might have an explicit representation, even a rather permanent one, without having that role.

Although the core/derived distinction is not the explicit/implicit distinction, the former can help illuminate the latter by putting it into context, as illustrated.

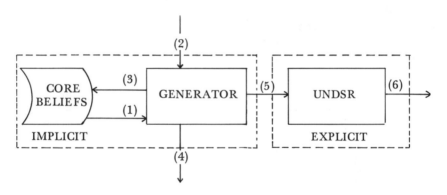

The generator produces representations of belief contents, either by generating consequences of core beliefs (1), or by generating consequences of other input (2) (e.g., perceptual, rational). Some of these may be stored as core beliefs (3). Others may be outputted to other parts of the system (4) (e.g., the perceptual system, the dream weaver, the affect repressor). Still others are output to the UNDERSTANDER (5). It is plausible to suppose this coincides with (but is not identical with) becoming conscious (perhaps the UNDERSTANDER is, or is part of, what Dennett calls the speech center, 1978, ch. 9), but this may be a mistake. In any case, the UNDERSTANDER connects with, or is part of, or just *is,* whatever it is in (or about) S that is properly analyzed in terms of explicit belief (6).

The thesis, put picturesquely, is just that only channels (5) and (6) carry the sort of stuff that requires intentional characterization; everything else is explicable without going beyond propositional interpretation, for nothing else presupposes that the representations have any role beyond the explanatory one involved in interpretive analysis. We shall shortly see reason to suppose that most of what is generally thought of as cognitive explanation requires only semantic interpretation, because it doesn't implicate the UNDERSTANDER.

If we are to take this thesis seriously, we must either stop calling implicit beliefs "beliefs," since attribution of an implicit "belief" isn't intentional characterization, or we must allow that some belief attributions don't involve intentional characterization but only propositional interpretation. I prefer the second alternative, which, I think, was an unnoticed corollary of the old distinctions anyway. Implicit belief just isn't an intentional state; it's a disposition to get into an intentional state. (Or rather: an implicit belief is instantiated as a state such that if you are in it, you are disposed to get into an intentional state the content of which is given by the sentence interpreting the state instantiating the implicit belief.) I can't help conjecturing that this rather obvious fact has been obscured by the intensionality of implicit belief attribution. But the intensionality of an attribution doesn't make the state attributed intentional. (We are not merely switching from the formal to material mode when we put a "t" for the "s.") Intentional characterization always assumes UNDERSTANDING; many intensional attributions do not. For example, consider

> S stores the information that George knows more about computers than chess.

This is an intensional attribution—i.e., a sentence whose attributing general term contains an intensional context. But evidently it isn't an intentional state that is attributed, for *this page is in the relevant state.*

The next step is to generalize the implicit/explicit distinction to propositional attitudes generally. It *might* be instructive to find out which, if any, of the usual verbs of propositional attitude yield only a degenerate form of the distinction—i.e., a case in which the implicit side is empty. "Judge that" is a plausible candidate, as is "have the thought that." A liberal distribution of such cases would indicate that the rudiments of the implicit/explicit distinction are already there in "ordinary language," for whatever that's worth. In any case, I will assume that the distinction can be applied across the board, and cover my tracks by allowing for degenerate cases. A cheap trick, no doubt, but nothing I want to say hangs on it, so far as I can tell.

Here is what we have so far:

1. The problem of intentionality—i.e., of intentional characterization—is a problem only for explicit propositional attitudes.

2. Psychological theory, therefore, need traffic in intentionality only insofar as it needs to traffic in explicit propositional attitudes.[25]

In the next section I will argue that much of what is generally thought of as cognitive explanation in psychology does not traffic in explicit propositional attitudes—i.e., much cognitive explanation does not involve intentional characterization. This is welcome, for we already have an account of the explanatory role of semantic interpretation, whereas, so far, we have no account at all of intentional characterization.

III.5. COGNITIVE EXPLANATION AND EXPLAINING COGNITION

A psychological theory might belong to cognitive psychology either because it is (1) a theory designed to explain a cognitive capacity,[26] or (2) a theory that explains a psychological capacity by appeal to cognitive subcapacities (or by appeal to instantiation in a cognitive system). Often it is both, for the best candidates for explanation by cognitive analysis are themselves cognitive capacities.

I think most of the explanatory successes of cognitive psychology are actually cases of *cognitive analysis, not cognitive analysis. Since *cognitive analysis is not obviously sufficient for the explanation of cognitive capacities, it should come as no surprise that the least controversial explanatory successes treat psychological capacities, or aspects of them, that are not cognitive. Of course, any capacity subject to *cognitive analysis is *cognitive, so if you are not careful about the *cognitive/cognitive distinction—and few are—successful *cognitive analysis will seem to reveal the cognitive character of prima facie noncognitive capacities. This is pretty seriously misleading. Really successful *cognitive analysis of a capacity often shows that it isn't cognitive at all. For example, *chess challenger's* capacity to play chess is revealed as *mere* *cognition when we see how that capacity is analyzed.

Illustration One: Shrinking After-Images

A visual after-image such as that produced by a flashbulb will be "seen as" a spot on a wall by a subject reasonably close to the wall (within five yards, say). If the subject approaches the wall, the spot appears to shrink, in spite of the fact that the relevant "spot" on the retina remains unchanged (and in spite of the fact that the subject knows this).

This capacity ("disposition" sounds better here) to see after-images as shrinking spots on approach I dub the capacity to shrink after-images, or "AI" for short. Here is an explanation. If there were a real spot on the wall, its image on the retina would expand on approach, unless the spot were itself shrinking. A real spot, shrinking at the right rate (i.e., as the square of the distance to the retina), would produce a retinal image of constant size. Since the retinal "(after-) image" remains constant in size, the subject sees a shrinking spot on approach. [27]

I find this explanation irresistible, so I will call it The Irresistible Explanation and simply assume that it is the (or a) correct explanation of the capacity to shrink after-images. The actual truth of The Irresistible Explanation doesn't matter much, it's the explanatory role of analyses like it that's at issue here: are they cognitive analyses or *cognitive analyses? Let's begin by trying to get clear about what The Irresistible Explanation requires us to assume.

The first point to note is that The Irresistible Explanation is *at least* *cognitive analysis, for it treats AI as an inferentially characterized capacity (ICC) *par excellence:* It interprets exercise of AI as an inference to the conclusion that the spot is shrinking from the premises that the retinal image is not shrinking and that the distance to the spot is decreasing.

Second, a tacit but important assumption is that the inference appealed to is a general procedure for determining apparent object size. What makes the Irresistible Explanation so appealing is just that it allows us to see AI as a special case of a much more general capacity: we can see that the reasoning invoked will generally get object size right but will fail in the case of an after-image. The Irresistible Explanation is plausible largely because it represents the shrinking after-image as the result of normal functioning.

Third, the inference is plainly not made consciously by the subject, for the subject knows there is no spot on the wall, and that the experience is an after-image. This information would plainly block the inference assumed by the Irresistible Explanation if it were "available."[28] Since the subject doesn't consciously infer that the spot is shrinking, we must assume one of the following:

1. The inference central to the Irresistible Explanation is made by something else—call it the subject's visual system—that does not have (or can't use) the information the subject has.
2. The inference is made by the subject unconsciously,[29] and this somehow insulates it from consciously available information.
3. The inference isn't "made" at all in the sense in which this involves intentional characterization; AI is a *mere* discursive capacity no input to which is interpretable as the inference blocking information known to the subject.

The fourth point to be made about the Irresistible Explanation is that it assumes that exercise of AI does require information about the distance to the wall/spot, about changes in size of retinal images via patterns of retinal stimulation, and about the relation of image size to object size and distance (viz., that image size is proportional to object size and inversely proportional to the square of the distance). None of this need be covered by any of the subject's explicit beliefs.

Fifth point: according to the Irresistible Explanation, the after-image is treated as (assumed to be, taken to be, seen as) a spot on the wall, (a) in spite of the subject's explicit belief to the contrary, and (b) in spite of the fact that the spot's location "on the wall" varies with eye movement. (a) means that the belief (if that's what it is) that there is a spot on the wall is implicit at best. (b) means that AI is insulated not only from the subject's explicit beliefs, but from a good deal of important and standardly utilized visual information as well. AI begins to look rather like a tropism; a *cognitive tropism.

Sixth point: the Irresistible Explanation assumes that what the subject sees is a function of the conclusion that the visual system (or whatever instantiates AI) produces. This is generally the hardest part to swallow, but it shouldn't be. The Irresistible Explanation doesn't pretend to explain the capacity for visual experience. It explains only why visual experience has certain features under certain circumstances—namely, why the after-image shrinks. It is entirely silent on what it is to *have* an after-image, or a shrinking after-image. The Irresistible Explanation explains why and how the visual system (or whatever) winds up with the information that the after-image is shrinking, but says nothing about how that information gets manifested as a visual experience. Since we have no idea at all what to say about this matter, it is tempting to say that it can't happen. "How could a conclusion—at a subpersonal level at that—produce (or be?) any aspect of a visual experience?" we ask rhetorically. The only answer, I think, is that no one knows how to answer this question, but AI, as Irresistibly Explained, shows that it *does* happen somehow.[30] So the Irresistible Explanation really contains two distinct steps. Step *two* explains after-image shrinkage as a function of a conclusion. This is unblushing deficit spending. Step *one* explains the disposition to draw the relevant conclusions.

The Irresistible Explanation thus reverses the empiricist strategy of explaining "seeing that" in terms of simple seeing, and that's what makes it a cognitive explanation of a visual capacity: it represents AI as an implicitly *cognitive/cognitive capacity. This strategy has been advocated by Gregory (1970, 1980, 1981) for many years. Percepts are hypotheses, according to Gregory; hence, to explain perceptual capacities is to explain cognitive capacities. This cannot be quite right, for it ignores step *two*. A more cautious claim is that *cognitive analysis explains why percepts represent what they do (e.g., shrinking spots) rather than something else.

With these five points in mind, let's return to our problem: Does the Irresistible Explanation involve intentional characterization, or is it merely propositional interpretation? By now, it should be clear that intentional characterization enters the picture only in phase two. Phase one invokes no explicit beliefs. Indeed, a striking fact about AI is the extent to which it is unaffected by explicit beliefs. Moreover, the premises of the inference invoked by the Irresistible Explanation evidently need not figure among even the implicit beliefs of the subject, let alone among the explicit beliefs. Phase one is a straightforward case of interpretive analysis.

We can make the point more obvious by expressing the analysis of phase one as a simple flow-chart, P-1, and imagining P-1 executed by the subsystem vs-1 of the visual system. Since vs-1 executes P-1, we can see why outputs of vs-1 will be sentences specifying appropriate size changes, hence why the visual experiences of the subject will represent (to the subject) the size changes they do rather than some others. This is all the Irresistible Explanation explains, and this much is evidently available at the level of propositional interpretation. Of course, it is obvious that phase two does involve intentional characterization, but we have no explanation of phase two. Hence, whatever explanatory progress is made, is made at the level of propositional interpretation.

One example does not a thesis prove, of course, and this example is pretty trivial. Still, there is a valuable lesson to be learned from this case. Cognitive explanation often exhibits the two-phase structure implicit in the Irresistible Explanation. Phase one is a *cognitive analysis of a *cognitive capacity—an ICC—and phase two is the claim that some intentionally characterized capacity has some of the features it does because the system having that capacity instantiates the analysis detailed in phase one. Phase two is always a promissory note in this (excellent) ploy. It is this ploy that allows cognitive psychology to make progress in the absence of any theory of intentional characterization: cognitive psychology can proceed without an account of intentional characterization because it is *cognitive psychology plus promissory note.

Illustration 2: Grammar and Psycholinguistics

The capacity to use and assess[31] a language is analyzed by Chomsky (1980) into three faculties: (i) the Language Faculty, which provides syntactic and phonological analyses (structural descriptions) and relates these to representations of meaning (pp. 28-29); (ii) a conceptual system, which "involves the system

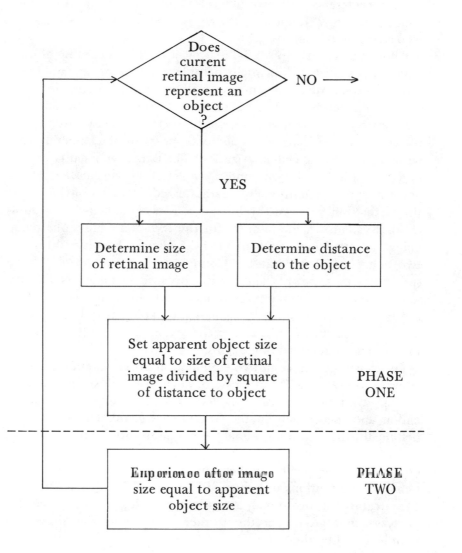

P-1: The Irresistible Explanation in flow-chart form

of object reference and also such relations as 'agent,' 'goal,' 'instrument,' . . ." (p. 22); and (iii) the use system, which performs and recognizes speech acts.

Chomsky suggests (pp. 23–25) that a system consisting of only components (ii) and (iii) might be able to communicate and enter into communicative conventions. Call this [i.e., (ii) and (iii)] the Communication System. Gricean characterizations of the Communication System (and what else is there?) are heavily intentional. By contrast, the Language Faculty appears to be characterizable without intentional characterization. The Language Faculty cranks out structural descriptions, and these determine certain features of performance as intentionally characterized. It seems obvious that the distinction between the Language Faculty and the Communication System is made to order for the Two-Phase Ploy, phase one being an interpretive analysis of the Language Faculty and phase two being the claim that the Communication System is able to spot syntactic ambiguity and the like because the Language Faculty is interpretable as a grammar-cruncher.[32] Looked at this way—and I don't see any other—psycholinguistic explanation is analogous to the Irresistible Explanation: the explanation ends where the intentional characterization begins.

Obviously not all cognitive explanation avoids intentional characterization. A paradigmatic case of cognitive analysis that doesn't even pretend to avoid it is provided by the literature on communication and speech acts in the Grice-Lewis genre. The whole idea behind this literature is to analyze communicative and speech-act capacities into utterance capacities and intentional capacities, especially the capacity to have intentions and to recognize the beliefs and intentions of others.[33] The Great Cognitivist Dream is to integrate propositional attitude psychology with *cognitive analysis, thus grounding the former, and paying the phase two debt incurred by the latter.

III.6. INTENTIONALITY: SEMANTIC INTERPRETATION AND INTENTIONAL CHARACTERIZATION

What is it to "give an account" of intentionality? What I should *like* is to relate intentional characterization to semantic interpretation in something like the way I've already related semantic interpretation to physical description. (This is what I taxed Dennett for not doing in my review of *Brainstorms*, 1981.) When we build an adding machine, what we do is realize a physical description D such that any system satisfying D instantiates an addition algorithm—i.e., such that any system satisfying D merits a certain semantic interpretation. Slogging through a problem like this enables us to understand how the physical facts—i.e., the facts seen through the lenses of a noninterpretive vocabulary—can make a semantic interpretation true and appropriate.

I think we would feel we understood intentionality, or at least understood its explanatory role, if we could come to see how the facts seen through the lenses of semantic interpretation (or something else not involving intentional characterization) can make an intentional characterization true and appropriate. This would not *reduce* intentional characterization to semantic interpretation, any more than we have reduced semantic interpretation to noninterpretive characterization, but reduction was never a serious possibility here, any more than it was for semantic interpretation.

Of course, there is no guarantee that this sort of explication of intentional characterization is possible any more than a reduction is possible. Many philosophers and scientists have held that intentional characterization is autonomous, not only in the weaker sense, in which this means that a reduction to the nonintentional is not possible, but also in the stronger sense, in which this means that even the sort of nonreductive explication I've suggested is impossible.

Actually, we can distinguish a strong and weak version of the program I've suggested.

> Strong Thesis: intentional characterization can be explicated via semantic interpretation, i.e., an intentionally characterized capacity can be instantiated as an information-processing system—e.g., a system of discursive capacities.

> Weak Thesis: intentional characterization can be explicated via some nonintentional concepts—i.e., an intentional capacity can be instantiated as a nonintentionally characterized system.

Denial of the weak thesis is, I take it, a form of dualism. To deny the weak thesis is to hold that there can be no instantiation of an intentional capacity; for to deny the weak thesis is to hold that sufficient conditions for intentional characterization cannot be stated in nonintentional language. This is equivalent to the mystery theory of intentionality, and I will therefore dismiss it—not because mystery is impossible, but because there's nothing to say about it.

The strong thesis is another matter. What makes the strong thesis so strong is the fact that just about any heap of junk is subject to semantic interpretation. Since hardly anything merits intentional characterization, the strong thesis entails that intentionality must, finally, be a matter of the complexity of the junk: something merits intentional characterization when it merits an especially ritzy semantic interpretation. This is hard to swallow because:

1. It seems to put systems having explicit propositional attitudes on a continuum with AND-gates;

2. It amounts to the claim that more and more representation for *us* will eventually be representation for *something else*—the subject of the intentional characterization.

So the strong thesis is hard to swallow. Yet I think we had better try hard to swallow it, and digest it too, because, to echo Fodor, there just isn't any other definite proposal in the offing.

The strong thesis is equivalent to the claim that intentionally characterized capacities are instantiated as capacities to execute information-processing programs. In the current jargon: intentionally characterized capacities are computationally instantiated. Computationalism is hard to swallow, as we've seen, but it is equally hard to spit out. The only alternatives are dualism, which is not an alternative theory but the claim that theory is impossible, and "neuronalism"—i.e., the doctrine that intentionally characterized capacities are realizable only as neurophysiological capacities.[34] Neuronalism strikes many as implausible precisely because it ties intentionality essentially to the chemistry-physics of the brain: it just seems a longer step from neurophysiology to intentional characterization than from semantic interpretation to intentional characterization. I cannot program explicit belief, and neither can anyone else, but if I had to write the program in the language of neurophysiology, I wouldn't even know how to begin. This doesn't tell against the truth of neuronalism, but it does tell against its viability as a research strategy. For me, anyway: I just haven't any neuronalist ideas to pursue, and I suspect the relative unpopularity of neuronalism is due to others finding themselves in a similar state. Henceforth, I shall adopt the strong thesis as a working hypothesis, exploring its consequences and mitigating its weaknesses.

III.7. COMPUTATION AND INTENTIONAL CHARACTERIZATION

In this section I will canvass five strategies for defending the strong thesis—i.e., five strategies for promoting semantic interpretation into intentional characterization. None of the five is successful, but they are not trivial either; there is something to be learned by getting clear about how each goes wrong. Moreover, I think that most discussion in the literature of the thesis I am calling the Strong Thesis focuses on one or more of these five strategies, though I won't try to document this claim.

First Strategy: Analyzing Homunculi

Intentional analysis—analyzing a capacity into intentionally characterized capacities—has been dubbed homunctionalism by William Lycan (1981). It's a good name: the idea is that when we appeal in analysis to an intentionally characterized capacity, we appeal to a characteristically human capacity; hence, appeal to such capacities is like postulating a little person in one's head. My UNDERSTANDER is obviously an homunculus in this sense, as are the capacities to recognize the communicative intentions of speakers assumed in Gricean analyses of communication. The methodological probity of homunctionalism has been defended by Dennett (1978) and Lycan as follows. There is nothing wrong with ringing in homunculi as long as they don't "duplicate entire the talents they are rung in to explain" (Dennett, 1978, p. 124), for we can keep replacing our homunculi with committees of dumber and dumber homunculi until we are left with homunculi so stupid they can be "replaced by a machine"—i.e., are so stupid that they have known computational instantiations.

This move creates the appearance of promoting computational capacities (semantic interpretation) into intentionally characterized capacities (intentional characterization) by confusing two distinct problems. One problem is the analytical explanation of intelligence. There is every reason to believe that intelligence is explicable by *cognitive analysis: an intelligent system is a well-organized army of (nonintentional) idiots. But the homunculi are out of place here: explaining intelligence is a matter of analyzing sophisticated discursive capacities; intentional characterization is quite beside the point.

Homunctionalism as a doctrine about intelligence is a case of substituting the convenient idiom of inferential attribution for the cumbersome idiom of inferential characterization: the homunculi aren't real ones. This is harmless, I said, as long as one doesn't forget what one is doing.

The simple move that works with intelligence won't work with intentionality, for, unlike intelligence, intentionality isn't a matter of degree. If we have real homunculi—i.e., intentionally characterized capacities—making them dumber won't make them less intentional, and making a system smarter won't make it intentional. Homunctionalism as a theory of intentional characterization may yet succeed—that's the strong thesis in one form—but it is a mistake to take the defense of fake homunculi in the analysis of intelligence as a defense of real homunculi in the analysis of intentionally characterized capacities. For when it comes to real homunculi, we have no idea how to achieve the crucial last step: we don't know how to computationally instantiate a real homunculus, however stupid, or even if such instantiations are possible.

Intentionally characterized capacities can be explained by analysis into other intentionally characterized capacities. But the analyzing capacities will not be less intentional than the analyzed capacity. The most we can hope for from this strategy is that the strong/weak thesis will ultimately have to face only a small number of noncomplex cases that are the primitive building blocks for intentionally characterized capacities generally. Thus the capacity to plan is plausibly analyzed into the capacity to believe and to intend. Further analysis of these would be welcome (don't hold your breath, though), but ultimately we must look to instantiation: analysis will only identify the critical targets.[35]

Second Strategy: Intensions and Intentional Characterization

A very common idea about intentionality is that intentional states are just representational states, states with (usually propositional) contents. On this view, if we could just understand what it is for a state of a system to *represent*—e.g., to represent grass as green or the Fountain of Youth as in Florida—we would understand intentionality. (This idea seems to be at work in Dretske, 1981, and sometimes seems to influence Fodor, e.g., in 1980.) It's a plausible idea. The paradigmatic cases of intentional characterization are attributions of propositional attitude, e.g.:

(1) Cummins believes that intensionality is a red herring.

A very natural and perhaps correct assumption about (1) is that it asserts a relation between a person and a representational state of that person having the content *intensionality is a red herring*. This much, I think, is on the right track. It is tempting, however, to go on to think of the representational state *as the belief*—i.e., to think of the belief as something Cummins *has,* viz., the representational state—rather than thinking of the belief as the *relation* between Cummins and the representational state. If one goes on in this way, the intentionality attributed in (1) will seem to lie in the representational state itself, rather than in the relation to it, for the intentionality surely lies in the belief, and this has been identified with the representational state. Hence, the problem takes this form: what is it about representational states such as belief that makes them intentional? Once one has got to this point, the only available suggestion appears to be that intentionality is a matter of how the representing is "done," how the state refers, as it were. In short, the intentionality of belief seems to resolve itself into the semantics of belief. Since 'believes' introduces an intensional context, the problem becomes that of explaining how a representational state could be intensional.

Perhaps the line of reasoning just sketched is not the only route (or even very common) to the conclusion that the problem of intentionality is just the problem of mental representation, the conclusion that we will understand intentionality when we understand how a state of a brain (or computer) could have a propositional content. But it is *a* route to that conclusion, a route, moreover, that repays study. (Often the conclusion is simply assumed, or inherited from predecessors, but that sort of route doesn't repay study.) I have already indicated why I think the conclusion should be avoided: explaining how a state of a system can represent is only half the story; we must also explain what it is for a representational state to be a representation for the system that has it. The point here is not whether to avoid the conclusion, but how. And the answer is not far to seek. The trouble starts when we suppose that the belief is the representational state rather than the relation to it asserted by the likes of (1). Once this move is made, the intentionality of belief is bound to be identified with the intensionality of the representation, for the belief and the representational state have been identified. If we suppose instead that belief is a relation to a representational state, we are free to separate questions about the semantics of mental states from questions about intentionality, hence free to suppose, for example, that UNDERSTANDING the representation is as crucial as the fact that there is some representation to be understood.

Third Strategy: Behaviorism

When we have a true intentional characterization, we have a system that UNDERSTANDS some of its own representations, for that is surely the point of saying that the system's representations are representations *for it.* Let us call a system that can UNDERSTAND some of its own representations an intentional system.[36] Our working hypothesis (the Strong Thesis) is that intentional systems are computationally realizable; that is, there is a computational description of the system—an interpretive functional analysis—satisfaction of which is sufficient to make the system an intentional system.

I have been talking all along of UNDERSTANDING representations, for that is the heart of the matter, but, clearly, a system that UNDERSTANDS its own computations is also an intentional system. Although it seems that UNDERSTANDING a computation must boil down to, or at least involve, UNDERSTANDING the representations manipulation of which constitutes the computation, the strategy I want to discuss is brought out more clearly by focusing on computations. UNDERSTANDING a computation is UNDERSTANDING representations in the context of doing something else, hence is a case in which immediate systematic context might enforce some constraints on what UNDERSTANDING amounts to.

Let's begin by understanding UNDERSTANDING as plain old understanding. What do *I* understand when *I* understand a computation? For example, when I do a truth-tree for *modus ponens,* I do a computation I understand, but a student may do the same computation and not understand it: Wherein lies the difference between us?

1. I know, but S does not, that every branch ends with an 'x' iff instances of the schema are valid.

2. I know, but S does not, why the biconditional in (1) holds.

(2) is too stiff: it rules out most first-semester logic students, and an analogous requirement will rule that most people don't understand long division. (1) seems about right: if I know that every branch ends in 'x' iff instances of the schema are valid, I can *use* the computation because I know what to conclude from the various outcomes. A similar remark applies to long division.

Weak as it is, (1) is, *prima facie,* still too strong, for (1) *intentionally* specifies a condition for understanding a computation. We might try to wriggle out of this by claiming (with Wittgenstein?) that *knowing that* the tree closes iff instances of the schema are valid is a matter of *knowing how* to use the tree method to test inferences; that this in turn is a matter of being disposed to display behavior conditional on inference validity; and finally that having this disposition is a matter of executing a program, P. If there is a standard way of solving the problem, I suppose this is it. I will call it the Standard Solution.

A curious feature of the Standard Solution is that it reverses the typically mentalist gambit of explaining knowing how in terms of knowing that. Indeed, the Standard Solution is philosophical behaviorism of sorts, for it holds that understanding a computation is at bottom a behavioral capacity, with the addition that the behavioral capacity in question is computationally instantiated. Since every version of computationalism I can think of is committed in one way or another to something similar, it is important to get clear just how behaviorism enters into the Standard Solution. There are four steps: (i) understanding a computation is equated with knowing what the point of the computation is; (ii) knowing what the point of the computation is is equated with knowing how to use the computation; (iii) knowing how to use the computation is equated with being able to use the computation; and (iv) being able to use the computation is explained as program execution—i.e., via computational instantiation.

Step (iv), though empirically serious, is conceptually straightforward: explaining behavioral capacities is what programs do best. Step (i) is a bit more controversial. Still, there is a long tradition of explaining understanding as knowledge—e.g., understanding a word is knowing what it means. Whatever the defects of this move, it plays no tricks with intentionality. The main problem with step (i) is deciding which knowledge goes with which understanding. If this were the most serious problem facing the Standard Solution, computationalism wouldn't even be controversial.

Steps (ii) and (iii) are the heart of the matter, for they are plainly *reductionist*. Taken together, (ii) and (iii) replace an apparently intentional characterization by a nonintentional one, and therefore embody the claim that, e.g., 'S knows that the tree closes iff instances of the schema are valid' doesn't intentionally characterize S at all! I'm not sure this is impossible, but I *am* sure that making the reductionist claim embodied in (ii) and (iii) plausible will undermine confidence in (i): if the knowledge-that attribution in (i) isn't intentional characterization, (i) loses its plausibility. This tension in the Standard Solution doesn't demonstrate its falsehood, but it does demonstrate its explanatory bankruptcy. Implementing the Standard Solution will inevitably leave us wondering what we've achieved, and that is just the sort of doubt a good philosophy of psychology should resolve.

The most obvious failing of the Standard Solution is its reductionism. A plausible solution will not eliminate intentional idiom, but rather explain how satisfaction of a computational description can guarantee satisfaction of an intentional description, while leaving intentional description more or less autonomous in the way that we left information-processing description (and functional description generally) autonomous.

The reductionism of the Standard Solution is not just implausible: There is also a deeper problem. Our explication of semantic interpretation involves an essential appeal to intentional characterization. A system is an adder, I said, just in case the numerals interpreting outputs represent sums of the numbers represented by the numerals interpreting inputs. The crucial phrase here is, "the numerals . . . represent sums": to whom? To the theorist, of course. Given the general strategy of explaining linguistic reference via speaker reference, we are committed to explaining numeral reference by appeal to intentional characterization. So semantic interpretation is explained via intentional characterization, and computationalism attempts to explain intentional characterization in terms of semantic interpretation. This isn't a vicious circle, even on the face of it, since intentional characterization of S is explained by appeal to intentional characterization of T (theorist). This is quite consistent with computationalism, but it isn't consistent with *reductive* computationalism. At the very least, a reductive computationalism must abandon the strategy of explaining 'symbol s refers to r' via 'subject S refers to r' and that would be to abandon most of the real progress that has been made on the problem of reference.

We must eschew reductionist computationalism, then. But it is curiously difficult to recognize nonreductionist solutions. If we haven't *eliminated* use of intentional characterization, the suspicion will remain that we haven't explained it from a nonintentional perspective. We want a computational description D_C of S satisfaction of which will guarantee satisfaction of an intentional description, D_I.[37]

But how are we to verify the guarantee? If I provide a D_C and a D_I, how do you decide whether satisfaction of D_C guarantees satisfaction of D_I? Reduction would provide a clear sufficient condition, for then we could deduce D_I from D_C: if D_C entails D_I, then satisfaction of D_C guarantees satisfaction of D_I. Reduction is plainly not in the cards, however, so we need another criterion of success.[38] I think this is part of why the problem is so hard. We all know reductionism isn't going to work, but abandoning it leaves us fresh out of clear criteria by which to judge of success or failure. So reductionism keeps creeping in by the back door.

*Fourth Strategy: Intentional Characterization is to
Semantic Interpretation as Semantic Interpretation
is to Physical Description*

Actually, we might get D_C to entail D_I without reduction. This is
how we establish that an information-processing capacity is physically instantiated. Let D_p be a physical description of S, and D_f be
an information processing description. If both are expressed in
program form, then

> (1) S satisfies D_f (i.e., executes D_f) if S executes D_p and
> D_f is isomorphic to D_p.

This will allow us to deduce satisfaction of D_f from satisfaction of
D_p (and isomorphism), but will not license a reduction. We can
even get a necessary and sufficient condition for satisfaction of D_f:

> (2) S satisfies D_f iff there exists a D_p such that S executes
> D_p and D_f is isomorphic (within idealization) to D_p.

(2) gives us a necessary and sufficient condition for the truth of
a functional description of S, for variable S, and the condition uses
no functional language. But (2) is certainly not a reduction of the
functional to the nonfunctional, for the condition supplied provides no hope of specifying a nonfunctional natural kind term
of physics (or anything else) satisfaction of which is necessary and
sufficient for satisfaction of a functional description.[39] What (2)
provides is an explication of instantiation/execution for functionally analyzed capacities.

It would be helpful to come up with an explication analogous
to (1) and (2) for intentional descriptions—i.e., with an explication
of instantiation for intentionally characterized capacities. I think
many workers in artificial intelligence tacitly or explicitly assume
that something strictly analogous to (2) will do the trick, e.g.,

> (3) S satisfies D_I if there exists a computational descrip-
> tion D_C such that S satisfies D_C and D_I is (within
> idealization) isomorphic to D_C.[40]

(2), especially when it is carefully distinguished from (3), is uncontroversial *modulo* fine details of formulation, hence provides us
with a way of deciding whether S satisfies a functional description
in virtue of satisfying a physical description. (3) can't play this
role, however. Suppose I have a program D_I written in intentional
language. D_I has instructions such as

(i) If you believe P, and want G, do A.

The computational isomorph will say something like,

(ii) If P is stored in B, and G is stored in W, then execute E_A.

Now the only thing that could make us think that storing P in B is believing P would be the discovery that (ii) instantiates (i), and that's just the issue. We have a kind of open-question argument here: given that D_I is isomorphic to D_C, and given that S executes D_C, it still makes sense to ask whether S executes D_I. The analogous question doesn't make sense for D_f and D_p. Thus, even if (3) or something like it is true (which I doubt), it isn't obvious enough a priori to have the sort of normative force (2) has.

Philosophical reflection establishes (2), but not (3)—at least not yet—and the prospects look dim. I think that the prospects are dim for a *philosophical* defense of *any* explication of instantiation that will allow us to deduce satisfaction of D_I from satisfaction of D_C. Not that such an explication isn't possible: I think it is possible. But no one knows what it will look like. As of right now, D_C is not going to entail D_I via some philosophically defensible explication of intentional system instantiation, so we need another solution—a kind of *pro tem* solution—to the problem of deciding whether a given D_C instantiates a given D_I.

Strategy Five: An Experimental Defense

The only remaining possibility for defending a computational instantiation of an intentionally characterized capacity is an experimental defense. We've ruled out

(A) reductionism (as false);

(B) a philosophical explication of instantiation that will license derivation of D_I from D_C (as currently unavailable).

So far as I can see, this exhausts the a priori possibilities. What's left is:

(C) An experimental demonstration that systems satisfying D_C are very like systems satisfying D_I—i.e., very like people.

This is the sense in which, for now, computationalism is "behavioristic": it must rely on similarity of behavior to infer instantiations which, lacking (B), it cannot claim to understand. There is bound to be strong pressure, visible in contemporary cognitive science, to cover up the lack of understanding by taking the behavioral similarity to be criterial for instantiation, thus reverting to (A). There are powerful forces behind the Standard Solution.

If this is on the right track, then our problem is to determine what sort of experimental results would most support the strong thesis.

I argued in Section III.1 that we will be forced to see *cogitation when we find a capacity that cannot be characterized except by specifying a rationale. An analogous move here would go as follows. Consider a capacity whose analysis is essentially intentional—e.g., the capacity to communicate as this is understood in the Gricean tradition, or, more generally, the capacity to enter into a Lewis-type tacit convention. Now suppose we devise a computational program P whose instantiations communicate or enter into tacit conventions. Then we shall have to conclude either that a device executing P merits intentional characterization, or that communication isn't essentially intentional. Of course we could also say that P-executors, being merely computational, don't really communicate, but merely imitate communicators.

Generalizing from the example, we have three possible lines of interpretation. Given that systems executing a computational program P simulate systems (persons) exercising an intentionally characterized capacity C, we may:

(i) conclude that systems executing P merit intentional characterization;

(ii) conclude that C isn't really intentional—that the intentional characterization of C is a case of substituting the convenient idiom of intentional characterization for the cumbersome idiom of semantic interpretation;

(iii) Conclude that the simulation is mere imitation on the grounds that mere computation couldn't be understanding a representation or a computation.

Evidently (iii) begs the question unless it can be independently established. In the absence of sound arguments for (iii), we should stick to (i) and (ii). (I shall consider whether there are any independent grounds for (iii) in the next section.)

But how to decide between (i) and (ii)? In Section III.1 we faced an analogous problem: when a symbol cruncher simulates something with a discursive capacity, are we to conclude (a) that the discursive capacity is instantiated as the symbol cruncher, or (b) that the target capacity isn't really a discursive capacity? The solution was to ask whether the symbol cruncher was the rationale "in disguise": if it is, then we pick (a); if not, we pick (b). This made sense since there is a clear criterion for answering the question: the cruncher is the rationale in disguise if they are isomorphic (within idealization). But here the analogy breaks down. D_C cannot be D_I "in disguise." Any reason to think this would be a better reason for supposing D_I not genuinely intentional.[41] If, therefore, we try to settle on (i) or (ii) by asking whether D_C is D_I in disguise, we shall always have to pick (ii). If D_C *is* D_I in disguise, D_I isn't intentional; if D_C *isn't* D_I in disguise, then the excellence of simulation demonstrates that the target capacity needn't be described in intentional terms. Opting for (ii) every time—i.e., on principle—is plainly perverse because it makes the existence of intentionality turn on the failure of simulation.[42] We were spared this problem in Section III.1 because a symbol-crunching program can be a rationale specification in disguise, for symbol crunching can sometimes be interpreted as the steps of a rationale. But reinterpretation will not make a semantic interpretation into an intentional characterization; it will just create a new semantic interpretation.

So how are we to decide whether (i) or (ii) is the correct interpretation of a given simulation? Perhaps all philosophy can do here (for now) is point out that (ii) can't always be right. The truth of intentional characterizations doesn't entail the impossibility of computational simulation.[43] If (i) is sometimes the right interpretation, then (always assuming (iii) can be eliminated) we could have experimental evidence for the strong thesis via experimental evidence for particular computational instantiations of intentionally characterized capacities.

Nevertheless, an experimental demonstration would leave the demonstrated instantiations empty of deep explanatory power. We would know *that* intentional capacity C_I is instantiated as computational capacity C_C in S, but we wouldn't know *how* that could be the case. Formally, we wouldn't be able to derive the characteristic transition law specifying C_I from that specifying C_C together with other facts about S, and this would block explanation of C_I in S. We have a theory—a philosophical explication—of instantiation for information-processing capacities. That theory tells us what it is for such capacities to be instantiated, and this is why we can explain a capacity of that type by specifying its instantiation. The theory explains, in advance, how a system of flip-flops *could* be an adder, leaving only the details—which flip-flop systems are which adders—to be settled on a case-by-case basis. We have no comparable theory of instantiation for intentionally characterized capacities. Lacking such a theory, computationalism will fail as an explanatory strategy even if its truth is experimentally beyond serious doubt. I think the experimental evidence is already significant, if not overwhelming. It seems quite possible that we will shortly be in the position of knowing that the strong thesis is probably true without having more than the vaguest idea of how that is possible. Such situations have been frequent in the history of science, and they have, in retrospect, turned out to be symptomatic of conceptual poverty. One can only hope that in the process of devising computational systems that simulate intentional capacities, we will develop concepts that will allow formulation of a defensible theory of instantiation for intentional capacities. Until then, our textbooks will have to be content with such statements as this: You can (explicitly) believe because your brain can compute, but no one yet understands this fact, and perhaps no one ever will.

Let's pause to consolidate. The strong thesis requires some way of defending claims to the effect that an intentionally characterized capacity is computationally instantiated. Reduction of intentional capacities to computational capacities would do the trick by allowing us to deduce an intentional description D_I from a computational description D_C. But reductionism is blocked by the possibility of diverse instantiations. An explication of instantiation for intentionally characterized capacities would also do the trick by allowing us to deduce D_I from D_C, but no such explication is available. Finally, an experimental defense might be possible, but the relevant experiments will be seriously ambiguous: given good computational simulation of an intentionally characterized system, we shall be left wondering whether we have computationally instantiated an intentionally characterized capacity, or demonstrated that the target capacity isn't really intentional. It would be perverse to hold out for the debunking interpretation on principle, for that would make the existence of intentionality turn on the failure of simulation. But accepting the first interpretation supports the strong thesis without conferring any explanatory power on its applications. Without an explication of instantiation for intentionally characterized capacities, computational systems will not explain the intentional capacities they instantiate. We can only hope that in the process of devising good computational simulators of intentional systems, we will develop concepts adequate to formulating the needed explication.

III.8. THE CHINESE ROOM

In this section I want to examine the prospects for a philosophical explication of the concept of instantiation for intentionally characterized capacities. My stalking horse will be Searle's Chinese room argument (1980). I think this argument does not, as Searle supposes, defeat the strong thesis, but I think it does show that it is hopeless to attempt to relate intentional characterization to semantic interpretation in the same sort of way we related semantic interpretation to physical description. I think the argument also bolsters my contention that semantic interpretation is only half the problem of intentionality; that semantic engines that are not UNDERSTANDERS are not genuine intentional systems. Indeed, it was Searle's argument that initially led me to distinguish cognition from *cognition, hence to wonder what one has to add to a semantically interpreted system to get a genuine cognizer.

Searle's argument is extremely simple. Imagine Searle locked in a room with a set of rules for manipulating Chinese symbols. The rules specify manipulations solely on the basis of symbol shape, so applying them will be computation. Assume that Searle understands no Chinese. We shove Chinese text under the door to Searle, who applies the rules and shoves the result under the door to us. Now suppose that, unknown to Searle, this system—Searle-plus-rules-in-room—simulates a Chinese person exercising his/her capacity to speak and understand Chinese. Should we

(i) conclude that we have computationally instantiated the intentional capacity to speak and understand Chinese, or

(ii) conclude that the capacity to speak and understand Chinese isn't intentional, or

(iii) conclude that the simulation is *mere imitation,* not instantiation meriting intentional characterization.

Searle says we should opt for (iii) on the grounds that (ii) is silly and (i) is ruled out because the system does not understand any of the Chinese symbols.

Let's begin by granting that (ii) is silly. The contest is between (i) and (iii). To make sense of (iii) we must assume that exercise of a genuinely intentional capacity C_I can be imitated by exercise of a computation capacity C_C that does not instantiate C_I or any other intentional capacity. I shall call this the *Imitation Thesis.*

> *Imitation Thesis:* Exercise of any intentionally characterized capacity C_I can be imitated by exercise of a computational capacity C_C.

When I say that exercise of C can be imitated by exercise of C′, I mean that C and C′ are input-output isomorphic (within idealization).[44] The usual word here is "simulated," but since that word is used in a variety of ways, I have introduced "imitated" and given it a technical sense to avoid ambiguity.

Searle appears to be committed to the Imitation Thesis, for he wants the Chinese-room argument to establish the quite general conclusion that intentionally characterized capacites cannot be computationally instantiated. He envisions variations on the Chinese-room argument for any intentionally characterized capacity, e.g., the deliberation-room argument, the perception-room argument, the pain-room argument, etc. A Searlian x-room argument always assumes that the intentionally characterized x-capacity can be computationally imitated—i.e., imitated by Searle in a room performing formal manipulations on symbols he does not (or need not) understand. Since we are supposed to be able to construct such an argument for any intentionally characterized capacity, it seems that Searle is committed to a computational imitation for every intentionally characterized capacity.

This is a misleading way of viewing the argument, however. It is the computationalist who is committed to the Imitation Thesis, for if C_I is instantiated as C_C in S, then exercise of C_C by S will imitate any exercise of C_I; imitation is a necessary condition of instantiation. Now the computationalist who envisions an experimental defense of the claim that C_I is instantiated as C_C in S envisions S imitating exercise of C_I by exercising C_C. The Chinese-room argument is an attempt to upstage this move by arguing for the "Mere-Imitation" Thesis:

(S1) Imitation is not sufficient for instantiation: S may imitate exercise of C_I by exercising C_C yet not instantiate C_I, or any other intentionally characterized capacity.

(S2) Even when exercise of C_C imitates exercise of C_I, exercise of C_C is essentially irrelevant to instantiation of C_I.

(S1) is more or less uncontroversial, though I'm not sure it should be. We have seen reason to reject an analogous claim about discursive capacities. If exercise of a nondiscursive capacity I seems to imitate exercise of a discursive capacity, R, we should assume that I is R is disguise, and hence not really a nondiscursive capacity, and if that won't work we should assume that R isn't a genuine discursive capacity. It isn't obvious to me a priori that exercise of C_C could *ever* imitate exercise of C_I, let alone that exercise of C_C could imitate exercise of C_I without C_C being an instantiation of C_I. Gedanken experiments such as Searle's Chinese-room argument make (S1) look plausible because it seems we can imagine that (i) Searle-plus-rules is imitating the capacity to speak and understand Chinese, and (ii) Searle is exercising a purely computational capacity but not understanding Chinese. But perhaps this is just not possible in actual fact.

Both Searle and his computationalist opponents help themselves to the Imitation Thesis (IT hereafter). (IT) is plainly an empirical claim, and the evidence for it is shockingly weak. When we do have apparent imitation, there is a strong tendency to suppose that the imitated capacity isn't really intentional. For example, the fact that cheap machines—about forty dollars currently—can imitate the capacity to play (decent if not great) chess tempts one to suppose that the capacity to play (decent if not great) chess isn't intentional. Chess playing appears to require intelligence, but not intentionality. Of course, as pointed out in the last section, the debunking strategy has its limits: to reject intentionality as a matter of principle whenever we get successful computational imitation is to make the existence of intentionally characterizable capacities contingent on the falsehood of (IT), and that is surely perverse. Successful computational imitation of a number of "core" intentionally characterized capacities—*capacities where it is UNDERSTANDING, not intelligence, that is the heart of the matter*—would constitute powerful evidence for (IT). Once we are careful to distinguish intelligence from intentionality, I think it is clear that no powerful evidence of this kind exists. I accept (IT) because it is entailed by the Strong Thesis, and I accept the Strong Thesis because I can't think of any other way to approach the problem of intentionality. This is reason enough, but it is a programmatic reason, not an empirical defense.

Searle can side-step this issue. He can grant (IT) to the computationalist for the sake of argument and argue for (S1): even *if* we had computational imitation of intentionally characterized capacities as the Strong Thesis requires, we wouldn't have computational instantiation of intentionality.

It is important to see that the Chinese-room argument provides no reason to accept (S1) that is independent of (S2). Searle gets (S1) from (S2) by arguing from (a), the Chinese-room does not merit intentional characterization in virtue of its computational capacities, to (b), the Chinese-room doesn't instantiate the capacity to speak and understand Chinese. I have no quarrel with the move from (a) to (b): If S doesn't merit intentional characterization in virtue of having C_C, then C_C doesn't instantiate C_I in S. If we reject this move, computationalism has no *point:* the point of computationalism is the claim that systems merit intentional characterization in virtue of exercising (certain special) computational capacities.

So far as I can see, this leaves the computationalist with only two lines of criticism.

First Line of Criticism

We may argue that (a) is false—i.e., that the Chinese-room does merit intentional characterization in virtue of its computational capacities. This is a favorite ploy of Searle's opponents (see the comments printed with Searle, 1980), but I don't think it will work. In the previous section I argued that the only strategy currently available for defending the claim that C_C instantiates C_I is experimental: S imitates exercise of C_I by exercising C_C. We beg the question against Searle if we trot out *this* strategy here, for the point of Searle's argument is to show that computational imitation is irrelevant. The computationalist claim that C_I is instantiated as C_C may be right, but computationalists need to *defend* the capacity of imitation to support such a claim.

Notice that the only representations that must be understood in the Chinese room are the rules: Searle must understand the rules (though not their purpose or rationale) to apply them. This is a spurious feature of the example, however. The rules are an internal manual in the sense of Chapter II, and Searle is the "little man" who reads them. He may be eliminated from the picture, and with him any suggestion that the rules must be read and understood for the system to function, by automating the functions he performs. *Searle* must understand the rules to apply them, but they needn't be understood to be applied, and so we can assume that they are applied without being understood. Once we've taken this step, there is no longer any *obvious* place for intentional characterization to take hold. Indeed, if there were an *obvious* place for intentional characterization in the Chinese room, we wouldn't have imagined a computational imitation.

Lacking an account of what it is to instantiate an intentionally characterized capacity, the computationalist has no nonquestion-begging strategy for arguing that the Chinese-room *does* understand Chinese characters.

Second Line of Criticism

A more serious objection to the Chinese-room argument is that it begs the question against computationalism. Lacking an account of what it is to instantiate an intentionally characterized capacity, the computationalist has only the imitation inference to fall back on. But the lack of an account of instantiation is equally embarrassing to Searle. For, lacking such an account, how is Searle to argue that the Chinese-room *doesn't* understand Chinese characters? The fact that Searle doesn't understand them is surely irrelevant, as his presence is immaterial anyway. And it is equally irrelevant that the Chinese characters needn't be understood to apply the rules. That, after all, is the point of the computational account: applying the rules to the characters is supposed to instantiate understanding them. So why is Searle so sure the Chinese-room doesn't understand Chinese?

Searle actually has only one argument for this conclusion. We can imagine, he says, that Searle has memorized the rules. Under this condition, Searle claims, he would instantiate the computational capacity, but still wouldn't understand Chinese. This is quite correct, if executing the unmemorized rules leaves Searle ignorant of Chinese, so would executing the memorized rules. So it seems that Searle is right to say that a system may imitate exercise of C_I in virtue of executing C_C, yet not have C_I.

A natural reply is that Searle may not have C_C "in the right way." Perhaps conscious execution of the rules from memory doesn't instantiate C_I. But what if the rules were wired into Searle's brain, so that their execution was nonconscious? Tempting as this is, it is quite beside the point: if computationalism is correct, the details of C_C's instantiation shouldn't count: neuronalism is being smuggled in the back door.

A more sympathetic reading of the objection is possible, however. The details of C_C's instantiation can't matter, but C_C's relation to other computational capacities of the system that executes it may matter a great deal. When we imagine Searle memorizing the rules, we imagine him endowed with C_C all right, but C_C is almost totally isolated from Searle's other capacities. In the spirit of functionalism we might insist that C_C instantiates C_I in S only if C_C is properly integrated with other computational capacities in S. Implementing one of these in isolation may not instantiate C_I, but perhaps if C_C is installed in a sufficiently ritzy neighborhood of other computational capacities, all properly integrated, then the whole computational network will instantiate a variety of intentionally characterized capacities. Perhaps intentionally characterized capacities cannot be instantiated one at a time. According to this "contextualist" line of thought, the Chinese-room indeed does not have the capacity to understand Chinese. What the Chinese room has is a capacity that *would be,* or, rather, *would instantiate,* the capacity to understand Chinese in the proper (computational) setting.

An analogous point can be made about semantic interpretation. Suppose we ask what makes a circuit an AND-gate? It is this: there are types of events identified as inputs, and types of events identified as outputs, and a rule for interpreting these as representations of truth-values such that an output represents 'true' iff each current input represents 'true.' This is enough to make something an AND-gate, but not enough to make it important or right to treat it as such. Assuming it is relative dc levels that are interpretable as representations of truth-values, why look at relative dc levels rather than mass, or temperature, or shape? Well, if we hook a lot of these and kindred circuits together in fancy ways, we will have a system whose most striking capacities are explicable only by analyzing them into simple capacities such as the capacity to compute a truth-function. Thus it is the need to explain the capacities of a containing system that makes truth-functional characterization useful—"the right thing to do." Indeed, only systematic context can make it right to say that it is an AND-gate and not a resister or a heat-sink, and we might put this point by saying that only in an appropriately ritzy neighborhood is it *actually* an AND-gate; otherwise it is only potentially an AND-gate, a would-be AND-gate (the sort of thing that would be an AND-gate in a better neighborhood).

So perhaps the Chinese-room is a would-be Chinese understander. This seems possible, at any rate. This line of reply to Searle actually concedes quite a lot, for it concedes that (1) an imitation experiment can at best establish only that a system with C_C has a would-be C_I. That is bad enough, but the point is recursive: The concession will extend to any network of C_C's no matter how broad a range of related C_I's they imitate unless we can say independently of imitation experiments what contexts will turn a given would-be C_I into the real thing. This is just a slightly more informative version of the conclusion reached earlier: we need an account of instantiation for intentionally characterized capacities. What we've added here is simply the suggestion that such an account will not treat C_I's one at a time.

Thus the Chinese-room argument does not refute computationalism, but it does seriously weaken the force of experimental defenses via imitation.

Having said all this, I would be dishonest if I didn't lodge a protest against the flights of dubious imagination we are required to take in following this argument. We have imagined a computational engine that takes Chinese characters as inputs and gives Chinese characters as output such that its input-output behavior imitates that of a Chinese speaker in conversation. Now the output side is just a gift to Searle. *No one,* not even Skinner, supposes that understanding what is said to you will suffice to determine what to say in return. To be a successful imitator of a conversationalist, this set of rules will need a lot of other input of a nonlinguistic kind, plus a ton of background (would-be) knowledge and a large and varied set of nonlinguistic (would-be) motives. *At least.* A computational engine that could play the conversation game would, in fact, imitate a whole integrated network of intentionally characterized capacities. Faced with such an engine, I couldn't take Searle's doubts seriously. Lacking an account of instantiation for intentionally characterized capacities, I would have to admit that I *might* be witnessing *mere* imitation, but I wouldn't believe it. I would believe the capacity to understand Chinese (among others) had been computationally instantiated, and I would also believe that this and similar technology would eventually—if it hadn't already done so—give rise to the missing account of instantiation. Lacking such an account, our explanation of the C_I's of this engine would be crucially incomplete, but I would dismiss out of hand any suggestion that such an account was impossible. My own view is that withholding intentional characterization from such a system would be a kind of neuronal chauvinism. Surely a child is right to engage in intentional characterization before knowing (or even considering) that everyone has the same kind of mush inside. When it comes to understanding intentionality, we are all children, and we'd do well to imitate their open-mindedness on the subject.

III.9. UNDERSTANDERS

In Section III.7, I canvassed five strategies for defending the Strong Thesis:

1. The first strategy was to analyze humunculi—things meriting intentional characterization—into armies of homunculi so stupid that they have known computational instantiations. This doesn't work because it confuses UNDERSTANDING with intelligence. The strategy works for intelligent *cognition but not for cognition, because a system that merits intentional characterization will merit it no matter how stupid it is.

2. The second strategy was to explain semantic content in non-intentional terms. This, though important, is only half of the story. Semantic engines that are not UNDERSTANDERS are not full fledged cognizers.

3. The third strategy—the "standard solution"—was to explain understanding a representation as knowing that it means so-and-so, then to explain this knowledge as a kind of knowing-how, and, finally, to explain knowing-how as a behavioral capacity. This strategy is simply a seductive form of reductive behaviorism, and inherits all of that doctrine's difficulties.

4. The fourth strategy was to explain intentional characterization in terms of semantic interpretation—propositional interpretation in particular—in a way strictly analogous to the way I earlier explained semantic interpretation in terms of nonsemantic characterization. This strategy fails as well: given a flow-chart of intentionally characterized capacities and an isomorphic chart of inferentially characterized capacities, we have no reason to suppose that the various inferentially characterized capacities instantiate the corresponding homunculi. In the allegedly analogous case—a flow-chart of inferentially characterized capacities isomorphic to a flow-chart of physically characterized capacities—the isomorphism itself is enough to underwrite propositional interpretation of the physically characterized system. But isomorphism of analytic structure will not underwrite intentional characterization of a nonintentionally characterized system.

5. Finally, I considered the prospects for an experimental defense of the Strong Thesis. I concluded that such a defense, though not at present available, could make the Strong Thesis practically

irresistible but would not endow it with any explanatory force. That is, an experimental defense of the Strong Thesis would not put us in a position to explain intentionally characterized capacities via computational instantiation.

Review of Searle's Chinese-room argument bolsters the sharp distinction I have been drawing between semantic interpretation and intentional characterization, and it is this distinction, at bottom, that undermines the five strategies just rehearsed. Reflection on the Chinese-room argument suggests further that a persuasive experimental defense is likely to involve simulating something close to a "whole" cognitive agent, an accomplishment that is just not in the cards for the immediate future. We are thrown back, then, on the need for a theory of intentional characterization, or, in other words, of UNDERSTANDERS in the rather special sense I have given that term.

I don't have a theory of UNDERSTANDERS, but I do have a kind of theory schema in the form of a set of increasingly explicit necessary conditions that a system must satisfy in order to merit intentional characterization. We may begin by setting down the two necessary conditions we've been assuming throughout the previous discussion.

(1) A state sigma of S is an intentional state of S only if sigma is a propositionally interpretable state of S—i.e., a state of S that has a semantic content and is individuated by it.

(2) A state sigma of S is an intentional state of S only if sigma is a representation *for* S—i.e., only if S UNDERSTANDS sigma.

Propositional interpretation, as we have seen, is often merited, even mandated, where intentional characterization is not, but condition (1) rules out the converse possibility that intentional characterization might be merited in cases in which propositional interpretation is not. This reflects a strategic decision more than a substantive claim. Such things as *fearing death* might conceivably be intentional states that are semantically interpretable but not propositionally interpretable, but this could so obviously be argued either way that it seems best to restrict attention initially to those states that do have a propositional content, since they are clearly the core cases.

Condition (2) tells us that what is common and essential to intentional states is that they are UNDERSTANDINGS: what makes an explicit belief that p, an explicit desire that q, and an explicit pondering of r all intentional states is that they are, respectively, UNDERSTANDINGS of p, q, and r. Put this way, the condition expressed in (2) is simply a consequence of the way I've introduced the terms 'explicit' and 'UNDERSTANDING', but I think it is nevertheless suggestive to put it this way, if only because it gives us a name for the missing common factor, a name that does not even suggest that we are looking for some further *semantic* property. Obviously, however, substantive progress requires some account of what it is for a system to UNDERSTAND its own propositional states.

I propose to pick up a thread that formed part of the "standard solution" scouted in Section III.7—viz., the idea that to UNDERSTAND a propositional state is to know what it means. This idea is, as I noted earlier, circular as it stands, because knowledge is (presumably) an intentional state itself, hence requires—by (2)—UNDERSTANDING of *its* semantic content. Following an earlier convention, I will call a state of a system a "would-be" or implicit knowledge state if it would be a knowledge state of that system if only it satisfied condition (2)—i.e., if only the system UNDERSTOOD the propositional content of the state. (Implicit knowledge is what Dretske has (perhaps) succeeded in analyzing in *Knowledge and the Flow of Information*.) Using this notion, we can formulate the idea that UNDERSTANDING a propositional state is "knowing what it means" without circularity.

(3) Sigma is an intentional state of S only if S implicitly knows what sigma means.

This amounts to the claim that sigma is an intentional state of S only if there is a propositional state sigma' of S such that sigma' would be knowledge of the meaning of sigma if only sigma' satisfied (2)—i.e., if only S UNDERSTOOD sigma'.

Condition (3) introduces a kind of regress of implicit knowledge, a regress reminiscent of the hierarchy of metalanguages encountered in formal semantics (Tarski, 1956, chapter viii): in order to formulate the semantics of (a truth definition for) a language L, we have recourse to a metalanguage, ML, that can

of Section III.1.) I see no reason to suppose that an intentional system could not be capable of such states; indeed, such states might be essential to a wide variety of the system's *cognitive capacities. Perhaps the vast majority of our own *cognitive capacities rest on our capacity for propositional states that are quite outside the range of our UNDERSTANDING, hence of our intentionality. If it turns out that we are not intentional with respect to many or most of our important *cognitive states, we shall simply have to revise our estimates of the relative importance of the capacity for intentional states.

The Role of Intentionality

Given the drift of these last remarks, one may be led to wonder what the capacity for intentional states is *for*. Depending on how we understand this question, it is either very easy or very hard. The easy answer is that the capacity for intentional states is necessary for the capacity to communicate, to deliberate, to premeditate, and a host of others, for each of these is analyzable into intentionally characterized capacities. This sort of top-down perspective makes the capacity for intentional states seem central and essential to mental life as we know it—the cognitive side of it in any case.

But there is another perspective from which the capabilities required by (1)-(4′) seem almost epiphenomenal. When we imagine the UNDERSTANDER doing its stuff—representing the semantics of a state of the system—it's hard to see what *use* the system could make of the results. For it does *seem*—and this is an intuition Searle relies on computationalist opponents to have—that we could simply eliminate the UNDERSTANDER, hence intentionality, from the system with no noticeable consequences. From this perspective, in other words, it seems the Mere-Imitation Thesis of Section III.7 must be true. Such a system (with the UNDERSTANDER eliminated) wouldn't *be* an intentional system, of course, but it would be (like the systems Dretske describes) a passing fair imitation. And if a nonintentional system can imitate an intentional system, what good is intentionality?

This last question is a bit unfair: it is only because we don't see what intentionality is for that we think the Mere-Imitation Thesis might hold after all. Or rather, it is only because we don't see what the system's capacity to represent the semantics of its own states is for that we take seriously the suggestion that a system not satisfying (1)-(4') could imitate one that did. After all, we *do* know what *intentionality* is for: communication, deliberation, etc. That was the easy answer, and it is surely right in spite of being easy. It is just that intentionality *conceived of as satisfaction of (1)-(4')* seems epiphenomenal because we don't know why, from a programmer's point of view, a system should need to be able to represent the semantics of its own states in order to communicate, deliberate, etc. Intentionality seems essential when we analyze the capacity to communicate, but when we analyze the capacity for intentional states, we don't see how it *could* be essential or even important.

This situation might be thought to show that (1)-(4') don't get at intentionality precisely because (1)-(4') don't explain why intentionally characterized capacities should be essential to such things as the capacity to communicate. For all I know, this may be the correct diagnosis. If so, then (1)-(4') are on the wrong track, and the Strong Thesis, at least in my hands, is in trouble. But there is another possibility. The fault may lie instead with our insufficient understanding (analysis) of such intentionally analyzed capacities as the capacity to communicate. Perhaps if we really try to build a system that instantiates the Grice-Lewis-Bennett analysis of communication, for example, we will come up against the need for the capacity specified by (4'). It is this possibility that has prompted me, at any rate, to attempt just this sort of project. (See Cummins and Dietrich, 1982.)

CHAPTER FOUR

Historical Reflections

In this chapter I am going to examine several episodes in the history of psychology with an eye toward making good my claim that most psychological explanation makes little sense construed as causal subsumption. Rather than try to cover a large number of cases, I am going to discuss three widely different cases in some detail. In Section IV.1 I will consider the introspectionist program of E. B. Titchener. In Section IV.2 the topic will be the system developed by Clark Hull in *Principles of Behavior.* Section IV.3 is a frankly speculative attempt to reconstruct Freudian explanation as a species of interpretive functional analysis methodologically on a par with current *cognitive psychology.

This chapter is not to be construed as history of science. My concern is not so much with historical accuracy as with providing a somewhat anachronistic reconstruction of certain theoretical episodes in the hope that this will clarify the significance of those episodes for current theorizing, while at the same time illustrating the theory of explanation sketched in Chapter I, above. My own view is that this sort of approach can be helpful in sorting out the historical issues as well. For example, exposing logical and conceptual problems in Hull's treatment of intervening variables helps us to understand Hull's ambivalent and sometimes confused attitudes toward his own constructs. Similarly, I think formulating a clearer version of the behavioristic critique of introspection than

Watson did (or could) formulate helps us to understand why the critique seemed so devastating at the time. Behaviorists "knew" the argument was "there," even though what they actually wrote at the time was often vague and polemical.

IV.1. THE INTROSPECTIONISM OF TITCHENER AND THE BEHAVIORIST CRITIQUE

Unquestionably the most significant introspectionist program in the United States was the "structuralism" of E. B. Titchener. Titchener was concerned to establish the claim that the "new psychology" imported from Germany had made psychology a rigorous empirical science. Lacking a nontrivial account of science, Titchener supported his claim by emphasizing the analogies between psychology as he saw it and an established experimental science—viz., physical chemistry. To understand Titchener's vision of psychology, therefore, we do well to examine his model briefly.

The core of physical chemistry in Titchener's time was the periodic table. The periodic table allowed one to explain analytically an enormous number of the chemical properties of compounds. It provided a list of chemical elements—i.e., components whose further analysis is not theoretically significant for the explanation of properties in the intended domain—together with a specification of the chemically important properties of those elements. With these resources, it was possible to derive laws of composition—which compounds are possible—and laws of instantiation for a large number of the empirically established chemical properties of substances. Titchener's idea was to provide for psychology what the periodic table provided for chemistry, thereby making it possible to explain the properties of mental events and processes by analyzing them into psychological "elements"— mental events that could not be further analyzed. Since Titchener's elements are not things or substances but events, his program requires some account of the origin of elements. He needed a general recipe for answering such questions as: Why do we have just these elements present (in consciousness) at this time rather than some others? Two kinds of answer were available: either a current element is the effect of one or more previous elements, or it is the effect of extramental stimuli. Titchener allowed both possibilities, but he concentrated mainly on the second, probably because (i) extramental events are more open to experimental manipulation, and (ii) under the influence of empiricist philosophy, Titchener believed that perception is the most significant source of events in the mind.[1]

The object of psychological theory, then, is to explain the origin and properties of the contents of consciousness—e.g., feeling anger, the visual image of a pouncing cat, or the experience of voluntary action. Suppose the feeling of anger has properties P, Q, and R (as revealed by introspection). We are to proceed by analyzing this feeling into its elements—call them x, y, and z. Then, appealing to the properties of these elements and the laws of composition, we endeavor to show why anger must have the properties P, Q, and R—that is, we endeavor to derive an instantiation law for these properties. To explain why S is angry at t, we explain the occurrence of x, y, and z, tokens of the mental element-types that make up anger, as effects of previous mental events and/or current extramental stimuli. (Perhaps we shall also need to explain why conditions were propitious for the combination of x, y, and z into anger. Compare: many chemical combinations require a fair amount of heat, or a catalyst, to take place.)

The project, then, was to discover the fundamental and introspectively unanalyzable elements of consciousness and to formulate the principles of combination whereby these elements are synthesized into the complex and familiar experiences of ordinary life. Every compound mental state or process was to be explained componentially, the characteristics of the whole derived from the characteristics of the parts and mode of combination. The central part of this program—analyzing familiar conscious experiences—was an extension of the project Locke initiated in Book Two of his *Essay Concerning Human Understanding.* The simple ideas of sense and reflection became the extramentally produced mental elements and the mentally produced elements, respectively, and the principle of association became the central law of mental bonding. Not surprisingly, introspectionists spoke of mental valences, of mental equilibrium, and of mental elements neutralizing each other. The fundamental issues of mental analysis and synthesis never got significantly beyond Locke, however, and the reason is fairly clear. There were simply no well-focused experimental procedures; nothing like qualitative analysis in chemistry. Lacking anything comparable to titration, centrafuges, solubility tables, oxidation, and analytical balances, the student of introspective psychology was, in the end, simply left to compete with Locke at more or less well disguised linguistic analysis. Notable improvements on the *Essay* were not forthcoming.

So the analysis of consciousness bogged down for lack of analytical tools. But the correlative project to explain the elements as responses did not, for here introspectionists had an experimental paradigm in the Weber-Fechner experiments. Here is Titchener's textbook description of a typical variation.

Method—to find the numerical expression of Weber's law for noise—An ivory ball is let fall from two different heights, upon a hard-wood plate. The difference of intensity between the two sounds (i.e., the difference between the two heights of fall) must be slight. The two sounds are given in irregular order in different experiments (to avoid the influence of expectation), and the subject is required to say, in each case, whether the second is louder than the first. In 100 experiments, he will give a certain number of right answers, and a certain number of wrong.

The method assumes that if the two sounds are just noticeably different in intensity, the subject will give about 80% right and 20% wrong answers. This proportion is calculated by what mathematicians call the 'law of probability.' Now suppose that a certain difference gave 70 right and 30 wrong answers in 100 experiments. We could calculate, by aid of the Integral calculus, how much larger the difference must have been to give 80 right and 20 wrong—i.e., to be just noticeable. The calculated difference (difference of height of fall) is the numerator, and the original intensity (height of fall) of the weaker sound, the denominator, of the fraction which expresses Weber's law. [Titchener, 1897, pp. 81–82]

Here is a different and more fundamental description:

Suppose that we are investigating the intensity of noise. We shall begin with a stimulus of moderate intensity: say, the noise made by the fall of an ivory ball upon a wood plate from a height of 90 cm. We will call the intensity of this sensation 1. If we gradually increase the height of fall, we shall reach a point at which the noise of the fall is just noticeably greater than the original noise. We may call the intensity of this second sensation 2. If we further increase the height of fall, we shall presently get a noise, 3, which is just noticeably louder than 2; and so on. Now what are the different heights of fall—i.e., intensities of stimulus—necessary to arouse sensations of the intensities 2, 3, 4, etc.? . . . An addition of 30 cm. suffices to raise the intensity of sensation from 1 to 2; but if we are affected by the stronger stimulus 120 cm., we must add more than 30 to it to change intensity 2 to intensity 3. In other words: change in the intensity of sensations does not keep even pace with change in the intensity of the stimuli which occasion them.

Experiment enables us to replace this general statement of the relation of sensation intensity to stimulus intensity by a definite scientific law. If sensations are to increase in intensity by equal amounts, their stimuli must increase by relatively equal amounts. [Titchener, 1897, pp. 79–80]

This sort of experiment, begun by Weber (1834) and refined and expanded by Fechner (1860), led to Fechner's law (mistakenly called Weber's law by Titchener and Fechner—compare Gregory, 1981, pp. 500–505). Here was a law—a transition law—and a procedure for testing and refining it. Does the law hold for all sensation? What are the values of the constants of proportionality for each case? Work on these matters proceeded apace.

But this apparent bright spot in the program proved to be an Achilles' heel. Although the analysis of consciousness languished, the fact was that there were no generally accepted or clearly articulated canons for the evaluation of analytic explanations, especially as applied to consciousness. Hence there was no way to determine whether the trouble was merely practical or deeply conceptual. On the other hand, there did exist well-articulated and generally accepted canons for the evaluation of the sort of explanations Fechner's law was used to construct, since the idea is to explain an event in consciousness—e.g., a discernible difference in loudness—as an effect of an external cause—a change in stimulus strength.

We can bring out the problem in a few lines. The canon requiring independent access to causes and effects applies to the Weber-Fechner experiments as follows. Suppose we find a subject whose responses don't fit the law? Is the subject (A) misdescribing his/her sensations, or (B) psychologically idiosyncratic? For that matter, how do we know that a subject responding normally is not in fact (C) psychologically idiosyncratic but systematically misdescribing experience, rather than (D) psychologically normal? We cannot compare a subject's descriptions with what is supposed to be described. Our only access to the sensations of the subject are (i) inference from established connections with responses, including verbal reports, and (ii) inference from established connections with stimuli. Obviously we cannot establish connections of the sort required unless we can, at least sometimes, distinguish (A) from (B) and (C) from (D). But we cannot make these distinctions unless we can establish the connections.[2] Since the accuracy of introspective observation cannot be checked, it seems it cannot play the role required of scientific observation. With introspection ruled out of court, the only way to measure sensation intensity is to measure stimulus intensity and then calculate sensation intensity using Fechner's law, but if we do this, we are using Fechner's law to define sensation intensity, and we cannot then turn around and pretend to explain the intensity of a sensation by appeal to stimulus intensity and Fechner's law. Once introspection is disqualified, we have no access to sensation intensity other than the very law that is supposed to explain it.

Thus it was that introspectionists became vulnerable to a powerful methodological attack. The methodology of explanation by causal subsumption had been well entrenched by Bacon, Berkeley, Hume, Mach, and Mill. The empiricist doctrine was (and is) that causal laws have no explanatory power unless the causes and effects they subsume are knowable independently of each other. It is ironic that this doctrine was so fatal to introspectionism, for introspection was held to be the only avenue to noninferential knowledge by the very empiricist philosophers who developed the line of argument that killed introspectionist psychology. Locke's inverted spectrum problem returned to haunt those who attempted to pick up where Book Two of the *Essay* left off. The inverted spectrum problem turned on the conceptualist assumption that linguistic training would inevitably disguise sufficiently systematic "psychological" differences. This is just the possibility raised by (A) and (C).

Whatever we may think of this critique,[3] the mere certainty that it could be formulated was eventually enough to kill any psychology based on introspection. And just as Berkeley's critique of representational realism seemed to point inevitably to a single alternative (if we know about tables and can know only about ideas, then tables are ideas), so this critique of introspectionism seemed to point inevitably to a single alternative. Introspection isn't genuine observation, so the Weber-Fechner law cannot be about consciousness. It is obviously about something, though, for experimenters certainly observe and record something in the sort of experiment described by Titchener in the passages above. What? Since experimenters record what their subjects say, the Weber-Fechner law must correlate stimuli with "introspective behavior." This is verbal behavior, *per accidens,* in the usual experimental set-up, but button pressings would do just as well.

This bit of diagnostics would probably have sufficed to produce behaviorism eventually, but a number of other factors conspired to guarantee a quick takeoff. Two, I think, are especially worthy of note. First, pragmatism was in vogue in United States philosophical circles, and pragmatists emphasized the importance of understanding connections with action to the understanding of traditional philosophical problems involving mental states and processes. According to Dewey, for instance, the central mistake of empiricists and rationalists alike is the supposition that knowledge and belief can be understood independently of action, and treated as antecedent conditions to be investigated in their own right. Refuting this supposition was always a central theme in Dewey's writings. It isn't a long step from this to the doctrine that talk of mental states is just shorthand for talk of identifiable behavioral patterns. Watson was a student at Chicago at a time when the influence of Dewey's pragmatism was very strong there.

The other significant factor was Pavlov's discovery of stimulus substitution. This was an important discovery in its own right, but in the intellectual climate I have been describing, it had a special significance, for it seems to account for the sort of phenomenon generally attributed to the association of ideas, without recourse to ideas. Someone taken with the empiricist critique of introspection, and the pragmatist treatment of doxastic states, could hardly have failed to conclude that Pavlov had shown that it was stimuli and responses, not ideas, that were associated. This had to seem a major breakthrough, for association was the only principle of learning on hand.

Introspectionist psychophysics was accessible to methodological scrutiny because it was a case of subsumption, an explanatory strategy the structure and logic of which were clear and familiar to Introspectionist and Behaviorist alike. In sharp contrast, the analytical strategy, though regularly applied, had not been clearly articulated as a strategy. The logic at the core of Titchener's program was, therefore, largely invisible, hence inaccessible to serious scrutiny. With the benefit of hindsight, however, we can see that Titchener's central explanatory program was naive in the extreme, and this gives us a measure of the extent to which the structure of property theories was tacit (at best) rather than explicit.

Titchener conceived the objects of psychological analysis as processes. This was the standard Wundtian line, a line that appears to go back to the empiricist conception of mind as a series of events in consciousness. Processes can be analyzed, of course, and so can properties of processes, just as chemical compounds and their properties can be analyzed. Chemists sought to discover what water is—namely H_2O—and this is naturally thought of as an analytic question. When we analyze water, what do we get? This, I think, is how Titchener and the introspectionists generally tended to think of their questions. They asked, "What is anger made of?"

Analysis of a compound, though often intrinsically interesting, is of theoretical interest mainly as a step toward explaining the dispositional properties of the compound. Similarly, Titchener's interest in analyzing anger was that such an analysis would be (hopefully) a necessary and useful step toward explaining the properties of anger—most importantly, its dispositional properties. But Titchener must have lost sight of this fact, or at least failed to note its implications. To see this, recall the schematic illustration of a Titchenerian explanation of anger. We are to imagine the feeling of anger analyzed into mental elements x, y, and z, and each of these explained as effects of previous disturbances. Now, the obvious question is: How does throwing x, y, and z together make anger? Is their mere coincidence in consciousness enough? This is surely naive in the extreme, for the whole program would then depend on the assumption of a "bushel basket" theory of consciousness (i.e., the theory that consciousness is simply a receptacle for elements that do not interact). On the other hand, if there is serious mental bonding, so that x, y, and z form a mental compound, then (i) we need an account of the capacities of x, y, and z to form this compound, and/or of the capacity of the mind to so compound them, and (ii) we can no longer seriously suppose that we can discern the components in the compound simply by "looking" at it. (Imagine someone supposing that one could tell what was in a chemical compound simply by examining it: this is surely a confusion between compounds and mixtures.)

Introspection as a method thus sorts ill with the explanatory goal of the theory. This goal was to explain analytically the properties of the complex contents of consciousness, and perhaps the capacities of the mind required for it to have such contents. Since introspection is at best a form of observation it *can* hope to yield *data*—the properties of conscious contents—but it *cannot* hope to yield analyses. The elements and their properties will not be "visible" when compounded unless we assume that there is no serious composition at all. If we assume a bushel basket theory of consciousness, a step even Hume did not take, then the properties of anger, say, will simply be the union of the properties of the elements in consciousness when one is angry. Analysis in such a case is morphological analysis at best. Morphological analysis certainly has significant applications, but the idea that the properties of complex, conscious experiences can be explained by morphological analysis is implausible in the extreme. "Implausible" is not the same as "false" or even "disconfirmed," of course, but if this implication of the program had been clearly perceived, the program would surely have looked much less attractive than in fact it did. It is evident that neither Titchener nor his critics were aware of this implication. It was thus the introspectionist's use of subsumption (in their psychophysics) that was vulnerable to well-focused criticism, and since their use of psychophysics was peripheral to their main project, the net result was more or less unsatisfactory to everybody concerned. As it happens, however, it is the use of introspection that is critical in both cases—though for different reasons—and therefore the general conclusion that introspectionist psychology fails because it is (exclusively) introspectionist is basically sound. Notice, however, that a critique of the role of introspection in the analytical part of the project does not point to a behaviorist alternative, as does the critique of the use of introspection in the subsumptivist part of the project. In the former case, the problem is not at all that introspective reports are unverifiable but rather that (i) the objects of introspection (the mental compounds) are not what need to be observed (the mental elements), and (ii) introspection, being a sort of observation, isn't an analytical tool (looking at anger won't take it apart any more than looking at sugar will take it apart). Now that verificationism is out of style, reliance on introspection in psychophysics seems less problematic than its role in Titchenerian analysis.

Analysis in the Behaviorism of Watson

The Pavlovian law of stimulus substitution owes whatever explanatory force it has to subsumption. The most important explanatory progress behaviorism made, however, was not via more and better subsumption, but via analysis. Thus the official explanatory strategy of introspective psychology became the unofficial explanatory strategy of behaviorism, and the unofficial explanatory strategy of introspective psychology became the official explanatory strategy of behaviorism. Official methodology is tailored to the official explanatory strategy, hence the empiricist methodology of explanation by subsumption under causal generalization became the official methodology of behaviorism. Introspective psychology made its living by exploiting an unofficial strategy in a way that sorted ill with the methodology universally associated with it. Behaviorism makes its living by exploiting a strategy to which its official methodology does not apply at all. But behaviorism has an advantage over introspectionism, for when practice is distinguished from preaching, we find that behaviorism exploits an explanatory strategy associated with *no* clear or widely accepted methodology. Behaviorist practice, therefore, proceeds in the absence of any clear or widely accepted standards of criticism, though this fact is disguised by adherence to the view that behaviorist psychology is subsumptive.

By itself, stimulus substitution has no chance of explaining complex behavior, or the introduction of new responses. Pavlovian conditioning can simply link new stimuli to responses already in the organism's repertoire, and experimentation quickly revealed that the stimuli and responses involved had to be rather short and simple. The new Pavlovian principle of association, though experimentally demonstrable, seemed to be no more explanatory than the old version.

Watson brightened this dim scene with a simple strategy: analyze an extended behavioral pattern into a sequence of responses to stimuli produced by execution of the previous response. Consider playing a tune from memory on the piano. Initially we have a set of connections between perceiving a written note (stimulus) and striking the appropriate key. Now striking a particular key produces a corresponding stimulus—visual and kinesthetic—that always immediately precedes striking the next key specified by the score. Thus repetitious playing from the score should produce stimulus substitution—perception of a previous response substituting for perception of the next note in the score. When substitution is complete, the score will be unnecessary.

This analysis fails for a number of rather boring reasons—e.g., it runs afoul of the fact that people can play more than one tune from memory without difficulty even though the different tunes share notes. But the *strategy* was promising and exciting because the problem of explaining acquisition and exercise of a complex behavioral capacity is reduced to the problem of analyzing the capacity into simple antecedently explained capacities. A compellingly general picture of psychological change emerges. An organism begins with a genetically determined endowment of S-R connections, some of which, perhaps, emerge only at certain maturation stages. This basic endowment is expanded via stimulus substitution. The resulting connections are then combined in more or less complex sequences to yield an organism with a respectably complex behavioral repertoire.

This picture is still the operative picture underlying behaviorist psychology. The shifts have been shifts in detail. First, contemporary behaviorism is far more liberal about genetic endowment than was Watson—the *tabula* isn't nearly so *rasa*. Second, and more important, classical Pavlovian conditioning is supplemented by operant conditioning. Since operant conditioning builds on emitted behavior rather than on preexisting S–R connections, this change affects the assumptions about genetic endowment. Also, since operant conditioning produces "shaping," contemporary behaviorism has a source of novel, unanalyzable, behaviors available as building blocks. But the basic Watsonian picture remains: significant psychological change is the result of composition of antecedently explained (via genetics or shaping) behaviors. Hence, psychological explanation must proceed by analyzing observed behaviors into more tractible components. Thus it is analysis, not subsumption under causal law, that is the central explanatory strategy of behaviorism.

Watson conceived of an organism as a transducer the input-output characteristics of which could be altered over time. To characterize the organism psychologically at a moment in time is to specify the current input-output properties—a bundle of S–R connections. The goal of psychological theory is to specify transition laws that subsume successive changes in momentary input-output properties—e.g., the law of stimulus substitution. It is therefore ironic that Watson never introduced a single principle of this type. Instead, his major achievement was the introduction of the analytical strategy into behaviorism in the guise of the response chain. Watson was fond of saying that the point of scientific psychology is the prediction and control of behavior. But Watson's analysis of habit, even had it been sound, would not have increased the power of psychology to predict or control responses at all, though it would have greatly increased its explanatory power. For example, the problem about playing a tune from memory was not that it was unpredictable: whether or not a subject could do this was predictable from the amount of practice (in so far as it was predictable at all). Watson's analysis did not alter this situation at all, for Watson did not isolate a stimulus, or stimulus history, that has as response playing a tune from memory. What Watson did was explain the capacity to play a tune from memory by analyzing it into antecedently understood (or anyway antecedently present) capacities of the organism. This in turn allowed Watson to describe (inaccurately as things turned out) the conditions under which this capacity would be acquired, but these were already known, and, in any case, this is not *predicting a response.* [4]

Watson's presentation of his analysis of habit formation in *Behaviorism* (1924) is introduced as a response to his discussion of the sort of learning Thorndike studied; what we now think of as operant conditioning.

> . . . [L]et us put in front of the three-year-old child, whose habits of manipulation are well established, a problem box—a box that can be opened only after a certain thing has been done. . . . Before we hand it to him, we show him the open box containing several small pieces of candy and then we close it and tell him that if he opens it he may have a piece of candy. . . . Let us suppose that he has 50 learned and unlearned separate responses at his command. At one time or another during his first attempt to open the box, let us assume that he displays, as he will, nearly all of them before he pushes the button hard enough to release the catch. The time the whole process takes, we will say, is about twenty minutes. When he opens it, we give him his bit of candy, close the box and hand it to him again. The next time he makes fewer movements; the third time fewer still. In 10 trials or less he can open the box without making a useless movement and he can open it in two seconds.
>
> Why is the time cut down, and why do movements not necessary to the solution gradually drop out of the series? This has been a hard problem to solve because no one has ever simplified the problem enough really to bring experimental technique to bear upon it. [p. 204]

This is not even prima facie a problem of prediction and control; it is a problem of explanation. It isn't at all clear how Watson's analysis is supposed to help with this particular problem, but it is quite clear that we have a capacity that wants explaining, not a response that wants predicting, and that the explanatory strategy employed is analysis, not subsumption. [5] The learning curves obtained by Thorndike and others specify a capacity of organisms. It was this capacity that Watson sought to explain by analyzing it into the capacity for stimulus substitution and the antecedently available capacities characterized by the organism's pretrial S-R connections.

IV.2. ANALYSIS AND SUBSUMPTION IN HULL

The term *theory* in the behavioral or "social" sciences has a variety of current meanings. As understood in the present work, a theory is a systematic deductive derivation of the secondary principles of observable phenomena from a relatively small number of primary principles or postulates. . . . In science an observed event is said to be explained when the proposition expressing it has been logically derived from a set of definitions and postulates coupled with certain observed conditions antecedent to the event. [Hull, 1943, pp. 2-3]

A natural event is explained when it can be derived as a theorem by a process of reasoning from (1) a knowledge of the relevant natural conditions antedating it, and (2) one of more relevant principles called postulates. [Hull, 1943, p. 14]

The above quotations from Clark Hull's *Principles of Behavior* make it clear that Hull accepted a deductive-nomological model of explanation of the sort worked out by Hempel. I want to emphasize two features of Hull's view, for they will be crucial to what follows. First, Hull assumes that the explananda are *observable events*. Second, the observable events that are the explananda of a theory are also the data that test the theory. Together, these points dictate the form of Hull's theorizing: he is after a transition theory, for this is the only kind of theory his philosophy of science recognizes. He is well aware of this, for he writes:

Scientific theories are mainly concerned with dynamic situations, i.e., with the consequent events or conditions which, with the passage of time, will follow from a given set of antecedent events or conditions. The concrete activity of theorizing consists in the manipulation of a limited set of symbols according to the rules expressed in the postulates . . . in such a way as to span the gap separating the antecedent conditions or states from the subsequent ones. [1943, p. 382]

This is a description of the picture of a transition theory that I gave in Chapter I:

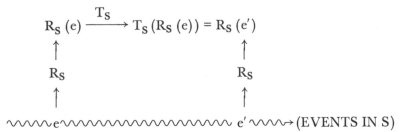

$$R_S\,(e) \xrightarrow{\ T_S\ } T_S\,(R_S\,(e)) = R_S\,(e')$$

Hull's Behaviorism

A Watsonian behaviorist thinks of an organism at a given instant as a bundle of S–R connections. These are altered over time by two factors: maturation, debilitation, injury and the like, and classical conditioning (stimulus substitution). Stimulus and response are, in principle if not in practice, to be described in psychologically neutral physical terms, preferably the terms of physics, chemistry, and anatomy. Sophisticated behavior is to be explained by analyzing it into a sequence of simple S–R connections, execution of the n*th* response producing conditioned proprioceptive stimuli for the n+1*st* response in the chain.

The basic picture Hull presents is not greatly different on the face of it. Classical conditioning is supplemented by operant conditioning (the law of effect), and since this presupposes that certain behaviors are simply emitted, and hence are not responses to identifiable stimuli, the organism is conceived not solely as a set of S–R connections, but as a set of S–R connections plus a set of relatively weighted tendencies to emit certain behaviors. Define an organism's behavioral repertoire at a time as the set of behaviors it can emit at that time together with its associated probability distribution: an organism is then characterized at a moment by a set of S–R connections and a behavioral repertoire.

What is distinctive at first sight about Hull's psychology is the use of "intervening variables" to characterize the internal psychological condition of the organism. No one has ever thought that perception of food causes salivation in dogs, or that pecking is emitted in pigeons without the mediation of internal processes. If we ask why perception of food causes salivation, or why pecking is emitted, the answer must be that the organism is internally structured in a way that accounts for these facts. With this, of course, other behaviorists agree. What is controversial is Hull's claim that internal states and processes can and should be characterized not physiologically or introspectively, but in terms of their psychological functions. A glance at the summary diagram on p. 383 of *The Principles of Behavior* (Fig. 1) clearly reveals that, though Hull assumes that his constructs characterize physiological mechanisms, the characterization is not in terms of physiological properties but of what philosophers of mind call their functional role—roughly, their contribution in context to the causation of behavior.[6]

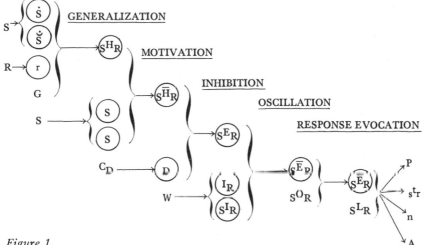

Figure 1.

Because of this, Hull is sensitive to the charge that he is introducing constructs that are in principle beyond observational verification. "Reaction potential," for instance, could not be observed even if we could "look into a person's head," unless we already knew what physiological process instantiated the function characteristic of reaction potential. And if we knew *that*, we wouldn't be worried about observational verification of the psychological reality of reaction potential. To avoid the charge of introducing unverifiable entities, Hull insists that intervening variables must be "anchored at both ends."

It is worth pausing to make this precise. To introduce an intervening variable sigma, we must (i) specify a function f that allows us to calculate a value for sigma given values for one or more independent variables representing stimuli or other observable antecedent conditions, and (ii) we must specify a function g that allows us to calculate a value for a response given a value for sigma.

Now, given f and g, it is evidently possible to eliminate reference to sigma in the theory by simple composition of functions. For suppose we have $f(s) = \text{sigma}$ and $g(\text{sigma}) = r$. Then we may replace these two equations with $g(f(s)) = r$, which refers only to s and r. Thus Hull's requirement that intervening variables be anchored at both ends amounts to the requirement that they be eliminable: intervening variables are allowable only if they aren't necessary!

So why have them? Neal Miller (1959) gives the following explanation (see Fig. 2). If there are more than two independent variables and more than two dependent variables, then a theoretical economy is achieved by introducing an intervening variable. Here is his argument. Suppose we have two stimulus variables, s_1 and s_2, and two response variables, r_1 and r_2. If we do not introduce intervening variables, we have to state four functional relations as indicated in Fig. 2.1. If we introduce an intervening variable, sigma, we still have four functional relations to state, as in Fig. 2.2 Now compare the situation involving more observables (Figs. 2.3 and 2.4). Without sigma, we have nine functional relations; with sigma, only six. Introducing sigma introduces economy, says Miller.

This argument is unsound. The number of functions—i.e., state equations—we need to specify to represent the relations between independent and dependent variables is always equal to the number of dependent variables. For Fig. 2.3, we need three equations:

$$f_1(s_1, s_2, s_3) = r_1$$
$$f_2(s_1, s_2, s_3) = r_2$$
$$f_3(s_1, s_2, s_3) = r_3$$

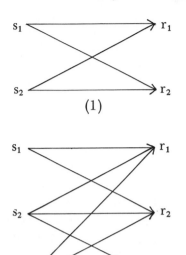 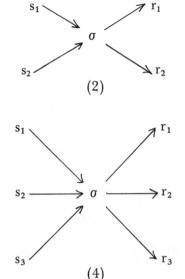

Figure 2.

For Fig. 2.4 we have:

$$f(s_1, s_2, s_3) = \text{sigma}$$
$$g_1(\text{sigma}) = r_1$$
$$g_2(\text{sigma}) = r_2$$
$$g_3(\text{sigma}) = r_3$$

which, by composition of functions, gives us:

$$g_1(f(s_1, s_2, s_3)) = r_1$$
$$g_2(f(s_1, s_2, s_3)) = r_2$$
$$g_3(f(s_1, s_2, s_3)) = r_3.$$

Miller seems to have confused the number of lines of causal influence (the arrows) with the number of equations needed to represent them, no doubt because the phrase "functional relation" is used in both senses by psychologists.[7]

Whatever intervening variables do, they don't achieve theoretical economy. What *do* they achieve? Since the causation of behavior is mediated by internal states and processes, the obvious answer is that intervening variables are introduced to describe these states and processes in a way that affords an explanation of behavior.

In order to clarify the role of intervening variables, it is useful to consider how we might explain the behavior of a machine or factory the insides of which, let us assume, we cannot directly observe—e.g., the Ford factory at River Rouge. This plant takes iron ore, wages, power, etc., as input and gives Fords as output. Now we could, if we wished, attempt to express precisely various measurable features of the output as functions of measurable features of the input. The resulting set of equations would yield predictions of the plant's "behavior." Since, however, the contribution of the factory to the character of output is large compared to the contribution of input, the features of output we could expect to predict (or control) in this way would be severely limited: what output will be made of will be largely unpredictable, let alone (let WAY alone) such features of the output as acceleration capacity and mileage. I suspect tonnage is about all we'll be able to handle, plus latency (we could radioactively tag in-going ore and thereby determine production time), probability of output (Fords vs. M-16's), and number of units producible after wages stop. Pretty limited fare.

Hull buffs will recognize that these outputs are analogues of Hull's dependent variables. For 'tonnage' read 'amplitude'; for 'probability of output' read 'probability of reaction evocation'; for 'latency' read 'latency'; for 'number of units producible after wages stop' read 'number of unreinforced reactions to produce extinction.' It seems clear that if Hull introduced intervening variables in order to theorize about the contribution of the organism, the gambit failed to yield more than the rather boring response variables achievable without the gambit. This should come as no surprise: the requirement that intervening variables be eliminable *guarantees* that they will add *nothing* to output predictability. The point of theorizing about the contribution of the organism or factory would *seem* to be to expand and enrich the predictable and explicable features of output, but Hull's methodological requirement effectively undermines this motivation.

Let's pause to consolidate. Why intervening variables? Not for theoretical economy. Perhaps to enrich and expand the explanatory and predictive scope of the theory then? But the eliminability requirement blocks that possibility. And finally, we must wonder about the explananda: a theory that purports to be a general theory of behavior should endeavor to explain more than Amplitude, Probability of Reaction Evocation, Number of Reactions to Experimental Extinction, and Latency. All of these except n (number of reactions to extinction) characterize particular responses, and science is almost never in the business of explaining particular events. "Why did that white stuff disappear in your coffee?" is not a scientific question; it calls for no theory, but for a particular cause (it dissolved) and, perhaps, some back-up justification of the causal claim (the white stuff is sugar, and sugar is soluble in water, which is mostly what your coffee is). "Why does sugar (or anything) dissolve in water (or anything)?" does call for theory precisely because it is not an individual event but a capacity that is the explanandum. A general theory of behavior should at least address questions about striking behavioral capacities, questions such as these:

—Why are organisms subject to the Law of Effect?

—Why does an after-image perceived as a spot on a wall shrink when the wall is approached?

—Why do people regularly commit the gambler's fallacy?

—Why does alcohol affect memory, and how?

Are recall and recognition reasonable tests of what is remembered, or are they just two of many special tasks for which memorized information is selectively made available?

—Why does the complexity of an English description of a color predict the memorability of colors for non-English speakers with no color vocabulary?

—Why is it easier to learn concepts of the form (A & B) than of the equivalent form -(-A v -B)?

Derivation of values for A, $_s t_r$, p, and n couldn't possibly answer these questions.

The problem is Hull's philosophy of science—his adherence to the doctrine that explanation is nomological subsumption of data. It is not. That doctrine confuses scientific explanation with scientific testing. One consequence is that the explananda of a theory are misidentified with the data that support it, i.e., with the data it subsumes. Hempel pointed out years ago that (narrow) inductivism fails to distinguish theory construction from theory testing. Since testing is inductive in character, narrow inductivism left no room in science for theories that are not generalizations of the data. We now require a comparable distinction between theory testing and theoretical explanation. To assimilate the logic of explanation to the logic of testing leaves us no conceptual space to delineate the difference between the data that support a theory and its intended explananda.

Let us, therefore, abandon the idea that the explananda of Hull's theory are the dependent variables of the theory: it is obvious that intervening variables are supposed to have an explanatory function in Hull's theory, and it is equally obvious that they add nothing to the nomic subsumption of the dependent variables, nor do they serve to enrich or expand the scope of those variables. So long as we suppose that the explananda of the theory are the dependent variables, the explanatory role of intervening variables will remain mysterious.

So what does Hull's theory explain? Once we take off the blinders of the D–N model Hull pushed so hard, I think the answer is obvious: the theory is not a general theory of behavior, but an analytical explanation of the capacity to be operantly conditioned. (Hereafter, I shall refer to this capacity as COC.) The summary diagram of the system we looked at earlier is a flow-chart analysis of COC (see Fig. 3). It would be a tedious but conceptually trivial task to use this flow-chart in conjunction with the glossary at the back of *The Principles of Behavior* to construct a computer program, hence to realize COC, as analyzed by Hull, on a computer. We could then test the analysis by (i) specifying values of the theoretical parameters, and (ii) comparing output with experimental findings.

This, of course, is just what Hullians did, although the simulation was not automated but done with pencil and paper. But thinking of it as simulation helps us focus on the explanatory role of the theory; it brings out several points of importance.

First point. Thinking of the theory in this way has the advantage of putting the dependent variables in their place: they are data, not explananda. The explanandum is COC. So the theory has a serious point, and so does its distinctive feature—the use of intervening variables—for these now appear as analyzing capacities. The Eliminability Requirement even makes a kind of sense: it becomes the requirement that analyzing functions be functionally specified—i.e., specified in terms of their connections to other functions.

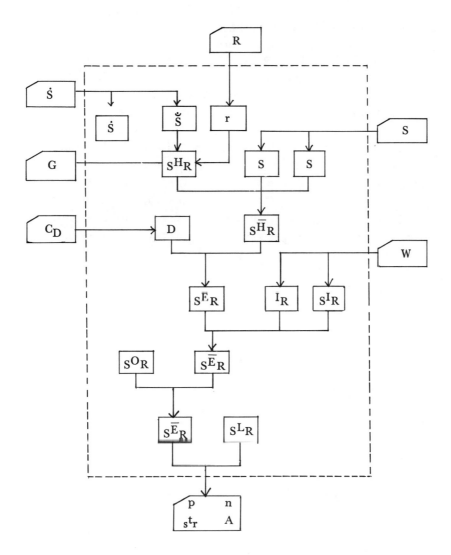

Figure 3.

Second point. COC is a capacity, and a capacity is defined by an input-output function. This is what the Hullian state equations that Miller was confused about do: they specify the capacity to be operantly conditioned. Intervening variables are utterly irrelevant to this specifying role of S-R functions. What *is* relevant is whether the equations fit the data, for that is what tells us whether the capacity we have *specified* is a capacity the organism *has*.

Third point. From this point of view, it is clear that A, $_st_r$, p, and n are measures of output—i.e., that a set of values for these variables is supposed to identify an exercise of COC. There is a theoretical commitment here: the idea is that the empirically possible values for the quadruple $<A, _st_r, p, n>$ for a given organism identify and distinguish the empirically possible exercises of COC in that organism. A, $_st_r$, p, and n no longer figure as general response measures, but simply as measures of exercises of COC.

Fourth point. A corresponding point can be made about the independent variables, $\dot{S}$, R, G, S, C_D, and W, with this difference: whereas we can motivate the inclusion of some of these (e.g., R and S) on the grounds that a capacity without something comparable to these as inputs wouldn't be COC at all, others are motivated solely on the grounds that they are needed to predict output. Inclusion of W, for example, is motivated on these grounds, hence rests on the thesis that specifying $< A, _st_r, p, n>$ is the right way to specify an exercise of COC.

Fifth point. For the theory to be a general theory of COC, not just a theory of COC in rats, or some particular rat, it must contain parameters that we can "tune" for particular organisms or species. It is obvious enough that these *are* present in Hull's theory. I have two comments about them:

(i) Consider $_sE_R$ (excitatory potential). This is calculated as follows in *The Principles of Behavior:* $_sE_R = _{s_1} + _{s_D}\bar{H}_R((\dot{D}+D)/(\dot{D}+M_D))$. Now obviously, changing the slash (division) to an "x" (multiplication) would be changing the analysis, not tuning it. On the other hand, $_sH_R$ is a function of an empirical constant, -j'. The force of saying it is an empirical constant is precisely that it has to be experimentally determined, hence might differ from organism to organism, or from species to species.

(ii) -j', of course, is an intervening variable in the sense of not being a measure of an observable. On the other hand, we cannot calculate -j' from independent variables, and we need it to calculate a value for $< A, {}_st_r, p, n>$. Hence, -j' cannot be eliminated as can genuine intervening variables; mathematically it is an independent variable. This is just what identifies it as a "tuning parameter": it is empirically determined but not a measure of an observable. How do you empirically determine the value of something like this? You pick the value that gives you the best fit between the state-equations and the data. If the state-equations prove difficult or impossible to tune in this way, they are just wrong. Conceptually, this is clear enough. Practically, it is sometimes messy because of the use of statistical techniques in the analysis of data. It is difficult to tell whether a borderline fit means bad tuning or a wrong model. The fact that the fit can be improved by tuning may not mean much unless God or another experimenter tells us how well one can do with a different model altogether.

In practice, the problem of finding a set of state-equations (including tuning parameters) that fits the data is so difficult that it is easy to lose sight of the fact that the ultimate explanatory point of the enterprise is not to predict the data but to explain COC. This seems to me precisely what has happened in learning theory generally, not just in Hull. But it is easier to diagnose in Hull because the idea that the dependent variables are the explananda of the theory is evidently inconsistent with (i) the descriptive scope of the theory, and (ii) the use of intervening variables together with the Eliminability Requirement. The same thing is happening in certain circles in cognitive psychology: the problem of specifying cognitive capacities—i.e., of constructing a set of state-equations that matches input-output data—is so difficult that people have lost sight of the point. The state-equations don't explain anything: the input-output data they subsume are not the explananda; the state-equations are a specification of the explanandum, viz., the capacity they specify. Capacities are not explained by specifying them, be it oh-so-carefully-and-mathematically. They are explained by analyzing them and, ultimately by exhibiting their instantiations in the systems that have them. Specification of a capacity can be a fascinating and challenging scientific problem, but it is not explanation. To the extent that psychology limits itself to this sort of problem—the specification problem—it forfeits its claim to be an explanatory science. To his credit, Hull did insist on his intervening variables, hence did have a shot at explaining something worth explaining—viz., COC—though his adherence to the D–N model of explanation kept him from seeing this clearly. (The explanatory attempt failed, of course, because COC is not to be analyzed into motivational capacities such as drives, but into inferential capacities: a capacity to be operantly conditioned is a capacity to make a certain kind of inductive inference. But that is another story altogether.)

What emerges is that the kind of psychology Hull was trying to do can be pictured as a kind of three-phase project. Phase one is the specification problem, phase two is functional analysis, and phase three is instantiation. This is the standard form of a property theory that has a capacity as explanandum. The three-part division should not be taken to mean that the phases are independent of one another. In practice, one should play both ends against the middle, functional analysis being a sort of middle man, adjusting the requirements of phase three and phase one to each other in a way that makes significant explanation possible. We should never forget that science is something we do in order to increase our understanding, and that it is explanations that do the job. True theories are not always helpful in this regard. It is therefore perfectly in order to reject well-confirmed theories in favor of competitors on the grounds that the competitor allows the construction of an explanatory picture. Looked at in this way, it is clear that neurophysiology (instantiation) constrains psychology no more than psychology constrains neurophysiology. The trick is to get one of each that can be glued together into a coherent explanatory whole by employing the strategy of analysis.

IV.3. FREUD AS FUNCTIONAL ANALYSIS

I was led to write this section because students in my philosophy of psychology courses—which dealt mainly with behaviorism and cognitivism—wanted to hear about Freud. I told them

Freud wasn't worth studying *qua* explanatory theory. They asked why not. When I began to tell them, I realized I was saying just the sort of things about psychoanalysis that behaviorists say about cognitive psychology. And this led me to hypothesize that Freud and cognitivists employ the same explanatory strategy. Philosophers—especially English philosophers—used to debate the claim that psychoanalysis is an elaborate attempt to apply an extended belief/desire psychology—explanation by rationalization—to abnormal behavior. I think there is a kernel of truth in the claim, provided we think of the extension along the lines suggested by contemporary cognitive science.

Is Freudian theory explanatory? It all depends on what you take Freudian theory to be. If it is simply the set of Freud's theoretical statements, then the answer is clearly "no," for this set is inconsistent. This approach, though admirably objective, leads to a boring dead end. Evidently, we must focus on a tidied-up or reconstructed substitute for the textual reality. But which one?

In this section I will propose a way of understanding Freudian explanations which make them precise, empirically testable, and very nontrivial. It may make them false as well, but that's a question for the scientists.

Before I begin, I must enter two caveats: first, let me repeat that this exercise is not to be understood as a contribution to intellectual history: as philosophers or scientists we can, unlike the historian, take the view that some interpretations of Freud are intrinsically interesting whether or not they are what Freud had in mind. This is the merit I claim for the approach described here. If we can find a way of understanding Freudian doctrine that results in an intrinsically interesting and fruitful theory, we need not apologize if our interpretation does not contribute to good intellectual history.

The second caveat is this: Freudian explanations can be understood as part of a therapeutic process, or as an application of a scientific theory. It is the latter perspective I wish to adopt here. I freely confess to having no idea how my approach would fit into a therapeutic setting.

There is a long, if not flourishing, tradition in the philosophy of science of passing methodological judgment on Freudian theory. Almost without exception, attempts in that tradition have led to quick and fairly convincing rejections of all psychodynamic theory as methodologically unsound. It is therefore quite in order to ask why we should go through the whole song-and-dance again. My answer is that previous treatments have all operated under the assumption that all scientific explanation is or should be subsumption under causal law. This assumption pervades even Clark Glymour's recent heroic attempt to reconstruct the epistemological logic of the "Rat Man" case (1980).

It is my contention that psychological explanation generally, and psychodynamic explanation in particular, is typically *not* a species of subsumption under law, but of functional analysis. If we treat Freudian explanations as applications of a transition theory, we are inevitably led to ask: (i) To what psychodynamic laws does Freud appeal? (ii) Are these laws causal? (iii) What sort of inductive warrant does or could Freud have for these laws? (iv) Could there be, in principle, independent epistemic access to the causes and effects subsumed? It is *clear* by now, that Freudian theory does not stand up well to this line of questioning: it simply does not meet the methodological constraints appropriate to the strategy of causal subsumption. Intellectual honesty leaves us with only two alternatives. We must junk Freud, or find a different way to understand Freudian explanation.

My proposal—i.e., that psychodynamic explanation as practiced by Freud and reported in the case histories is best understood as a species of functional analysis—is interesting because the methodological constraints appropriate to functional analysis are quite distinct from those appropriate to causal subsumption. Hence, the demonstrable failure of Freudian explanation to meet the latter constraints may not be very significant.

Very roughly, the idea is (i) to reconstruct individual psychodynamic explanations as function-analytical explanations of neurotic symptoms, and (ii) to reconstruct Freudian theory as a partial functional analysis of the mind, or rather of certain mental capacities. Less roughly, the idea is this: each case history consists of a causal story and an interpretation of it. The causal story consists of a chronological narrative of events in the public domain, and in the conscious and unconscious mind of the subject, together with a specification of causal linkages between these events. An interpretation consists in a systematic mapping of "meanings" or functions onto this causal structure, the mapping being effected by a functional analysis. Freudian theory thus stands to the causal story as a program stands to the hardware that executes it. Neurotic behavior, then, is construed as the exercise of the capacity analyzed, given the conditions or "inputs" specified in the patient's history.

There are five very general considerations that persuade me that this is a workable suggestion.

(1) Leaving therapy aside, the point of a psychoanalytic interpretation is to explain "symptoms." Now to have "symptoms" is to have dispositions to produce anomolous behavior—e.g., a disposition to react irrationally to your father's affair with a friend. This is evidently a sophisticated disposition, and functional analysis is a strategy for explaining sophisticated dispositions. Moreover, that strategy centrally involves appeal to subdispositions and it is obvious enough that Freud explains symptoms by appeal to such things as the disposition to repress unconscious material, the disposition to represent unconscious wishes, the disposition to displace sensations upward, the disposition to convert psychical excitation into physical terms, and so forth.

(2) The crucial explanatory claims in Freud are plainly interpretive: Freud explains a symptom by telling us what it "means," how it got that meaning, and why something or other was bound to get that meaning. On reflection, this seems analogous to explaining the disposition of an adder to add by specifying the meaning of each ink-mark, internal state, button-pressing, etc., and showing that, on the given interpretation, the causal structure realizes an addition algorithm. For the interesting thing about adders is not that they have the capacity to produce funny little patterns, but that they have the capacity to produce patterns systematically interpretable as numerals representing sums of the numbers represented by the numerals that are the interpretations of the 'inputs'. Similarly, it is of no interest to Freud that Dora has the capacity to cough; what interests him is the fact that Dora has the capacity to produce behavior systematically interpretable as a symbol representing an unconscious fantasy involving oral sex.

(3) If the proposal is on the right track, we should be able to read a case history on two levels: (i) a causal story, consisting of

a chronological history of events and their causal connections, and (ii) a principled attempt to fit a coherent interpretation to the causal story. I think it's obvious that this is possible, and that this distinction of levels is one of the most striking features of case histories.

(4) Freud complained that case histories present special organizational difficulties: "Consecutive presentation is not a very adequate means of describing complicated mental processes going on in different layers of the mind" (1920). And Philip Rieff makes a similar point about organizational complications in his introduction to *Dora* (p. 9). This is naturally explained on the hypothesis that we're dealing with systematic-interpretive functional analysis, for the salient feature of that type of analysis is precisely that the analysis cannot be fitted to the causal structure piecemeal. This also explains the usual reaction readers have to a case history such as *Dora:* each claim is incredible, but the whole thing is, somehow, inevitable.

(5) Fundamental questions about Freudian theory and about particular analyses are naturally couched in functional language: (i) When we ask what repression is, we want to know how a repressor would function, i.e., what its input-output properties would be. (ii) Once we grant that repression occurs, the next question is, why? Here, what we want to know is: What is the function of repression? (iii) Freud's basic strategy is to explain symptoms by appeal to their "meanings"—i.e., by appeal to the claim that they represent certain unconscious wishes, hatreds, loves, etc. This raises a fundamental question: *Why* are these things represented in symptoms? Here, what we want to know is, What is the function of symptomatic representation?

These considerations are quite enough, I think, to justify an attempt to construe psychoanalysis as a case of functional analysis of the systematic-interpretive variety. Having explained the proposal, and argued for its prima facie feasibility, it remains to illustrate the proposal in a concrete case.

For purposes of illustration I choose the case history of Dora (1905, page numbers from the Collier Edition of 1974), mainly because it is readable and readily available in paperback. Our first task is to recover the causal story (see Fig. 4). This consists of a chronology of the events mentioned by Freud in the course of the book, divided into events in the public domain, events in Dora's conscious experience, and events in Dora's unconscious. (Some of these, especially the latter, are hypothetical in the sense that Freud is led to suppose their existence in order to explain Dora's symptoms and remarks.) From time to time Freud asserts the existence of causal links between these events, and these links are indicated by connecting arrows. The chart shown here is by no means complete, and some aspects are more soundly grounded in the text than others. Still, it gives a fairly good view of the "plot," as Freud saw it.[8] This stage, though time-consuming and tedious, is relatively straightforward.

The next stage is somewhat trickier: we must "flag" each interpreted event with the interpretation Freud gives it. What makes this tricky is just that it isn't always clear what Freud's interpretations *are*; sometimes it's not even clear what, exactly, he is interpreting. At this stage, the former problem doesn't matter much: we may simply retain Freud's own words.[9] The latter problem is rather unsettling, but this unclarity often disappears at the next stage, and, meanwhile, one just has to live with it. Some sample interpretations from *Dora* follow.

Abdominal pains represent childbirth.

A limp represents a "false step," hence getting pregnant.

Aphonia represents a lover's absence (since there is "no one worth talking to" when he is gone).

A cough represents: Dora's father's asthmatic breathing during intercourse; guilt over venereal disease (via a pun; a catarrh being both a cough and a vaginal discharge); oral sex (fantasized) with Dora's father.

Upper body pressure is said to be a displacement of a perception of Herr K.'s erection during an embrace, the memory of this perception being repressed.

Dora's obsessive rejection of her father's affair with Frau K. is said to be the means by which Dora represses her love for Frau K. and Herr K. It is also said to be a symptom or effect of this repression.

Having come this far, the drudge work is done, and the fun starts. The next stage is to construct a functional theory that will

map the causal story onto its (partial) assigned interpretation. In what follows I will illustrate this stage for a fragment only of the chart for *Dora*; indeed, I will discuss only one interpretation of one symptom. I will ignore corrections—perhaps massive ones—that would no doubt be required to bring what I say here into conformity with (i) a more complete treatment of *Dora,* (ii) a treatment of similar phenomena in other case histories, and (iii) Freud's explicitly theoretical writings on the subjects of repression and obsession.

Dora is obsessed with her father's affair with a certain Frau K. What marks her reaction to the affair as obsessive is the fact that her thoughts and actions are not under normal rational control. Her beliefs about the affair sort ill with her avowed belief that her father is impotent, with her affection for Frau K., and with her lack of affection for her mother. More significantly, her actions conflict with her love for Herr K., a love that would surely be promoted by encouraging the affair: Herr K. would be left alone, and Dora has substantial reason to hope for a divorce between the K's under such circumstances. Yet she opposes the affair in every way possible.

Freud tells us that Dora's love for Herr K. is repressed. What exactly does this mean, and how does it explain, or help to explain, Dora's obsessive behavior? Begin with the former question: What is the function of repression (of love of Herr K.) in this case? Evidently, it cannot be to restore coherence to the conscious belief-desire structure, for in this case repression is supposed to explain obsessive behavior, and obsessive behavior is identified precisely by its irrationality—i.e., by the fact that it manifests beliefs/desires that conflict with other conscious beliefs and desires. Indeed, even a cursory reading of *Dora* reveals that the inconsistency of a set of beliefs/desires is never regarded by Freud as a serious objection to their attribution at the conscious or unconscious level.

A more promising suggestion derives from the nature of obsessive behavior itself: the essential fact about obsessive behavior is that it is engaged in whether it is reasonable or not—i.e., it is produced instead of more reasonable alternatives. In the case at hand, Dora opposes the affair in circumstances in which the more reasonable alternative (for her) would be pursuit of Herr K. That is, Dora's obsessive behavior occurs in place of behavior that would be the natural manifestation of the love she is supposed to have repressed. This gives a valuable hint about the mechanism of repression—about how it's accomplished: Dora cannot both pursue Herr K. and seek to break up her father's affair. But her opposition to the affair is obsessive: she will oppose it whenever the opportunity arises no matter what. Hence, she never has the opportunity to pursue Herr K.: all such opportunities are inevitably and automatically monopolized by incompatible behavior.

But why is this necessary? What is the function of repression—by obsessive exclusion in this case? The natural suggestion is that pursuit of Herr K. is perceived as very undesirable in some way. But this suggestion won't do: if pursuit of Herr K. is perceived as highly undesirable, then it *won't occur,* and for the same reason that Dora will not step out of a third-story window—namely, that more reasonable alternatives—alternatives involving more desirable consequences—are bound to be available. It seems that any action plan that is perceived as so disastrous as to merit exclusion by an obsessive alternative won't require it: elementary, conscious, prudential considerations will exclude it.

This reflection suggests that only actions or action plans that would rationally rank very high could require exclusion by an obsessive alternative. For the special point about an obsessive alternative is that it will exclude incompatible alternatives no matter how desirable or reasonable those alternatives might be made to appear. Thus if obsessive exclusion is to have any role to play, we must suppose that when the opportunity arises, pursuit of Herr K. would appear very desirable indeed to Dora were she to consider it in comparison to other alternatives.

But if this is so, why is exclusion necessary? If this alternative would rank so high, why isn't it simply adopted? Looking at our chart, we find that Dora is frightened and disgusted by sex, at least by sex with men. Furthermore, we find that she regards Herr K. as a "deceiver": he used her former governess ill, it seems, and approached Dora at L. with the same line he used on the governess ("I get nothing from my wife"). What this all adds up to is that *Dora is afraid to do what she wants to do.* So we must conclude, in this case anyway, that the function of repression is to avoid a direct conflict between this fear—which is at least partially conscious, and her love for Herr K. The (or a) standard treatment of "vertigo" is analogous: dizziness prevents the subject from arriving at high places, thereby avoiding a conflict between the fear of falling and a (repressed) desire to jump.

Now this, by Freud's lights anyway, would doubtless be enough to explain Dora's obsessive reaction to the affair between her father and Frau K. But Freud gives us two more related factors. (i) Dora "recalls" her childhood love of her father in order to motivate and reinforce her jealous reaction to the affair (p. 75), and (ii) according to Freud, Dora's jealousy of her father "concealed from herself the contrary fact, which was that she grudged her father Frau K.'s love, and had not forgiven the woman she loved for the disillusionment she had been caused by her betrayal" (p. 80). This is a bit opaque: the main idea seems to be that Dora's love for Frau K. is repressed, as is her love of Herr K., in order to avoid conflict with her fear of betrayal. How opposition to the affair was supposed to accomplish this is not clear: it seems, that Dora's love for Frau K. would *reinforce* her opposition to the affair, and, indeed, this is the line Freud suggests first (p. 72). Looking at the matter in this way, Dora's love for Frau K. leads to jealousy, hence opposition to the affair, hence reinforces the repression of her love for Herr K. But then how is her love for Frau K. repressed? Surely it threatens to show itself here? Perhaps in order to deal with this point, Freud took a different line: Jealousy of her father serves to conceal jealousy of Frau K., hence helps to repress her love for Frau K. But even if we concede the internal coherence of this line (which I do not), it raises another problem. Freud claims that, though "recalled," Dora's love for her father is still repressed. And this sorts ill with Freud's claim that Dora's jealousy of her father conceals jealousy of Frau K.

Freud is aware that his treatment of this matter is not tidy. He introduces the topic thus: "The element to which I must now allude can only serve to obscure and efface the outlines of fine poetic conflict which we have been able to ascribe to Dora" (p. 77). I think he takes the line he does because he thinks he has adequate independent evidence of Dora's unconscious love for Frau K., yet finds no sign on Dora's part of overt jealousy directed at Frau K. This, perhaps, is fair enough. But his claim that Dora's jealousy of her father and her jealousy of Frau K. are *directly opposite and incompatible* seems strained at best.

We could pursue this matter a good deal further—perhaps indefinitely—but we have enough to go on for the illustrative purposes at hand. Let us, therefore, turn to theory-reconstruction.

Our main component is an AFFECT REPRESSOR. Its basic *modus operandi* is to repress an affect by introducing behavior execution of which excludes manifestation of the affect to be repressed (see Fig. 5). To succeed, the affect repressor must be able to find an excluding alternative and confer despotical power on it. Thus its typical output will be *obsessive* behavior. Since, in our case anyway, the function of repression is to avoid a conflict between a repressed desire and a more or less conscious fear, the input to the affect repressor must consist in information about existing fears and desires. Moreover, AFFECT REPRESSOR must be able to judge their relative *intensities*; it must be able to recognize potential conflicts, and to determine whether they are to be avoided by means of obsessive exclusion. So far, we've arrived at the following required components (see Fig. 6):

1. Fear-finder
2. Unconscious affect-finder
3. Conflict evaluator
4. Decider (should conflict be avoided by obsessive exclusion?)
5. Relative intensity measurer
6. (Arbitrary) intensifier
7. Alternative finder

The intensifier apparently does its stuff in part by choosing among candidate excluders one that can serve as an outlet for powerful existing but relatively conflict-free affects.[10] But this cannot be the whole story, for if it were, the excluding alternative would not appear obsessive, merely intense. In our case we have two powerful affects—Dora's love of her father and of Frau K.—reinforcing Dora's opposition to the affair. But neither of these, especially the second, is completely conflict free. Thus the outlet provided must be indirect enough to be compatible with Dora's ignorance of the "true nature" of the feelings she manifests.

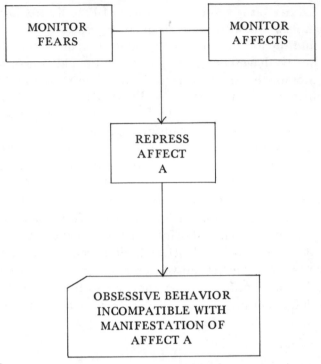

Figure 5.

Apparently, then, the repressor engages in a complex juggling act, using some repressed affects to aid in the repression of others, and vice versa. It must, therefore, be able to evaluate contexts (opportunities) for expression in behavior (and thought): it will exclude Dora's feelings for Herr K. being expressed in the context of *the affair,* by substituting feelings for her father and Frau K., feelings that are relatively unrecognizable in this context. But in the context of, e.g., her seven-year-old cousin's remark that she hates her mother and will marry her father on her mother's death, we must assume that Dora's feelings for her father would be excluded, perhaps even by her feelings for Herr K.!

This gives us the following addition to our list of components (Fig. 7):

8. Context evaluator

Putting all this together, we get the following (Fig. 8): This chart should be thought of as a fragment of a theory of the normal

1. Fear Monitor
2. Desire Monitor
3. Conflict Evaluator
4. Decider (Should conflict be avoided by obsessive exclusion?)
5. Relative Intensity Measurer
6. (Arbitrary) Intensifier
7. Alternative Behavior Finder

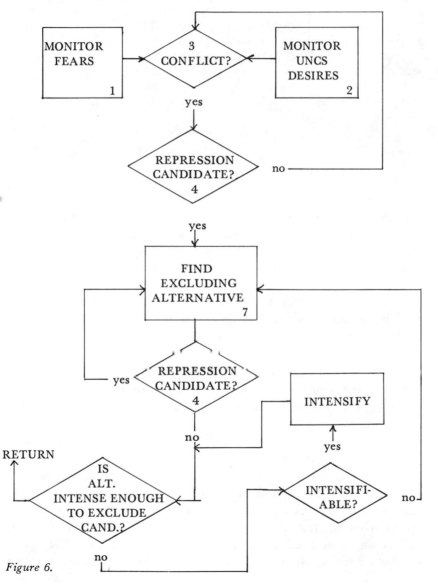

Figure 6.

8. Context Evaluator

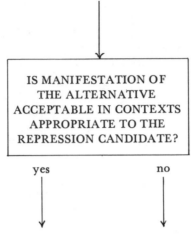

Figure 7.

mind, not as a theory of one neurotic, or even of all neurotics.
To give this idea some substance, if not plausibility, imagine
AFFECT REPRESSOR as a default subroutine in a general program for dealing with risk. Suppose you are being chased by a
bear, and you come to a chasm: what to do? You can jump, or
turn and face the bear. This is a forced option. The usual ways of
dealing with risk—what I call the bettor's options—are to alter the
payoffs or alter the probabilities. In this case, neither of these
options is available. Perhaps you will do the usual calculation and
behave accordingly. Or perhaps you will fool yourself about either
the bear or the chasm or about your abilities to fight or jump. If
you regularly dealt with a risky situation where the options were
not forced in a manner akin to any of these last, you would be be-
having neurotically.

Similarly for Dora. She could decide to pursue Herr K. She
could take up masturbation again. She could pursue someone else.
But the input to her *big* program is not compatible with these outcomes, for the information it has to work with indicates that the
risk involved in these alternatives is too high. Thus Dora is no different from the rest of us. She just got different input. If Freud is
right, we would all default to AFFECT REPRESSOR given
similar experiences. To put it very crudely, neuroses are like

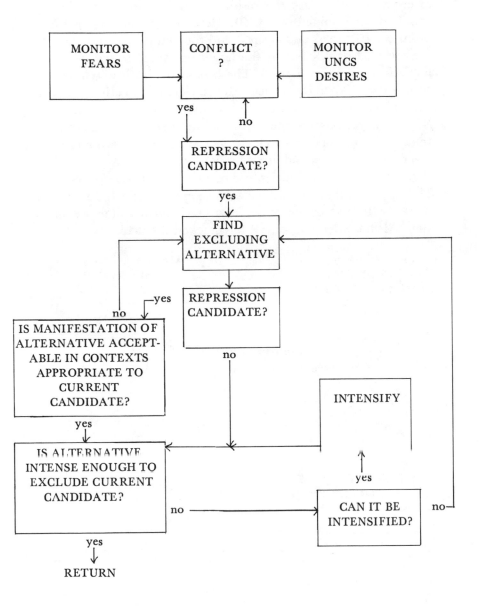

Figure 8.

after-images: they are the result of normal functioning in a non-standard environment (Fig. 9). Here we are supposing that the monitoring of fears and desires, and the determinations of conflict, are not part of AR but of the larger program. So we may stream-line AR a bit, as in Fig. 10. The box at the bottom will now take care of itself. When Dora encounters a Herr K.-pursuit opportunity, she will avoid it by manifesting love of another, her father, or Frau K., whichever is safest; for one way of making it clear to Herr K. that she is unavailable is to lavish her affections elsewhere. She will always pick this second alternative because that has been "intensi-fied"—i.e., the probabilities and payoffs have been skewed by AR. The upshot is that the ordinary decision process will do AR's dirty work for it. The ordinary decision mechanism will make the deci-sions AR has selected, for AR has stacked the deck.

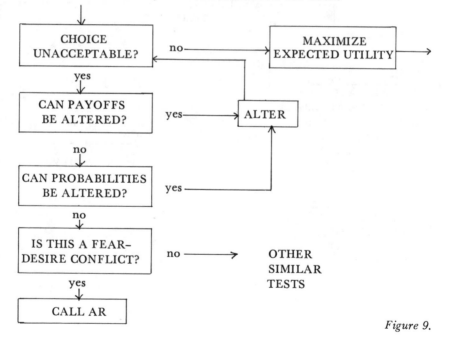

Figure 9.

Conclusions

Well now, is this theory testable? In one respect, it certainly is: we can ask whether it fits the causal story for Dora better or worse than various alternatives, and this question has, for some alterna-tives, perfectly clear answers. I'm sure most readers could suggest

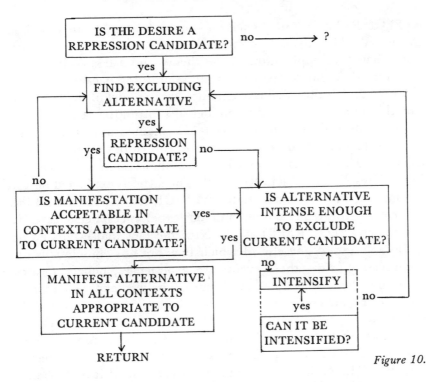

Figure 10.

improvements, and to do so would be to concede my point. But this approach clearly presupposes that the causal story is testable, and, indeed, that it is testable independently of theories such as the one just rehearsed. This is surely more controversial, for what Freud does, of course, is use a theory comparable to AFFECT RE-PRESSOR, together with events above the bottom line, to infer an interpretation of those events. Put abstractly like this, the unconscious does not appear to be implicated at all. But it *is*, because to interpret a symptom is to see it as the expression or representation of an unconscious process. Thus we have not separated the causal story from its interpretation at all: the process of interpretation *is* the process of assigning unconscious "determinations." So the right picture is this: given AFFECT REPRESSOR and the stuff above the bottom line of the causal chart, we infer the stuff below that line and its connections with the material above. This makes the situation look black: we use the theory and what we know about Dora to infer uncheckable conclusions!

What makes the situation *look* so black is that we have no way of getting at the unconscious determinants other than the use of

AFFECT REPRESSOR, hence no way of testing the theory. But this is actually a misunderstanding born of a failure to distinguish the explanatory application of the theory and a test of it. We are accustomed to think of these as the same thing because they *are* the same thing in the deductive-nomological model of explanation. But that model is evidently a model of subsumptive explanation, not of analytical explanation. What is explained in this case is the capacity to produce obsessive behavior, and Dora's exercise of this capacity. The former is explained on the assumption that she instantiates AFFECT REPRESSOR. The latter is explained on the assumption that she instantiates AFFECT REPRESSOR and has had certain conscious and unconscious experiences, hence actually executes AFFECT REPRESSOR. Now the fact that events go on in Dora and everyone else of which they are not conscious is uncontroversial. That these events are experiences, beliefs, desires, fears, and the like, is not.[11] And that the beliefs, experiences, etc., are what Freud says they are in Dora's case is not uncontroversial either. But given AFFECT REPRESSOR and the symptoms, Freud would be justified in inferring these unconscious determinants in order to explain the symptoms. This is not a test of AFFECT REPRESSOR, but an explanatory use of it that assumes its truth. To test AFFECT REPRESSOR, we would, of course, need some independent access to the unconscious occurrences that are supposed to be its "input." Opening up heads won't help much, for an unconscious belief is, at best, an event in the brain under a certain interpretation, and that interpretation could only be enforced by an interpretive functional analysis of the very sort in question. While such a test is possible in principle—as it is in practice with computers—it is not feasible given (i) the moral problems involved in opening heads, and (ii) the lack of an overall functional analysis of the mind. Instead, we would do better to do as Freud did. For example, we could develop a functional analysis of the capacity to have dreams and the capacity to express unconscious wishes in them. We could then test this theory against AFFECT REPRESSOR and vice versa. Better yet, we could develop a functional analysis of the capacity to resolve behavioral conflicts, and test AFFECT REPRESSOR in that context. But the obvious thing to do is to program AFFECT REPRESSOR on a computer, input the history Freud attributes to Dora, and see if it opposes its father's affair. This wouldn't prove that Dora and you and I work the same way, but neither does billiard table experimentation PROVE that car accidents are Newtonian. I, for one, would be impressed.

This is high-handed, of course, because computers don't have fathers. This in itself isn't too serious: we can supply the computer with access to an ersatz, a data structure called 'Dora's father.' And just as a chess-playing computer will upstage or hinder certain moves on the part of its opponents, so our ersatz Dora might upstage or hinder certain moves on the part of our ersatz Dora-father. In fact, we can be pretty sure it would: we've cooked up AR to do just that. So simulating Dora wouldn't be all that impressive. But if the system we *cooked up* to simulate Dora also successfully simulated a variety of other cases, then, I think we should have to buy it, at least pro tem. For we would have demonstrated that *if* people are functionally structured as AR specifies, they would have the neuroses they are observed to have. Most of atomic physics rests on exactly comparable grounds: if atoms are structured as Atomic Theory says they are, then molecules would have the properties they are observed to have.

I conclude that Freudian explanations can be understood as applications of hard-nosed testable and explanatory scientific theories. This is not to say that such theories are true, or even tested. My own view is that when they are tested, they will fail. But that's pure conjecture biased by hope.

Program Execution

A paradigm case of assigning symbolic significance to certain specified physical transactions is provided by the assignment of numerical significance to the states of certain electronic circuits familiar to computer designers. For purposes of illustration, and also in order to crystallize intuitions, consider a typical four-bit counter. The basic circuit in the counter to be considered is the complementing flip-flop, for which a schematic diagram appears in Figure 1.[1]

We distinguish two states of such a circuit: (i) x-state: the terminal labeled 'x-output' is positive relative to the terminal labeled 'y-output', and (ii) y-state: the terminal labeled 'y-output' is positive relative to the terminal labeled 'x-output'. A pulse at the terminal labeled 'input signals' will change the state of the circuit, which is always in one of the states specified. Since negative signals will back-bias the diods, only positive signals (of sufficient amplitude) will affect the circuit. Thus, suppose the y-output is relatively positive. Then T1 (a pnp transistor) is saturated and conducting freely, whereas T2 (a pnp transistor) is cutoff and T2 will begin to conduct. Hence the x-output is now relatively positive. Exactly similar reasoning shows that the next positive pulse will change the circuit back to its original state.

This circuit is represented in so-called *block diagrams* in the simplified form shown in Figure 2. T, for 'trigger', is the input

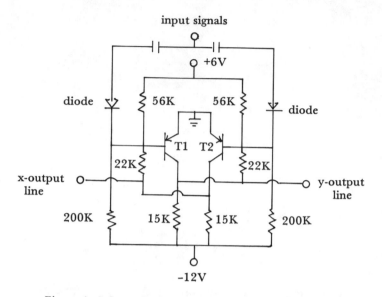

Figure 1: Schematic Diagram of a Complementing Flip-Flop

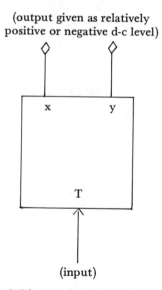

Figure 2: Block Diagram for a Complementing Flip-Flop

signal terminal; the x-output terminal and the y-output terminal
are indicated at the top. The diamonds on the output lines indicate
that outputs are taken as (relative) d-c levels. Using this notation,
we can now show how to construct a four-bit binary counter by
connecting four complementing flip-flops as in Figure 3. To understand the operation of this circuit, assume that the x-outputs are
relatively positive on each of the flip-flops A, B, C and D. When
the first input signal arrives, the y-output of A will go relatively
positive, and the x-output relatively negative. Since the input line
to B is the x-output line from A, and since negative signals have no
effect, B will remain unchanged, as will C and D. The second input
pulse will change the state of A again. This time, the x-line of A
will go relatively positive, and a positive pulse will appear at the
'trigger' of B, changing the state of B. The x-output line of B will
be relatively negative, so C, and hence D, will remain unchanged.
Continuing in this manner, the counter as a whole will successively
assume sixteen different states.

The device described is used to compute the successor function
(count) as follows. First, we assign a symbolic (in this case, numerical) significance to the two states of each flip-flop: the x-state
represents a zero, the y-state represents a one. We then interpret
the state of the counter as a whole by "reading" it from left to
right (D, C, B, A) as a binary representation of an integer in the
interval $[0, 15]$. Thus, just as '15_{10}' or '1111_2' are notations for fifteen, the state of the counter when all its flip-flops are in the y-
state is a notation for fifteen. So interpreted, it is clear that the
counter indeed counts. That is, it successively names (produces
notations for) the integers zero, one, two, . . . fifteen, each symbol
being produced on the occasion of some recognizable event.[2]

Suppose, now, that we are confronted with such a device and
asked to construct a theory of its behavior. Initially, what is required is a transition theory specifying the behavioral capacity of
the device. We require an interpretation I and a transition function
C such that C(i,s) is o, just in case if the device were to be in a
state x such that I(x) = s and an event y such that I(y) = i were to
occur, then, normally, an event z such that I(z) = o would occur.

A theroy of this sort has already been provided in the course of
describing the operation of the device. S, the set of internal states,
consists of the sixteen states of the device defined in terms of the

relative d-c levels of the x-output lines. OUT (the set of outputs) is the same as S. IN (the set of inputs) has a single member which is said to occur just in case a pulse occurs on the input line to the counter. The value of I on this member of IN is inconsequential (let it be a fixed symbol, 'p'). I takes the members of S and OUT into binary notations for the integers in the interval [0,15] in the obvious way. For example, the value of I on the state of the counter in which all y-output lines are relatively positive is '1111'. The transition function takes the binary notation for n onto the binary notation for n plus one, for $0 \leqslant n < 15$, and takes '1111' onto '0000'.

In specifying a satisfactory interpretation and transition function in this case, we are considerably aided by (i) the fact that the designer of the counter solved the difficult problem of choosing an appropriate domain for I, and by (ii) the fact that S and OUT are the same, the current internal state being simply the last response. The parallel which emerges here between the problems of design and the problems of theory construction was and is an important factor in the development of information processing theorizing in psychology. The problem of designing a counter is to design a device of which a certain transition theory will be true.

In this case, more particularly, the problem is to design a device such that there is a transition function C and interpretation I such that C and I constitute a true theory of the device, and C takes notations for integers onto notations for their successors. Now it is possible to design (and build) more than one sort of four-bit counter. That is, there are devices different in design from the counter of Figure 3 for which the interpretation and correlation defined in the last paragraph are perfectly satisfactory. One such is shown in Figure 4. We may think of the counter of Figure 4 as another solution to the same design problem (design a four-bit counter), or we may think of it as a solution to a different design problem, that of designing a counter whose storage units change states in sequence from left to right (units representing more significant digits changing before units representing less significant digits). The counter of Figure 3 may be thought of as a solution to the problem of designing a counter whose storage units change states from right to left (units representing less significant digits changing before units representing more significant digits). If, as

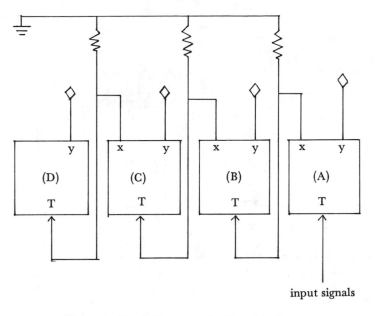

Figure 3: Block Diagram of a Four-bit Counter

suggested, to solve such design problems is to design a device of which a certain theory is true, the question arises as to what the two theories could be in this case.

Global transition theories will not discriminate between the counter of Figure 3 and the counter of Figure 4. This is because both counters have the same input-output properties and internal states.[3] But, although both counters "produce the same behaviors," they produce these behaviors in quite different ways. Our approach will be to attempt to capture these differences by producing two distinct programs, one of which is executed by the counter of Figure 3 and one of which is executed by the counter of Figure 4.

The required program will consist of a list of instructions whose execution in the specified order will replace a binary notation for an integer in the interval [0,14] by a binary notation for its successor, and a binary notation for fifteen by a binary notation for zero. Further, it must be the case that anything executing the program effects these replacements in the way the counter of Figure 3 effects them. That is, it must be the case that the counter of Figure 3 executes the program. Thus, we are searching for a particular

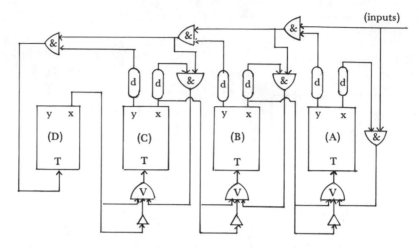

Figure 4: Four-Bit Counter Which Complements from Left to Right

The components labeled 'V' are OR gates. An OR gate passes a positive pulse just in case a positive pulse appears at one of its inputs. An AND gate—labeled '&'—passes a positive pulse just in case positive pulses appear at all its inputs. The components labeled 'd' delay a pulse. The components represented by triangles invert a pulse—change negative to positive and positive to negative pulses.

To understand the operation of this device, imagine that the x-lines of (D) and (C) are relatively positive while the y-lines of (B) and (A) are relatively positive. An input pulse will fail to pass the AND gate to the right of (A), but will pass the AND gate above (A). It will fail to pass the AND gate between (A) and (B), but will pass the AND gate above (B). The pulse will not pass the AND gate above (D), but will pass the AND gate between (C) and (B). The OR gate below (C) will be passed and (C) triggered, sending a negative "edge" down the x-line of (C). This will be inverted, and a positive "edge" will pass the OR gate below (B), triggering (B). This will send a positive "edge" down the x-line of (B) which will pass the OR gate below (A) and trigger (A). Result: x-lines of (D), (B) and (A) relatively positive, y-line of (C) relatively positive.

computation of the transition function C. The counter is known to (was designed to) compute C. We now wish to specify the instructions it executes in order to effect this computation.

The following is a program for replacing the binary notation for n by a binary notation for n+1, modulo 15—for "augmenting" the symbol which consists of the symbols, D, C, B, A in that order.

AUGMENT D͡ C͡ B͡ A[4]   (I)

(1) START.
(2) COMPLEMENT A.

(3) IF A CHANGES TO 0, CONTINUE; OTHERWISE, GO TO (9).
(4) COMPLEMENT B.
(5) IF B CHANGES TO 0, CONTINUE; OTHERWISE, GO TO (9).
(6) COMPLEMENT C.
(7) IF C CHANGES TO 0, CONTINUE; OTHERWISE, GO TO (9).
(8) COMPLEMENT D.
(9) STOP.

In this program, 'A', 'B', 'C' and 'D' are names for symbols—in this case variables—each of which may take either of two values. They will be called memory symbols. To complement a memory symbol is simply to change its value. If necessary, we could easily write a sub-routine for performing the complementing operation, regarding instructions (2), (4), (6) and (8) as instructions to execute this sub-routine.

COMPLEMENT X

(1) IF X = 1, GO TO (3): OTHERWISE, CONTINUE.
(2) SET X = 1, AND GO TO (4).
(3) SET X = 0.
(4) RETURN AND CONTINUE.

To execute instruction (4) in the main program, one executes the subroutine COMPLEMENT X, with 'B' for 'X'. Instruction (4) of the subroutine returns control to the main program, in this case to instruction (5). Whether or not we wish to include a sub-routine for executing the COMPLEMENT operation will depend on explanatory considerations that are not at issue here. The only question to be considered here is this: does the device execute these instructions? Or rather: under what conditions should the device be said to execute these instructions? By arguing on an intuitive level for a positive answer to the first question, I hope to tease out the beginnings of an answer to the second.

The assumption is that the device does execute some program or other, the problem being to discover which one. It will therefore be useful to compare the program above, which I will call Augmenter I, with a competitor, Augmenter II. Eventually, I shall argue that the counter of Figure 3 executes Augmenter I, the Figure 4 counter Augmenter II.

AUGMENT D͡ C͡ B A.   (II)

(1) START.
(2) IF A = 0, GO TO (11); OTHERWISE, CONTINUE.
(3) IF B = 0, GO TO (9); OTHERWISE, CONTINUE.
(4) IF C = 0, GO to (7); OTHERWISE, CONTINUE.
(5) COMPLEMENT D.
(6) IF D CHANGED, CONTINUE; OTHERWISE, GO TO (12).
(7) COMPLEMENT C.
(8) IF C CHANGED, CONTINUE; OTHERWISE, GO TO (12).
(9) COMPLEMENT B.
(10) IF B CHANGED, CONTINUE; OTHERWISE, GO TO (12).
(11) COMPLEMENT A.
(12) STOP.

Augmenter I and Augmenter II have the same input output properties. That is, given initial values for A, B, C and D, execution of each program results in the same terminal values. I will express this by saying that the two programs are output-equivalent. Further, if we regard 'A', 'B', 'C' and 'D' as names for the four flip-flops of the counter of Figure 3, or of Figure 4, interpret '= 0' to mean the same as 'has a relatively negative y-output line', and interpret '=1' to mean the same as 'has a relatively positive y-output line', then both programs are, in an intuitively obvious sense, adequate accounts of the input-output properties of both devices. That is, each program will, when executed, replace a true description of the state of a counter before an input pulse with a true description of the first state of that counter after that pulse such that the counter would normally remain in that state until another pulse were received.[5] This I will express by saying that the programs are *output-adequate* for the devices of Figure 3 and Figure 4 under the interpretations given. Since the notions of output-adequacy and interpretation will play an important role in what follows, we will need to stop in order to generalize them and make them precise.

Following Newell, Shaw and Simon (1957), the object under study will be assumed to have a number of distinct parts, called memories, each of which is capable of assuming a number of distinct states. A memory-interpretation I of a device d for a program c is a function having parts of d and states of those parts as domain and the set of memory symbols of C and their values as range.

> I : X $\underset{\text{onto}}{\to}$ Y is a memory interpretation of a device for a program C if and only if, (i) X = S $\cup$ P where P is a set of parts of d, S a set of states of those parts, (ii) Y = M $\cup$ V where M is the set of memory symbols of C, V the set of their values, and (iii) for all p in P, s in S, I(p) is in M and I(s) is in V and s is a state of p if and only if I(s) is a value of I(p).

It was the trick of providing memory-interpretations of the counters of Figure 3 and Figure 4 for Augmenter I and Augmenter II that allowed us to think of those programs as trafficking in descriptions of the counters. We can now use the definition just given to define output-adequacy.

Intuitively, the idea is to mirror the input-output properties of a device by the input-output properties of the associated program. But since a memory-interpretation only interprets parts and states of parts, we run up against a problem. Although the terminal value of a program's memory symbols—or some subset of them—appear to be a natural interpretation for outputs, a memory-interpretation provides no equally plausible candidates for interpretations of inputs to a device. The initial values of the memory symbols correspond to initial internal states of the device, not to inputs to the device. This can be seen clearly in the case of the counter of Figure 3. As was pointed out above, the "current" internal state is simply the last response—the terminal state of the counter after the last pulse.

The inputs to the counter are obviously the pulses on the input line. But these have no plausible interpretation in the program, at least via a memory-interpretation. Actually, on an intuitive level, it seems that giving an input to the counter—pulsing the input wire—simply corresponds to starting to execute the program. Thus we might consider the following correlations: interpret all inputs as instructions to start, interpret "current" internal states as initial values of the memory symbols, and interpret outputs as terminal vaues of the memory symbols (or some subset of these).

The problem with this approach is that it can make no distinctions between inputs. For the counters under consideration, this is not a difficulty since only one type of input is distinguished: only responses to positive pulses are considered, since interpretable transactions occur only on reception of a positive pulse. If an input of a different nature, a negative pulse, say, is tried, the counter will not respond at all; that is, nothing interpreted as a response will occur.

We can easily imagine, however, that this is not the case. Indeed, it is easy to design counters which accept both positive and negative pulses and which behave rather differently, depending on the sort of pulse received. Figure 5 depicts such a counter. This device is like that of Figure 3 except that negative pulses on the input line will "clear" the counter rather than have no effect.

There are two ways to treat this kind of problem. The first is to write several programs, one corresponding to each type of input, and interpret each type of input as the START instruction of the corresponding program. The second is to introduce a new memory symbol, the different values of which will correspond to the various inputs. A conditional or "branching" instruction will then direct control to appropriate sub-routines, depending on the value of the new memory symbol. In order to make this clear, both approaches will be illustrated for the device of Figure 5.

First Approach. We include two programs, one exactly like Augmenter I, and the other as follows:

>CLEAR
>
>START.
>SET A, B, C, AND D = 0.
>STOP.

Negative input pulses are then interpreted as instructions to start CLEAR, while positive input pulses are interpreted as instructions to start Augmenter I.

Second Approach. One program is specified as follows:

>(1) START.
>(2) IF E = 0, GOT TO (11). OTHERWISE, CONTINUE.
>(3) COMPLEMENT A.
>(4) IF A CHANGES TO 0, CONTINUE; OTHERWISE,
>   GO TO (12).

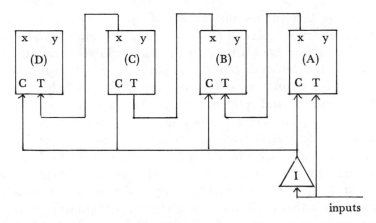

Figure 5: Four-Bit Counter Which Accepts Positive and Negative Input Pulses
The input terminals to the flip-flops marked "C" are called CLEAR input
terminals. A positive pulse at the CLEAR input will cause the y-output to go
relatively positive. As usual, a negative pulse has no effect at the flip-flop in-
puts, though, of course, a negative pulse on the input line to the counter will
clear the counter.

    (5) COMPLEMENT B.
    (6) IF B CHANGES TO 0, CONTINUE; OTHERWISE,
        GO TO (12).
    (7) COMPLEMENT C.
    (8) IF C CHANGES TO 0, CONTINUE: OTHERWISE,
        GO TO (12).
    (9) COMPLEMENT D.
  (10) STOP.
  (11) SET A, B, C, AND D = 0.
  (12) STOP.

The correct memory-interpretation will give the memory symbol E as value on the input line of the counter. A negative pulse in
the input line will be mapped onto the value zero (of E); a positive
pulse onto the value one (of E). The device will be considered to
have received an input if it receives one sort of pulse or the other,
and inputs to the device, so construed, will be interpreted as instructions to start.

Neither approach is "the correct approach." Indeed, there is no
such thing. Rather, we are faced with a largely arbitrary decision

about how to talk, in this context, about inputs. The first approach is perhaps the more natural in that it preserves the ordinary view that a device may have a number of distinct kinds of inputs, the behavior of the device depending, in part, on what type is actually received. The second approach, on the other hand, has certain formal advantages, and reflects the fact that, in many cases, to give an "input" to a device in the ordinary sense is simply to change the structure or state of the device and to start it going.[6] I will adopt the second approach, but, if it were convenient to do so, the definitions which follow could be altered to accommodate the first approach. The main feature of the use of the second approach in what follows is that it allows us to ignore the notion of input.

The initial internal state of a device will be interpreted in terms of initial values for the set of memory symbols. For a particular program C, the set of memory symbols will be called the *memory set* of C. A set of values for the members of the memory set of C will be called a *valuation* of C. Assuming an ordering of the memory set, a valuation of C may be thought of as an ordered n-tuple the kth member of which is the value of the kth member of the memory set, where n is the cardinal number of the memory set. The set of valuations for a program will be denoted by 'V_C'. A Valuation with which a given execution of a program begins is called the *initial valuation* for the execution.

The outputs of a program C are given by the values of certain of the memory symbols of C at the time the instruction to stop is executed. The set of the memory symbols involved will be called the *output set* of C. A set of values for the members of the output set of C will be called an *output* of C. Assuming an ordering of the output set, an output may be thought of as an ordered n-tuple the kth member of which is the value of the kth member of the output set. The set of outputs of a program C will be denoted by 'OUT_C'. The memory and output sets for a program need not be a proper subset of the memory set. The memory set of C should not be confused with V_C; and the output set of C should not be confused with OUT_C.

With a view to defining output-adequacy, I will now show how a memory-interpretation can be used to associate the initial valuations and outputs of a program with the (physically specified) behavior of an appropriate device.

Let I: $S \cup P \to M \cup V$ be a memory-interpretation of a device d for a program C. Let n be the cardinal number of the memory set of C,

Memory set for $C = A_1, A_2, \ldots, A_n$.

Let N be in V_C; $N = (a_1, a_2, \ldots, a_n)$. d is in the I-state I^N if, and only if, a part p such that $I(p) = A_i$ is in a state s such that $I(s) = a_i$ for all i, $0 < i < n + 1$. Simiarly, let m be the cardinal number of the output set of C.

Output set of $C = B_, B_2, \ldots, B_m$.

Let O be in OUT_C; $0 = (b_1, b_2, \ldots, b_m)$. d is said to give the I-output I^O when a part p such that $I(p) = B_i$ is in a state s such that $I(s) = b_i$ for all i, $0 < i < m + 1$. I-states and I-outputs may be thought of simply as sets of states of parts of d.

If a program C gives the output O on the initial valuation N, I shall write 'N $\underset{C}{\rightleftarrows}$ O'. If C gives no member of OUT_C as output on N, I shall write 'N $\underset{C}{\rightleftarrows}$!'. Correspondingly, if it is the case that if d were in the I-state I^N and given an output, d would normally give the I-output I^O, then I shall write '$I^N \underset{d}{\rightleftarrows} I^O$'. If it is the case that if d were in the I-state I^N and given an input d would not normally produce any I-output, then I shall write '$I^N \underset{d}{\rightleftarrows} !$'.[7]

> C is an *output-adequate program for d* if, and only if, there is a memory interpretation of I of d for C such that for all N in V_C, O in OUT_C, (i) N $\underset{C}{\rightleftarrows}$ O if, and only if, $I^N \underset{d}{\rightleftarrows} I^O$; (ii) N $\underset{C}{\rightleftarrows}$! if, and only if, $I^N \underset{d}{\rightleftarrows} !$.

> Two programs C and C′ are *output-equivalent* if, and only if, (i) $V_C - V_{C'}$, and $OUT_C = OUT_{C'}$, and (ii) for all N in V_C, O in $OUT_{C'}$, N $\underset{C}{\rightleftarrows}$ O if, and only if N $\underset{C'}{\rightleftarrows}$ O; N $\underset{C}{\rightleftarrows}$! if, and only if N $\underset{C'}{\rightleftarrows}$!.

> Two programs C and C′ are *output-isomorphic* if, and only if, there are one-one functions f_1 and f_2, $f_1 : V_C \to V_{C'}$; $f_2 : OUT_C \to OUT_{C'}$, such that for all N in V_C, O in OUT_C, N $\underset{C}{\rightleftarrows}$ O if, and only if, $f_1(N) \to f_2(0)$; N $\underset{C}{\rightleftarrows}$! if, and only if, $f_2(N) \underset{C'}{\rightleftarrows}$!.

Evidently, by these definitions, Augmenter I and Augmenter II are output-equivalent. Also, under the interpretation given earlier, both programs are output-adequate for the counters of Figure 3 and Figure 4. Since the notion of an output of a device only makes sense relative to some memory-interpretation and program, we cannot simply conclude that the counters of Figure 3 and Figure 4 are output-equivalent: to say of two devices that they are output-equivalent *simpliciter* makes no sense. We can, however, make sense of the claim that, relative to a program C, two devices are output-equivalent: C is output-adequate for both. By this definition, it is clear that the counters of Figure 3 and Figure 4 are output equivalent relative to Augmenter I and relative to Augmenter II.

As far as output-adequacy goes, there is no reason to associate one program rather than the other with either counter. Nevertheless, it is obvious that the two counters operate differently. Our task is to formulate a definition of 'd executes C' so as to be able to capture these differences in differing programs. To begin with, I shall argue that differences between Augmenter I and Augmenter II capture the important differences between the counters of Figure 3 and Figure 4. After seeing how this is done, I shall generalize to the desired definition.

One important difference between the two counters has already been noted. The flip-flops of the Figure 3 counter change states from right to left, the unit representing the least significant digit changing first, while the opposite holds of the Figure 4 counter. This is reflected by the fact that in Augmenter I, the instruction to complement A is executed before the instruction to complement B, etc., whereas in Augmenter II, the instruction to complement D is executed before the instruction to complement C, etc.

This fact alone is enough reason to prefer Augmenter I to Augmenter II for the Figure 3 counter, and Augmenter II to Augmenter I for the Figure 4 counter. But there are differences other than differences in the order in which memory symbols change value. Compare the following program with Augmenter I.

AUGMENT D̂ Ĉ B̂ A.   (III)

(1) START.
(2) COMPLEMENT A.
(3) IF A = 1, GO TO (9); OTHERWISE, CONTINUE.
(4) COMPLEMENT B.
(5) IF B = 1, GO TO (9); OTHERWISE, CONTINUE.
(6) COMPLEMENT C.

(7) IF C = 1, GO TO (9); OTHERWISE, CONTINUE.

(8) COMPLEMENT D.

(9) STOP.

Augmenter I and Augmenter III are quite similar. Memory symbols are changed in the same order, with each change in a memory symbol other than A depending on the outcome of the previous change. Nevertheless, they are significantly different. Assume that A = 0 and B = 1. In both programs, the first instruction to be executed which effects a change in the value of a memory symbol is the instruction to complement A. Now suppose this instruction is fluffed in both cases. Augmenter I will simply stop, making no change in B. Augmenter III, however, will complement both B and C. Checking Figure 3, we see that the behavior of the device diagrammed there answers to Augmenter I and not to Augmenter III. For if flip-flop A is not triggered, no positive edge will appear at the trigger of flip-flop B. Augmenter I correctly captures the fact that a change in flip-flop B depends on a certain *change* in flip-flop A and not on the current state of flip-flop A.

Examining Augmenter II, we see that a change in the value of memory symbol B depends on both the initial value of A and, in some cases, on whether a change takes place in the value of C. So if Augmenter II is correct for the device of Figure 4, we should expect an examination of Figure 4 to reveal that changes of state in flip-flop B depend on both the initial state of flip-flop A and, in some cases, on whether a change of state occurs in flip-flop C.

This is indeed the case. That changes in flip-flop B depend on the initial state of flip-flop A is evident: the AND gate above A must be passed if B is to change at all, and that gate is only enabled when A is in the y-state. To see that a change in B sometimes depends on the occurrence of a change in C, imagine that flip-flops D and C are in the x-state, while flip-flops B and A are in the y-state. An input pulse will pass the AND-gates above A and B as well as the AND-gate between C and B, and the subsequent CR-gate. Now any change at all in C will cause a positive edge to appear at the trigger of B. But if no change occurs in C because of some malfunction, then no change will take place in B. It is this fact which requires the inclusion of instructions (6), (8) and (10) in

Augmenter II. If these instructions are deleted, then the initial valuation (0, 0, 1, 1) will lead to changes in the values of memory symbols B and A regardless of whether or not the instruction to complement C is mis-executed.

The points which have emerged are the following. Given an appropriate interpretation, a correct program of a device d must (i) mirror the changes in memories and the order of these changes, (ii) mirror the dependencies between changes in and states of one memory and changes in others.

Corresponding to the changes in individual memories are the changes in value of associated (via a memory-interpretation) memory symbols. Corresponding to the order of changes in memories is the order of instructions specifying changes in the values of associated memory symbols. Let us stop to make this precise.

In the case of the Figure 3 counter, we wish to interpret a change in the state of the left-most flip-flop from x-state to y-state as an execution of an instruction to change the value of I (flip-flop D) from I (x-state) to I (y-state), i.e., an instruction to change the value of memory symbol D from 0 to 1. Now on the face of it, there is no such instruction in Augmenter I. There is an instruction 'COMPLEMENT D', but this instruction, taken by itself, does not determine a value of the memory symbol D. Whether or not executing this instruction does effect a change from D = 0 to D = 1 depends on the value of D before the instruction is executed. And this in turn depends on the effect of previously executed instructions on the initial valuation which initiated the execution of the program. In general, it makes no sense to ask *simpliciter* whether or not a given instruction correctly interprets a given change in the memories associated with it by some memory-interpretation. Rather, we must ask whether an instruction as it comes to be executed in the course of executing an entire program on some particular initial valuation correctly interprets a given change in the memories associated with it by a memory-interpretation. In what follows the notion of the context of an instruction's execution is made precise in the definition of a memory-path. The requirement that a device execute all the memory-paths of a program is meant to capture in a precise way the requirement (i) above that a correct program of a device mirror the changes in memories and the order of these changes.

By a path in a program C we mean an initial valuation N together with the sequence of instructions whose execution is required for the execution of C on N. A path is "generated" by a particular execution or "run" of the program in the sense that, if each instruction is written down as it is executed, the resulting list, together with the initial valuation initiating the run, will be a path. Each initial valuation determines (belongs to) one and only one path and is said to initiate that path.

In general, an instruction taken by itself does not determine a definite value for the memory symbols involved. Thus, as lately pointed out, the instruction to complement D does not determine a value of D unless an initial value of D is given. But in the context of a path, instructions other than instructions to start, stop and branch (i.e., go to some specified instruction) do determine a specific change in the value of the memory symbols involved; the initial valuation providing a definite initial value of each instruction involving a given memory symbol for the first time, and the result of executing an instruction involving a given memory symbol providing a definite initial value for the next instruction involving that memory symbol.

The result of deleting from a path instructions to branch as well as 'START' and 'STOP' will be called a memory-path. It should be clear that Augmenter I and Augmenter III have the same memory-paths, though not the same paths, while Augmenter II has different memory-paths. Thus, as expected, the fact that a device executes all the memory-paths of a program will distinguish between Augmenter I and Augmenter II, but will not distinguish between Augmenter I and Augmenter III.

In the context of a particular memory-path, execution of an instruction x has the effect of fixing values for certain memory symbols (usually only one). I shall write 'x_i $^P(A) \Rightarrow (a)$' to abbreviate 'in executing the memory-path p, execution of the ith instruction in p[8] fixes the value of the memory symbol A at a'. Similarly, let '(p) $\underset{d}{\Rightarrow}$ (s)' abbreviate 'part p of d changes to state s'.

We are now in a position to attempt a definition of memory-path execution. Let p be a memory-path $x_1, \ldots, x_i, \ldots$ (possibly infinite) initiated by the initial valuation N in a program C. Let M be the set of memory symbols of C, V the set of values.

d executes the first instruction of p if, and only if, there exists a memory-interpretation I of d for C such that if d is in I^N and given an input, then subsequently,[9] for all A in M, a in V, $x_1^P(A) \Rightarrow (a)$ if, and only if, (p) $\underset{d}{\Rightarrow}$ (s) for some p and s such that $I(p) = A$ and $I(s) = a$.

d executes the first n (n>1) instructions of p if, and only if, there exists a memory-interpretation I of d for C such that if d executes the first n–1 instructions of p, then, subsequently,[9] for all A in M, a in V, $x_n^P(A) \Rightarrow (a)$ if, and only if, (p) $\Rightarrow$ (s) for some p and s such that $I(p) = A$ and $I(s) = a$.

If p has a finite length, say k instructions, then d executes p just in case d executes the first k instruction of p. If p is infinite, d executes p just in case for all $n > 0$, d executes the first n instructions of p.

Several problems arise in connection with this definition. The definition requires that the changes in the memories of d take place successively in the order specified, via I, by the memory-path. Nothing is said, however, about how long each transaction is to take, or how long an interval might separate the occurrence of two particular transactions. Suppose that the counter of Figure 3, beginning with flip-flops A and B in the y-state, C and D in the x-state, receives an input pulse: flip-flop A changes to the x-state, then flip-flop B does the same, but so far, nothing further has happened. So far, the counter has executed the first two instructions of the memory-path in Augmenter I initiated by (0, 0, 1, 1), but not the first three (the whole path). How long must w wait to be sure that the counter will not complete the path? In general, there is no answer to this question. In practice, we can be quite certain that the counter will not complete the path: the circuitry is such that any lag indicates a breakdown.

Obviously the question "Is such-and-such a sequence of transactions in d an execution of the first n instructions of the memory path p?" can, in principle be definitely answered in the affirmative. But the question cannot, in general, be definitely answered in the negative, for this would require trying all possible memory-interpretations of d for every program of which p is a memory-path. Indeed, as the example above shows, even if we fix the memory-interpretation, as was done implicitly in the example, no finite period of observation will guarantee a negative answer. Of course, the fortuitous occurrence of an unspecified change in memory can show that a given path is not executed (relative, of course, to some fixed memory-interpretation). But even discounting such fortuitous occurrences as well as possible independent knowledge of break-down or abnormal functioning, the situation is tolerably good. At any given moment, the question "relative to the memory-interpretation I, has d executed, as of this moment, the first n instructions of memory-path p?" has, in principle, a definite affirmative or negative answer. Later on, when we come to formulate a full-fledged definition of adequacy for programs, this clarity will disappear. For adequacy requires (among other things) not that a device actually execute the appropriate paths, but only that it have this capacity.

We have now laid the groundwork for capturing the requirement (i) above that a correct program mirror changes in memories and the order in which they occur. The next task is to deal similarly with the requirement (ii) that a correct program mirror the dependencies between changes in, and states of, one memory, and changes in others.

In arguing for the existence of a significant difference between Augmenter I and III, I pointed out that a mis-execution of the instruction to complement A sometimes has differing effects on their respective outputs. This is because, in Augmenter I, changes in value of B depend on the occurrence of a change in the value of A from 1 to 0. In Augmenter III this is not the case. In that program, if B is to be complemented at all, it is complemented regardless of whether or not the instruction to complement A is mis-executed. A similar point holds with respect to the other memory symbols of the two programs. Since it is obvious that the behavior of the Figure 3 counter answers to Augmenter I in this respect and not to Augmenter III, the straightforward strategy is to generalize the requirement that mis-executions of instructions by a device lead to deviations in operation as predicted by the program. This strategy will be adopted in what follows, keeping in mind that it is the difference in organization effected by the branching instructions that is at issue.

Mis-executions are of two sorts. An instruction may simply fail to be executed at all, or it may be wrongly executed, resulting in the assignment of an incorrect value to some memory symbol.[10] In either case, further execution of the program may be altered, and/or the output may be affected, because of the fact that some memory symbol may have an incorrect value, or an incorrect change may have taken place in the value of some memory symbol.[11]

In the context of a particular memory-path, the effect of an instruction is fixed. Thus, in the memory-path initiated by (0, 0, 1, 0) in Augmenter III, the effect of the instruction to complement A is to set A equal to 1. Any operation which doesn't have this effect is a mis-execution. Altogether, there are eight possibilities: no change is made at all, B is set equal to 1, or D is set equal to 1 or some combination of these last three occurs. In each case, the result is a change in the memory-path. The path which is actually executed, given a particular mis-execution, can be constructed as follows. Suppose the mis-execution in question amounts to setting C equal to 1. The effect of this mis-execution is to execute the instruction to complement C instead of the instruction to complement A. If we substitute this instruction for the original in Augmenter III we get a variation on Augmenter III. Call this new program C'. The memory-path initated by (0, 0, 1, 0) in C' is (COMPLEMENT C, COMPLEMENT B, COMPLEMENT C, COMPLEMENT D).

Similarly, assume the mis-execution in question to be the one considered earlier, namely, no change. The relevant variation on Augmenter III is constructed by deleting the instruction to complement A, or, in order not to effect the numbering, by substituting 'CONTINUE' for 'COMPLEMENT A.' The memory-path initiated by (0, 0, 1, 0) in this variation is (CONTINUE, COMPLEMENT B).

We rejected Augmenter III as a program for the Figure 3 counter because if that counter executes all the memory-paths of Augmenter III under a memory-interpretation I, then it does not execute the path just constructed under I when flip-flop A fails to trigger.

This suggests the following strategy. Assume d executes all the memory-paths of a program C under a memory-interpretation I of d for C. Now suppose d executes the first n instructions of a memory-path p initiated by N in C, and suppose x_{n+1}^p (A) $\Rightarrow$ (a).

However, instead of it being the case that $(r) \underset{d}{\Rightarrow} (s)$ for some r and s such that $I(r) = A$, and $I(s) = a$, suppose it is the case that $(r) \underset{d}{\Rightarrow} (s')$ where $I(s') \neq a$. This is a mis-execution of the n+1th instruction.[12] Corresponding to the fact that $(r) \underset{d}{\Rightarrow} (s')$ we should have had $x_{n+1}^{p} (A) = (b)$, where $I(s') = b$. So strike the part of the n+1th instruction which changes the value of A to a, and append to it the instruction to set A equal to b. Now consider the variation of C' of C which results from substituting the appended instruction for the original in C, and construct the memory-path p' initiated by N in C'. The suggestion is that, in all such cases, d must execute p'. Unfortunately, although on the right track, this suggestion will not do.

Consider the program of note 6, which I will call simply L.

> L
>
> (1) START.
> (2) SET A = A+1.
> (3) IF A< 10, GO TO (2); OTHERWISE, CONTINUE.
> (4) STOP.

If the initial value of A is n, n< 10, instruction (2) will appear 10-n times in the memory path initiated by (n). Now mis-execution of this instruction on one occasion is no guarantee that it will be mis-executed on another. Furthermore, the instruction may be fluffed in different ways on different occasions. These facts are ignored if we construct variations on paths in the way described above.

To see the consequences of this, assume an initial value of A = 8. The memory-path initiated by (9) is (SET A = A+1, SET A=A+1), or $((2), (2))$. We have that $(2)_1 (A) \Rightarrow (9)$ and $(2)_2 (A) \Rightarrow (10)$. But now suppose (2) is mis-executed the first time around, with a subtraction being made instead of an addition, but is correctly executed thereafter. According to the procedure sketched above, we construct a variant program as follows

> L'
>
> (1) START.
> (2) SET A = 7.
> (3) IF A< 10, GO TO (2); OTHERWISE, CONTINUE.
> (4) STOP.

and consider the memory path initiated in this program by (8), namely, (SET A = 7, SET A = 7, . . .). What is wanted, however, is (SET A = 7, SET A = A+1, SET A = A+L, SET A = A+1). Substitution of 'SET A = A-1' for (2) yields no better results.

One way out of this situation is suggested by the fact that the correct execution of instruction (2) in L the second time around is, from the point of view of the variant memory-path, a mis-execution of the second instruction of that variant. Proper execution of the path requires that nothing happen, but, by hypothesis, $(r) \underset{d}{\Rightarrow} (s)$ where $I(r) = A$, $I(s) = 7$, and then $(r) \underset{d}{\Rightarrow} (s')$, where $I(s') = 8$, then $(r) \underset{d}{\Rightarrow} (s'')$, where $I(s'') = 9$, then $(r) \underset{d}{\Rightarrow} (s''')$ where $I(s''') = 10$. The obvious suggestion is to construct a variant of the variant of p, using the same procedure as was used to construct the variant of p. But this suggestion clearly will not do. The procedures under study would have us substitute the instruction to set A equal to eight into L', but this results in the memory-path (SET A = 8, SET A = 8, . . .) which is not executed at all. In fact, it is evident that the procedure above will always yield memory-paths of the form (X, X, . . .) and no memory-path of this form is satisfactory.

The moral of this story seems to be that variations on memory-paths should be constructed by substitution in memory-paths, not in the original program. However, if we change the ith instruction of p, then we must return to the program to construct the rest of the memory-path. This is simply because, depending on the branching instructions in the program, the change effected by the ith instruction may lead to changes entirely different from those specified (via I) by the $i+1^{th}$, $i+2^{th}$, . . . instructions in p.

A variant p' of p from the ith instruction should be constructed as follows. Let p be a memory-path in C. p' is the same as p through the $i-1^{th}$ instruction. Execute the first $i-1$ instructions of p. Suppose the ith instruction of p has the reference number k in C. Instead of executing k, execute some appropriate substitute. Now continue to execute C beginning with $k+1$, and listing non-branching instructions as they are executed. The resulting list is a list of instructions $i+1$, $i+2$, . . . of p' in order. This procedure is the motivation behind the following definitions.

By a *memory-path segment* in C initiated by N at k is meant the list of instructions other than instructions to branch or stop generated by executing C on the valuation N beginning with instruction number k in C. By a normal instruction for a program

C is meant the instruction to continue, or an instruction of the form

SET M = v

such that M is in the memory set of C and v is in the range of values of M.

Now let p be a memory-path in a program C. p′ is a variant of p from the ith instruction of p if, and only if, (i) the first i-1 instructions of p′ are the first i-1 instructions of p, (ii) the ith instruction of p′ is some conjunction of normal instructions of C, and (iii) the rest of p′ is the memory-path segment in C initiated by N at k+1 where N is the valuation of C after the first i instructions of p′ and k is the number in C of the ith instruction in p.

One further problem must be dealt with before proceeding to a definition of 'd executes C'. Suppose p′ is a variant of p from the ith instruction of p. Now it may be the case that if a device were to mis-execute the ith instruction of p (under I) then d would *normally* execute p′, i.e., *provided no further mis-executions were to occur.* But, of course, they might. Consider L once again. It was pointed out above that one mis-execution of instruction (2) in L is no guarantee that (2) will continue to be mis-executed. If this *were* to happen, then the variant p′ from the first instruction in the memory-path initiated by (8) would not be executed. The obvious suggestion is that a variant p″ of p′ from the second instruction of p′ *would* normally be executed, *provided no further mis-executions were to occur.* And so on.

Although the revised definition of a variant memory-path disarms former objections to thus constructing variants of variants, the tactic might still be thought suspect. For if we simply require the execution of some variant of some variant of some variant . . . , we will have required nothing at all. Suppose d mis-executes the first instruction of p (under some memory-interpretation I). We examine d to see what it does do (as interpreted by I) and substitute the appropriate conjunction of normal instructions, creating a variant p′. Now, *of course,* d executes the first instruction of p′ —we rigged it that way. But suppose it mis-executes the second instruction of p′. We repeat the procedure, and construct a variant p″ of p′. *Of course,* d executes the first two instructions of p″—we rigged it that way. And so on. No matter what transpires in d, we will be able to mirror it.[13]

Fortunately, this trivializing procedure represents a corrigible misunderstanding of the requirement. This can be brought out by considering a concrete example.

If the requirement really is trivial, then it should fail to distinguish between Augmenter I and Augmenter III as theories of the Figure 3 counter. Assume once again that flip-flops D, C, and A are in the x-state, flip-flop B in the y-state. This corresponds, via the obvious memory-interpretations, to the initial valuation (0, 0, 1, 0) for both programs, and in both cases (0, 0, 1, 0) initiates the memory-path (COMPLEMENT A). Now suppose the counter receives an input, but flip-flop A does not change state. Flip-flops B, C, and D are assumed to be in normal working order. The appropriate variant memory-paths are the following.

p'_I (Augmenter I):   (CONTINUE.)

p'_{III} (Augmenter III): (CONTINUE, COMPLEMENT B, COMPLEMENT C.)

As pointed out before, the counter will in fact do nothing—it executes p'_I. But isn't this simply a mis-exectuion of the second instruction of p'_{III} from the point of view of that memory-path? If it is, we should construct a variant on p'_{III}.

p''_{III}: (CONTINUE, CONTINUE.)

And, since p''_{III} is executed by the counter, conclude that Augmenter III satisfies the requirement.

Although it is true that the counter executes p''_{III} it is not the case that it would normally execute p'_{III} if it were to execute the first instruction of p'_{III}. On the contrary, execution of p'_{III} would require an abnormal "spontaneous" change in flip-flop B. Intuitively, the instruction to complement B would not normally be executed since, if no change occurs in flip-flop A, no pulse appears at the trigger of B—flip-flop B would never get a "chance" to change states. And even if it did, the assumption was that flip-flops B, C, and D are functioning normally[14] so a pulse at the trigger of flip-flop B would result in a change of state.

We are now in a position to state precisely a definition of program execution incorporating output-adequacy,[15] execution of memory-paths, and execution of variant memory-paths.

Let C be a program for a device d.

d executes C if, and only if, there exists a memory interpretation I of d for C such that, with respect to I,

(i) for every initial valuation N of C, if d were to be in I^N and given an input, d would normally execute the first instruction of the memory-path in C initiated by N, and

(ii) for all memory-paths p in C, $n > 0$, if d were to execute the first n instructions of p, d would normally execute the first $n+1$ instructions of p, and

(iii) for all memory-paths and memory-path variants p of C, if d were to mis-execute the nth instruction of p, d would normally execute a variant of p from the nth instruction of p.

A word needs to be said about the use of 'normally' and the subjunctive conditional constructions. There are two reasons why they are there: they are needed, and I do not know how to eliminate them. They are needed in order to take account of devices which never perform normally at all, as well as those which perform abnormally on occasion.

As defined here, program execution is a dispositional concept. The reason for this is that information processing psychologists wish to account for behavioral *capacities* by appeal to programs. The strategy is to explain an organism's capacity to produce a certain behavior by appeal to the fact that the organism has a certain program in its repertoire. Adding, in the sense in which we say that adding machines add, is depositional in this sense. When we say of a device that it adds, we mean that it has a certain capacity, not that it is actually, at that moment, adding. If the machine adds by executing a certain program, then to say of the machine that it executes that program is to attribute a certain capacity to the machine, not a current activity. In the case in which the machine is now engaged in computing a sum, we say that it *is adding,* and that it *is executing* a certain program, and this is different from saying that it adds, or that it executes a certain program. A manufacturer of adding machines who publishes an explanation of how his machines add may publish the truth even though all his machines are destroyed in a warehouse fire before they ever add at all. Similarly, a psychologist who publishes an explanation of how people sneeze or how George solves logic problems may publish the truth even though no one ever sneezes, or George never encounters a logic problem.

An information processing theory is not automatically suspect because it never happens to be the case that the organism (or whatever) is executing the program, for the conditions under which the organism is supposed to actually be executing the program may never be satisfied. The subjunctive construction guards against trivial satisfaction of the definition in such cases.

But what if the appropriate conditions are satisfied and yet it does not subsequently come to be the case that the organism is executing the program? Is it not always open to the theorist to claim that things are not *normal;* that if things were *normal* the organism would be executing the program? This is equivalent to asking whether condition (iii) of the definition of program execution is not always trivially satisfiable. Although this question has already been answered in the negative, it is, perhaps, worthwhile to deal with it again in a more general way.

Condition (iii) is designed to capture the requirement that a program mirror the dependencies between events in memory. The idea behind the requirement is that, if these dependencies are properly mirrored, then the consequences of mis-executions, i.e., of unexpected but still interpretable events in memory, should be predicted by the program. From the point of view of a program, the occurrence of a mis-execution is the only way in which things can fail to be normal. Now events in memory which are interpreted as mis-executions can arise in two ways: either the memory in question is faulty, or the dependencies between events in memory are not what they are alleged to be. Only if these dependencies *are* correctly mirrored will it always be the case that, on the occasion of a mis-execution, some variant memory-path will be executed. Even so, that variant memory-path may not be executed, since a further malfunction of the same kind may occur. For this reason it is only required that that variant memory-path would normally be executed, ie., that it be executed unless some further breakdown in a memory occurs.

Thus, 'normally', as this expression occurs in the definitions of this section, means the same as 'barring any (further) failure in one or more memories'. In this sense of 'normally' it is possible in principle to discover whether a device is operating normally without reference to any particular program.

Of course, the memories and their states must be identified. We cannot determine whether the memories of a device are operating properly unless we know which parts the memories are, and which states of those parts are relevant: Determinations of normalcy are relative to a memory-interpretation domain. Mis-identification of a memory will result in a failure of a program to mirror (under the responsible memory-interpretation) dependencies between events in memory. Suppose that we wire an adding machine in such a way that a light goes on whenever the button marked '2' is pressed. To simplify matters, assume that, when pressed, buttons remain in the depressed position until the add or clear button is pressed. So we are supposing that the light is on just when the button marked '2' is depressed. Now, as long as the whole device, as altered, functions normally, there is no reason to choose the button over the light for the office of memory storing the symbol '2'. If we settle on the light, however, and the light burns out, then, from our point of view, the machine will no longer store the symbol '2' in that memory, but (presumably) will always be found to store the symbol '0'. According to our overall theory, this should have some consequences for output. But, of course, it won't, because it is the button not the light, which really is the memory in question.

A program which is executed by the adding machine under the proper memory-interpretation will fail to mirror the dependencies between events in memory under a memory-interpretation the domain of which includes the light instead of the button. Nothing depends on the state of the light, while a good deal depends on the state of the memory storing the symbol '2'. As a result, the device will not, assuming that other memories are operating properly, execute a variant memory-path under the faulty memory-interpretation, but will perform as if the memory in question were functioning normally, as indeed it is. In contrast, a failure in the button, for example its becoming stuck in the depressed position, will have consequences for output, and this will be, or may be, accounted for in terms of the execution of a variant memory-path under a memory interpretation which identifies the button as the memory in question.

The foregoing account of program execution is not meant to be perfectly general. It assumes a rather particular sort of device, and a rather particular sort of program. The goal was to find a level of generality that (i) is "low" enough to permit something approaching a rigorous definition and concrete discussion of cases, while (ii) "high" enough to be interesting. The point is to show that loose talk about realization can be made precise. *How* it is made precise in each case is, from a philosophical point of view, not so important as the fact that it can be made precise in *some* cases.

One respect in which the above account is *not* general deserves special mention, however. The approach illustrated here will not apply at all to cases involving execution of an information processing program that has an information processing instantiation. If the program has to be compiled or interpreted to run on the device in question, then, though the approach illustrated here will work for the "machine code," another approach is required to handle the idea that the device executes the source code. This is simply because control structure is, in general, obliterated in the compilation process. Referential structure is obliterated as well. If your source program in PASCAL, say, traffics in the types of outpatients in a typical week of hospital business, nothing in the approach illustrated here will help explain what condition of the machine executing the program represents, say, an outpatient as "psychiatric," the reason being that *nothing* in the executing device has that representational function. In such cases, we do not, as we do in the cases of the counters described above, have machine states with the same content as instructions in memory-paths of the executed program. Program execution involving dimension shift is a whole new kettle of fish.

The case discussed is, however, an example of the fundamental notion of program execution, a case in which the analysis effected by the program is descriptively instantiated. Information processing instantiations must ultimately ride "piggy-back" on descriptive instantiations. It is, perhaps, well to end by emphasizing the obvious: the fundamental notion of execution made precise here makes no place for the idea that the program is "stored," "read," and "obeyed." This is not due to the fact that the programs discussed are supposed to be "hardwired." The only difference, from the point of view of instantiation, between hardwired and softwired programs is that the latter sort are easier to change. But the situation brought about by hardwiring with a soldering iron is exactly the same as that brought about by softwiring with punch cards: what is achieved in either case is a device so structured that it executes a certain program in the sense lately made precise.

Notes

1. I do not mean to suggest that the applicability of the analytical strategy, or inapplicability of the subsumptive strategy, in any way distinguishes psychology from other social sciences or from science generally.

2. I don't know whether a law can be causal but not deterministic. It seems possible: a law might subsume cause-and-effect pairs and yet subsume more than one type of effect with a given type of cause. Such a law would, so far as I can see, be causal yet not deterministic. Whether/how such laws would be explanatory is a matter I leave aside but for this: such a law surely would not explain why an event of the one effect type rather than the other occurred.

3. See Cummins (1978a) and Scriven (1975) for related discussion.

4. We can represent this in first-order form as follows: $(e)(y)(u)(v)[(Py$
$\& \text{Leyuv}) \rightarrow (Ee^*)(Te^*y2\pi \sqrt{u/g} \ 2\pi \sqrt{v/g} \& Cee^*)]$, where

    Py: y is an ideal pendulum;
    Leyuv: e is a change in the length of y from u to v;
    Teyuv: e is a change in the period of y from u to v;
    Cee*:   e causes e*.

This representation [and the corresponding one for (5)] makes it clear that the representation of e and e*, and the calculation of the value of T given lh (or lh given T) are quite independent of the causal claim.

5. By a *nomic* correlation, I mean a correlation that is underwritten by natural law: it holds because certain natural laws hold. Nomic correlations (equivalently, lawlike correlations) are thus to be contrasted with accidental or coincidental correlations. The best rule of thumb for making the distinction

is, I think, that advocated by Nelson Goodman (1965): a correlation between F's and G's is nomic (lawlike) just in case knowing that a particular thing is an F is good inductive warrant for believing it is a G as well. "Everything in my coat pocket conducts electricity" is not a nomic correlation, by this test, because even if every time I have examined something in my coat pocket I have found it to be a conductor, this provides no warrant for thinking that the next thing I examine from my coat pocket will be a conductor. As Hume would have said, there is no necessary connection between being in my coat pocket and being a conductor.

6. There is a chicken-or-egg question here: perhaps it was focus on transition theories that gave rise to the deductive-nomological model. In any case the two go together.

7. It is Berkeley, not Hume, who deserves the credit. The essentials of the argument are in sections 18–20 of *The Principles of Human Knowledge* and in the last few pages of the *Three Dialogues Between Hylas and Philonous*. Hume's best-known use of this line of criticism is in the *Treatise of Human Nature*, I.IV.ii, "Of Skepticism with Regard to the Senses." For a discussion of Berkeley's contribution, see my review (1979) of Pitcher's book, *Berkeley*.

8. This is often confused with 'how does S acquire P?' Property *acquisition* is state change. I may know how I got poison ivy without knowing what poison ivy is.

The differences between property theories and transition theories are obscured by treating an event (following Kim, 1969, 1973) as a thing having a property at a time. On this construal, 'Pendulum P has period T at time t' is as much an event schema as 'The period of P changed from v to u at t.' Indeed, even 'System S is undergoing no change at t' is an event schema on this account. If instances of *this* schema are events, then there are certainly uncaused events.

We typically think of causation as a relation between events, as we should. But the Kim proposal has the effect of trivializing this idea, for it allows us to treat any singular statement as an event description, hence, like Hume, to see causation as a relation between objects.

9. Of course, an elementary part can change its relational properties—e.g., its momentum—and such changes can be the object of a transition theory. Indeed, it often happens that a property of a system is instantiated as relational properties of its components, allowing us to explain transitions in the former as transitions in the latter.

10. We might also undertake to explain, or rather explicate, the concept of property instantiation generally, but that isn't empirical science on anyone's view.

11. (6ii) is a (candidate) law when 'S' is replaced by a designation for a type of system—e.g., 'water,' 'human memory,' 'Z-80 processors.' When 'S' is replaced by a designation for a particular system—e.g., 'This computer' or 'The River Rouge Ford Plant'—we get a particular rather than a general statement. Laws are usually conceived as generalizations, but nongeneral instances of (6ii) are lawlike by the usual tests, so I will speak of all instances of (6ii) as laws.

It should be obvious that instances of (6ii) and (6iii) do not describe causes and effects to be subsumed by (6i).

12. Philosophers have often puzzled over the function (or "logical status") of such fundamental scientific laws as the law of inertia and the law of universal gravitation: are they definitions, rules of inference, specifications of fundamental causal connections, or what? I think a shift in perspective will help in some of these cases. It seems illuminating, for example, to construe the law of inertia as it functions in Newtonian mechanics as a nomic attribution specifying a fundamental property of bodies. Seeing it as part of a property theory makes it possible to understand how it could be central to the claim that continued motion (or rest) is not an effect, hence needs no cause to explain it. See Cummins (1976) for details.

13. I'm not sure that NA_2 should be treated as a fundamental nomic attribution *at this level of theory.* Without a fuller picture we are left wondering why energy is proportional to frequency (though it's easy to see why it isn't proportional to intensity). We must add other fundamental nomic attributions (e.g., that photons have a rest mass of zero) for NA_2 to lose its air of mystery.

14. Point (iv) is not, of course, a fundamental nomic attribution, since it attributes dispositional properties to particles ("at any instant, a particle has additive dispositions to accelerate").

15. Richard Boyd (1980) seems to have arrived at a similar conclusion. See especially his section 11.

NOTES TO CH. II: FUNCTIONAL ANALYSIS (PAGES 28–51)

1. Some would distinguish capacities and dispositions. It sounds odd to say, e.g., that sugar has the capacity to dissolve in water—as if it might "decide" not to, sometimes. But it doesn't sound odd to say that a calculator has the capacity to add: There is no hint here that it adds only when it "decides" to. I think we speak of a capacity of S rather than a disposition when we are selecting for attention one of several dispositions of more or less the same type (as we usually are in functional analysis). Thus, it doesn't sound odd to say water has the capacity to dissolve sugar and salt but not oil. I don't think there's anything of philosophical interest here, and I use the terms as stylistic variants.

2. This is the view I defended in (1975a) and I still think it is substantially correct. However, it is the analytical style of explanation, especially as applied to complex capacities, that interests me, not the proper explication of the concept of *function.* Thus 'functional analysis' can be understood here as no more than a technical term for a theory designed to explain a capacity or disposition via property analysis.

3. Proper analysis may nevertheless violate these conditions, at least on the surface. Faced with anomalous input, a perception program might call a more complex and sophisticated general problem solver. If so, the capacity to

perceive will involve a subcapacity that is, on the surface, more complex and sophisticated than the analyzed capacity. I say "on the surface" because, if we accept such an analysis, we will be accepting a revised (upward) view of the relative sophistication of perception. From this revised viewpoint, (i) through (iii) will be satisfied.

4. This, among other things, is why it would be wrong to say that a function of a submerged object is to displace liquid.

Nondispositional properties (as opposed to the systems that have them) are, of course, subject to analysis, but I know of no important explanatory use of this strategy in science—except, perhaps, in translation.

5. As I use the expression, 'S executes P' attributes a capacity to S, viz., the capacity to do what P says to do under some set of (perhaps vaguely—e.g., "when needed") specified conditions. 'S does what P says to do' should not be taken to imply that S does what it does because P so instructs. See section II.3 for a discussion of the pitfalls involved in ignoring this point.

6. See the Appendix for a simple but detailed illustration of this requirement.

7. Not always. Suppose we have:

      5   819   72
      0   211   76.

Taking the bottom half of the top line, and the top half of the bottom line, we have:

       כ   819   72
      0   211   76,

a perfectly respectable set of symbols. Once this sort of thing becomes a serious possibility, the whole game gets much harder.

Notice that cypher translation is a property theory of the interpretive variety for a nondispositional property. If the interpretations are context free, we have a morphological analysis; if not, we have a systematic analysis.

8. The distinction is borrowed (with some alterations) from Haugeland (1978, p. 220). His terms are 'intentional instantiation' and 'physical instantiation'. Since analyzing properties are dispositional properties in functional analysis, and since specifying a disposition of S is specifying a causal transition law for S, descriptively specified instantiations typically are "physical" in the ordinary sense of that word.

I use 'information-processing instantiation' rather than 'intentional instantiation' because instantiating a capacity as an information-processing system may not involve any intentionality. In Chapter III this point looms large.

9. Haugeland calls the shift effected by instantiation "dimension shift" to distinguish it from the more familiar shift in level effected by analysis, and he makes the important point that level and dimension are independent. Thus, at one dimension, a validity checker may be a symbol cruncher, but we cannot (in the case imagined) analyze the capacity to check validity into symbol-crunching capacities. See Haugeland (1978), p. 220.

10. I am ignoring here the possiblity of information-processing instantiations. Decimal adders are typically instantiated as binary adders, which are

in turn instantiated as truth-function computers. But they needn't be. Mechanical calculators and, for all I know, people physically instantiate decimal-addition algorithms.

11. If this is the only way to understand an information-processing capacity, and I think it is, then a materialist theory of information processing is the only alternative to a mystery theory of information processing. Hence, if being intelligent is a matter of having the right information-processing capacities, we must either be materialists or abandon the explicability of intelligence. I think dualists know this, and that this is what makes anti-materialism attractive to them.

12. "Indirect specification": we say, "Whatever it is that physically instantiates bringing down the next significant digit," rather than "closing relays A through D." Indirect descriptions of this sort may, of course, fail to refer.

13. We will see shortly that a system may execute a program it does not represent.

14. "Relatively permanent": If the system is reprogrammed, those features will disappear, of course, and this may happen often and easily. But the features must be *relatively* permanent: they must last as long as the capacity analyzed by the program lasts.

15. Typically, of course, what we do is cause S to E-represent an instantiation of P, and not P at all. See below.

16. This holds only if the compiler works like an interpreter, as compilers frequently do not. In general, there need be no routine in the ML compilation that is input-output isomorphic to any instruction in the PL source program.

17. Typically, of course, the source program is represented on a disk or deck of cards, but this is strictly for the convenience of users who may wish to read or edit it. The machine must compile the program—i.e., produce an input-output isomorphic program with different representational content—to execute it.

If we replace the compiler with an interpreter, the whole system, including the disk (or whatever) that stores the source program, bears a superficial resemblance to the situation envisioned by the internal manual model. In this case we have the interpreter—an ML program E-represented in the computer—taking an instruction of the source program as input and outputting an input-output isomorphic ML program that is then E-represented and executed. The interpreter then "reads" the next instruction, and so on.

The resemblance is only superficial, however, for in this case it is clear that the source program is E-represented in the system, though in a particularly ingenious way. Talk of "reading" here indicates only that the E-representation is also a user-representation. We have arranged things so that writing a command on the system alters it in such a way as to produce behavior interpretable as an execution of the command. The computer no more reads the instructions than a calculator reads a button-pressing; what happens is not even remotely comparable to what happens when a cook reads and follows a recipe. The cook must understand the symbols; the calculator or computer simply reacts to the rather subtle kick we give it.

Talk of interpreters "reading" source programs is, of course, useful and generally harmless, but there is no reason to suppose that this concept of reading will have a psychological use. No one supposes that brains contain representations of uncompiled programs—programs that aren't E-represented—that must be "read" to be executed. Brain programs are surely all E-represented. They are not "read" even in the weak sense in which interpreters read source programs; control simply passes to them.

Those who think that input-output isomorphic programs must be somehow representationally equivalent should consider this analogy: Imagine any set of directions D for getting from point A to point B in a city. D may contain representations of any landmarks and features you like. Now construct an alternate set of directions D* that specifies a different route between A and B. D* represents different landmarks and features. If D and D* are to be counted representationally equivalent because they are input-output equivalent programs, then we will have to count 'cross the bridge' as representationally equivalent to 'go through the tunnel'.

18. When we are dealing with a computing system, representation has a control function: we cause the system to do something interpretable as adding by writing 'add' on it in a certain specified way. This is extremely convenient for us; it is much easier than using a soldering iron. It has no significance for the system at all. It is irrelevant to the working of the system that causally altering it in the necessary way is also producing a token of the instruction to add in some language or other.

Representation also has an explanatory function: Learning which causal changes in the system lead to outputs interpretable as sums amounts to learning which causal changes in the system are interpretable as the instruction to add. But it is the explainer who does the reading, not the adder.

19. I have a small objection: reading couldn't be instantiated as any of the things that are called reading in computer-ese.

NOTES TO CH. III: UNDERSTANDING COGNITIVE CAPACITIES (PAGES 52–117)

1. It is important to see that whereas inferential characterization requires sentential interpretation of inputs and outputs, the converse is not true: a device instantiating a transformational grammar transforms sentential inputs into sentential outputs, but the inputs and outputs are not related via any pattern of inference. One should also keep in mind that sentence processors are only one kind of information processor. A device executing a program for constructing truth-trees is an information processor, but it doesn't process sentences.

It has become fashionable these days to run down sentential interpretation as a kind of linguistic chauvinism. But consider: What makes a *cognitive capacity (or a cognitive capacity, for that matter) *cognitive (or cognitive) is surely that its exercises are epistemologically assessable, and this commits one to the view that such exercises are amenable to sentential interpretation. The object of epistemological assessment has to be, or be closely tied to, a truth-value bearer. Information theory, for example, provides no room for epistemological assessment, precisely because it provides no room for truth values. Talk of cognition in the absence of actual or potential sentential interpretation of inputs and outputs is mere hand waving.

2. This needn't be a valid rule in the usual sense, but at least a more or less reliable rule in the context the instantiating machinery operates in. Otherwise, there will be no reason to think of the capacity as *cognitive.

3. Actually, this is something of an overstatement. We may have reason to suppose that we are dealing with an inferentially characterizable capacity without knowing how to characterize it, for we may be able to distinguish correct from incorrect output even though we can't state even an approximation of a rule of inference connecting input to output.

Suppose a space vehicle of unknown origin is dug out of a crater in Arizona. On board we discover a machine that makes accurate and precise astrological predictions—i.e., given someone's birthday and so on, and local astronomical data, it predicts that person's future ("headline events" anyway). We would certainly *suspect* this to be an ICC—indeed an explicitly *cognitive capacity—but the situation is strained by the fact that *we* can't specify a (set of) rule(s) of inference that characterize the capacity. We can distinguish correct from incorrect outputs, of course, but we cannot, without an explicit inferential characterization, distinguish cogent from non-cogent outputs. For suppose the device makes a false prediction: is this bad input (cogent) or bad design (non-cogent) or mal-function (neither)? We just can't tell. Since we can't tell, we don't know beyond a rough approximation what capacity we are trying to explain. In such a situation, solving the problem of characterization is easily mistaken for an explanation: if we do come up with some rule(s) that do the job, it will be nearly irresistible to suppose we've explained how the job is done. Evidently, however, we can't explain how a system conforms to a (characteristic) inferential pattern if we don't know what inferential pattern (if any) the system conforms to.

4. Many who balk at talk of inference are not so much balking at inferential characterization as at *inferential analysis*—see below.

5. This point requires careful treatment. I may figure out that XVII times XXI is CCCLVII by translating into decimal arabic numerals, multiplying by partial products, and translating back. Here, my capacity to multiply roman numerals is explained by analysis into the capacity to translate between roman and decimal arabic, and the capacity to multiply in decimal arabic. This is not information-processing instantiation, but analysis: inferential connections between steps remain obvious and intact. The deinterpretation aspect of an instantiation, however, obliterates inferential connections, since these are semantically determined. The point is obvious if we turn it on its head: interpretation is required in the first place to reveal the inferential structure that defines a particular ICC, so deinterpretation will "hide" that particular ICC again.

6. I'm concerned only with necessary conditions for being an intelligent

inference maker, not with necessary conditions for intelligence generally (if there's a difference).

7. One might suppose the contrary on the grounds that, say, an inverter's logical capacity can be flow-charted thus:

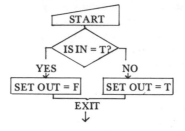

But a much better treatment does away with the branching.

A similar point applies to the logical capacity of the OR-gate. The baroque AND-gate is a very stupid machine.

It should seem obvious that the nonbranching chart is better, but here is an argument for the recalcitrant. A device instantiating the branching chart is susceptible to mal-functions to which a device instantiating the nonbranching chart is immune. If the former device regularly mis-executes "set OUT = F," it will mal-function only when IN = T. If the latter device regularly mis-executes its only instruction, it will always get it wrong. This will distinguish the two analyses, and I am assuming that the device instantiating the inverters in the baroque AND-gate can mal-function in the second way but not the first.

8. Perhaps it is worth remarking that this is a point about what it would take to make us understand intelligent *cognition, not a point about what is metaphysically possible. Perhaps there could be intelligent *cognition without *cogitation, but it would be incorrigibly mysterious to us.

9. Here I "may be" taking issue with John Haugeland, who explicitly rejects a version of the "what-else?" argument (1978, pp. 221–222). I say "may be" because my topic is *cognition, not cognition, but I think what he says can be taken in a way that runs counter to my claim here, for I think *his* topic is really *cognition. What I am calling ICC's, Haugeland calls (misleadingly, I think) intentional black boxes.

10. Actually, what we are committed to is the claim that C is isomorphic to some idealization or restriction of I. See Haugeland (1978), p. 217.

11. This doesn't mean that R has an information-processing instantiation as I: if I translates R, then I gives an inferential analysis of C—indeed, the very analysis afforded by R. I and R thus lie on the same dimension.

12. That is, few have disagreed with the claim that depth perception is an ICC of a fairly sophisticated sort. Many *have* disagreed with the claim—perhaps also Berkeley's—that visual judgments of depth are epistemologically inferential—i.e., with the claim that visual depth judgments are *justified* inferentially, but that is quite another matter. Most (all) epistemologically basic (immediate, noninferentially justified) judgments are the result of the exercise of sophisticated ICC's. When I judge that A is further away than B by looking, inferences surely get made, but I (as distinct from my subsystems) don't make them.

13. A device might play chess very well—indeed intelligently—without being an intelligent chess player, because one or more crucial components are instantiated as intelligent something-elsers. Good chess need not be intelligent *chess*, though it presumably involves intelligent *cognition about something.

14. The "same" capacity might eventually be "taken over" by (i.e., instantiated by) acquired structures, of course.

15. Suppose we replicate a computer. We may replicate it completely, as programmed, or only partially—e.g., without some data, without some programming, etc. Now imagine the only available input is FORTRAN, but we fail to replicate FORTRAN's compiling capacity. Then the "offspring" will not be able to "perceive."

16. By 'Information Theory' I mean the theory associated with Shannon, 1948. See *Knowledge and the Flow of Information* (p. 237, note 1) for some references relevant to the development of the theory.

17. Dretske also attempts to show how informational states of a system can exhibit a kind of intensionality comparable to that exhibited by belief sentences. I'm not convinced that this attempt is successful, but neither do I think the problem is terribly important. So far as I can see, there is no reason to insist that belief *states*—even explicit belief states—must exhibit anything comparable to the intensionality of belief *sentences*. Explicit beliefs must be intentional states, of course, but I will argue later that this is quite a different matter.

18. The expressions 'due to', 'can be accounted for in terms of', and 'depends on' should be understood as they are in statistics: r_j is "due to" s_i to the extent that there is a positive correlation between the occurrence of r_j and the occurrence of s_i. Even when such a correlation is perfect and lawlike, it does not follow either that s_i causes r_j or that the occurrence of s_i explains the occurence of r_j. The correlation might be a lawlike "artifact" of a common cause, for example.

19. To see this, imagine that $p(Fs/r)$ is less than one. Then it is possible that s is not F even though r occurs at the receiver. The signal is therefore equivocal: maybe s is F, and maybe not. Referring back to (2), we see that $I_{Fs}(r) = (I(Fs)$ – equivocation). If the equivocation is positive, then $I_{Fs}(r)$ is less that I(Fs).

20. Actually, this is a simplification of the definition Dretske gives on page 65: *Informational Content:* A signal r carries the information that s is F = the conditional probability of s's being F, given r (and k), is 1 (but, given k alone, less than 1).

k is intended to represent what the receiver already knows, antecedent to the occurrence of r. The idea behind this relativization can be brought out as follows. Suppose there are three possibilities at the source: s is F, G, or H. If the information that s is not F is already available at the receiver, then a signal r that eliminates the possibility that s is G suffices to determine that s is H, hence carries the information that s is H. But if the information that s is not F is not antecedently available at the receiver, then the occurrence of r carries only the information that s is H or G. See Dretske's discussion, pp. 78 ff.

21. Dretske also expresses this by saying that the semantic content of r (if it has one) is that informational content it carries in completely digital form (p. 184). Dretske's new and useful way of drawing the digital/analog distinction makes this formulation particularly illuminating. r carries the information that s is F in digital form just in case r carries no other information not nested in s's being F; otherwise, r carries the information that s is F in analog form (p. 137). Viewing matters in this way allows Dretske to bring out the important fact that digital coding always involves loss of information, for digital coding of the information that s is F makes unavailable information not nested in s's being F. This enables us to see how digital coding can amount to a kind of generalization or classification, for it amounts to focusing on certain features of the source to the exclusion of others—viz., the ones not nested in s's being F.

22. Dennett often cleaves to an instrumentalist treatment of intentional characterization, and would therefore (I assume) be prepared to characterize intentionally a system with reasonably sophisticated discursive capacities. Indeed, he is prepared to characterize plants intentionally.

23. I suspect something like this fuels the internal manual model. If we talk in a way that makes us see inferential interpretation wherever we have inferential characterization, then whenever we have discursive capacities, we will see representation *for the system*, with the consequence that the system must be credited with the ability to "understand" the representations!

24. This is why I feel some trepidation about my use of the phrase 'intentional characterization'. Propositional attitude attribution is the standard illustration of intentional characterization, and this makes it virtually impossible to argue, as I will shortly, that some belief isn't intentional in the sense staked out above.

25. Remark: I am ignoring nonpropositional cases of intentionality.

26. Recall that a transition theory that predicts and causally explains individual exercises is a solution to the "specification problem" only; it provides a precise specification of the capacity to be explained; it does not explain that capacity. Mathematical models of cognitive capacities are solutions to the specification problem, not to the explanatory problem.

27. Why doesn't the subject see a receding spot of constant size? Or a spot that both shrinks and recedes? Some people do, but it's rare, presumably because the after-image is seen as a spot on the wall and the wall is not perceived as receding. But some subjects do report seeing the spot "go through the wall" or "go back into the wall," so that it is perceived as, e.g., the

bottom of a hole in the wall. (Notice that the perceived size of the "spot" is not a function of perceived distance. Rather, changes in "spot" size are a function of changes in perceived distance.)

Do animals have AI, and if so, which ones? It would be easy enough to find out about any animal that can be conditioned to respond to shrinking spots.

28. Of course, we do sometimes make inferences (consciously) without taking into account obviously relevant information. But exercise of AI involves (according to the Irresistible Explanation) using information one is *not* aware of and ignoring the relevant information one *is* aware of. AI is not a corrigible (or incorrigible) tendency to sloppy thinking.

29. This is not the same as the subject not being conscious of making the inference. The inference invoked is beyond conscious reach.

30. It is tempting to say that having a shrinking after-image is instantiated, in part, as the visual-system drawing the conclusion that a spot on the wall is shrinking, or that the vs's drawing the conclusion causes the after-image to shrink (causes one's visual experience to be of a shrinking after-image?). Maybe one of these is true, but it's obvious that no one really understands either of these alternatives well enough to make it explanatory.

31. By the capacity to *use* a language I mean the capacity to communicate with it; to employ it in speech acts. By the capacity to *assess* a language, I mean the capacity to judge grammaticality, intersentential relations, and the like—the capacity to produce the "intuitions" that are the bread-and-butter of psycholinguistics.

32. Chomsky says the Language Faculty represents tacit knowledge of L. Tacit knowledge, as opposed to implicit belief, is best construed thus: S tacitly knows that P iff some subsystem of S is appropriately interpreted as having an ICC the exercise of which is equivalent to manifesting knowledge that P. I think this captures the explanatory role of appeals to tacit knowledge (though not to implicit belief), while making it clear that appeals to tacit knowledge are not appeals to intentional characterization or internal manuals. Perhaps not all appeals to tacit knowledge will bear this construal, but I think Chomsky's will, and he has de facto squatter's rights to the term.

33. I think it is pretty clear that many of the propositional attitudes invoked by Gricean accounts are implicit. But the *upshot* of a communicative episode is plainly an explicit propositional attitude.

34. Neutronalism is what you get by conjoining the Weak Thesis with the denial of the Strong Thesis. Computationalism is incompatible with neuronalism, for computationalism entails that the details of physical realization are irrelevant, while neuronalism is the claim that they are essential.

Searle, I think, is sometimes interpreted as a neuronalist, but he does not hold that intentionality can *only* be instantiated as it is in human (and other) animals. His view is rather that any system having the same "causal powers" as a human nervous system might instantiate intentionally characterizable capacities, but he insists that mere computational equivalence is not enough to ensure the required sameness of causal powers. Thus Searle is, perhaps, free to insist that his view does not tie intentionality to the chemistry/physics of the brain, but only to its causal structure. On one reading, this is just orthodox functionalism, understood as the doctrine that mental states have only their causal roles essentially. See, e.g., Churchland and Churchland (1982) for a recent defense of this position. (The Churchlands, however, take their position to be incompatible with Searle's.)

This understanding of Searle's position makes it more plausible than neuronalism, but not more practicable. I have no idea how to approach the problem of the instantiation of intentionality within the constraints this view enforces: "What causal powers—specified non-intentionally—must a state have to be an intentional state?" seems a dead-end question, at least for now. And in any case, it seems to me that Searle's position reduces to neuronalism on the plausible assumption that two systems have the same causal powers just in case they have the same chemistry/physics.

35. I don't want to give the impression that homunctional analysis—functional analysis with genuine homunculi—is a mistake: it isn't. I'm just warning against the attempt to get clear of intentionality by making the analyzing homunculi less sophisticated along some other dimension.

36. This use of 'intentional system' is to be strongly distinguished from Dennett's use of the phrase.

Davidson calls a system that can understand *another's* representations an *interpreter*. He claims not only that all interpreters must be understanders, but that all understanders must be interpreters. See Davidson (1975).

37. Talk of guarantees is really too loose. We want a D_C and a D_I of S such that S satisfies D_I in virtue of satisfying D_C. Pretend 'guarantee' is a technical term explained by the previous sentence.

38. Indeed, failure of the reduction functions as a kind of minimal test of intentionality. The Standard Solution gets D_C to entail D_I only at the price of making D_I nonintentional.

39. Thus, though (2) (or rather (1)) tells us that we can deduce D_f from D_p, it is consistent with the obvious fact that D_f tells us next to nothing about the physical constitution of systems that satisfy it.

40. I have expressed this as a sufficient condition only, since a sufficient condition is all the present problem requires.

41. This is just the dilemma faced by the Standard Solution: if understanding is a behavioral disposition ("in disguise"), then it isn't what we were after.

42. Suppose S simulates one of *my* cognitive (or *cognitive?) capacities in virtue of executing D_C. Then won't *I* know that (ii) is the wrong move? Won't *I* know that D_I genuinely applies to me? Of course: though such judgments will be fallible; they can't be dismissed as a classs, in advance. This just reinforces the present point, which is that choosing between (i) and (ii) is not to be done by analogy with choosing between (a) and (b)—i.e., by asking whether D_c is D_I in disguise.

43. Perhaps eliminative materialists such as Rorty (1979) would disagree, holding that sucessful simulation will eventually exorcize intentionality. For this to happen, the computational systems responsible would have to be rather

crude. Otherwise, a better move would be to adopt the Strong Thesis. Dennett's discussion of "debunking explanations" in "Skinner Skinned" (1978) is the relevant text. The Strong Thesis is surely more plausible than eliminative materialism if the computational systems required for respectable simulation turn out to be surpassingly complex.

44. 'C and C' are input-output isomorphic' can be defined as follows. Let t_C and $t_{C'}$ be the transition functions specifying C and C', respectively. Then C and C' are input-output isomorphic iff there exist one-to-one functions

$$I_D: \text{Dom } f_C \xrightarrow{1\text{-}1} \text{Dom } f_{C'}, \text{ and } I_R: \text{Ran } f_C \xrightarrow{1\text{-}1} \text{Ran } f_{C'},$$

such that $(x)(y)(f_C(x) = y \equiv f_{C'}(I_D(x)) = I_R(y))$. C and C' are input-output isomorphic within idealization if C is input-output isomorphic to some restriction of C' or C' is input-output isomorphic to some restrict of C. By a restriction of C, I mean the result of failing to distinguish some elements in Dom f_C and/or Ran f_C.

NOTES TO CH. IV: HISTORICAL REFLECTIONS (PAGES 118–162)

1. Since 'in the mind' meant 'in consciousness' for Titchener, as it did for Locke, this emphasis on perception as the source of mental elements is hardly surprising.

2. Appeal to abnormal ear structure is tempting but ultimately only a delaying tactic: how do we establish the needed connections between ear structure and sensation?

3. Perhaps the experimenter could avoid this difficulty by using him/herself as subject. Since the objects of introspective "observation" are events, one cannot look at the same object twice, hence, as Wittgenstein pointed out (1953, §§244–315), there is no guarantee that one is describing consistently over time. One simply has to assume that the same (type of) stimulus produces the same (type of) experience. With this assumption, one can check oneself and others for consistency.

What about the assumption? It certainly isn't safe as a general rule: experience and response vary with other factors besides stimulus conditions. But it seems one might remember: "Yes, that's just what it was like last time." Wittgenstein seems to have thought that this sort of thing isn't a genuine memory report because there is no way to check it. But have someone prick you in the back with a pin, then touch you with a finger, and ask yourself whether, so far as you can remember, the second felt like the first.

4. B. F. Skinner is even more insistent that the goal of scientific psychology is prediction and control, and he constantly represents psychology as seeking predictive nomic correlations. Yet his *Verbal Behavior* (1957) is a sustained attempt to apply a variant of Watson's analysis of habit to linguistic behavior. It is thus not even prima facie an exercise in prediction and control, and when Skinner tries to exhibit it as such, the results are ludicrous. See Chomsky's review (1959) for some amusing examples.

5. Watson's analysis of complex habits in fact makes the phenomenon he

describes in the long quotation above *more* difficult to understand. On Watson's view each action of the child is the response to some stimulus. If the child executes R_1, R_2, and R_3 in manipulating the box, then there must be corresponding S_1, S_2, and S_3. We should get kinaesthetic stimulus substitution here—K_i substituting for S_i. Since this is not observed, we must assume that the S_i do not recur at all, or not in the same order, from trial to trial. This makes it clear that, on Watson's view, it must be the S_i that drop out, for only this would account for the observed dropping of the R_i. But then Watson hasn't even identified these S_i, let alone a mechanism for ensuring their fortunate nonrecurrence over trials!

6. Here is a glossary of the symbols in the diagram:

$\dot{S}$	physical stimulus energy in learning
R	organism's reaction
$\dot{s}$	neural result of $\dot{S}$
$\check{s}$	neural interaction from 2 or more stimulus components
r	efferent impulse leading to reaction
G	reinforcing event
$_SH_R$	habit strength
S	evocation stimulus (same continuum as $\dot{S}$)
$_S\bar{H}_R$	generalized habit strength
C_D	drive determining event (deprivation)
D	drive strength
$_SE_R$	reaction potential
W	work in evoked reaction
I_R	reactive inhibition
$_SI_R$	conditioned inhibition
$_S\bar{E}_R$	effective reaction potential
$_SO_R$	oscillation
$_S\dot{\bar{E}}_R$	momentary effective reaction potential
$_SL_R$	reaction threshold
P	probability of reaction
$_St_r$	latency
n	number of reactions to extinction
A	amplitude

7. The points made here are touched on in Fodor (1965) and the ensuing discussion: Berlyne (1966), Osgood (1966) and Fodor (1966).

8. Freud's confidence concerning the unconscious processes posited is, of course, by no means prior to, or independent of, his interpretations of symptoms. Often, the existence of something in Dora's unconscious is inferred from the interpretation of a symptom.

9. My own technique is to keep the relevant quotations on file cards identified by numbers.

10. Freud misses a bet when he fails to notice that Dora's love for her father is relatively safe given her belief that he is impotent.

11. There seems to be no reason why the unconscious beliefs, desires, and so on implicated in AFFECT REPRESSOR need be explicit rather than implicit propositional attitudes. Indeed, this is one plausible way of construing the claim that they are unconscious. Freudian explanation is, therefore, largely *cognitive explanation rather than cognitive explanation.

NOTES TO THE APPENDIX (PAGES 163–192)

1. For a more detailed but elementary discussion of flip-flops and flip-flop counters, see Thomas Bartee (1960), ch. 4. The chapter includes a brief discussion of the components of these circuits as well.

2. Some philosophers would doubtless be unhappy about saying of any device which does this that it counts. They would prefer to say, for example, that such a device can be used to compute the successor function. In this appendix I shall simply ignore the issue raised by this objection.

3. That is, the same input-output properties relative to the correlation given. (See below.)

4. "D C B A": The complex symbol consisting of the symbol D followed by the symbol C followed by the symbol B followed by the symbol A.

5. By a "true description of the state of the counter" I do not, of course, mean any true description of the state of the counter, but a "canonical" one of the sort which results from interpreting expressions of the form

       (memory symbol) X = y

in the way indicated above.

Notice also that a definition of "is the output to pulse p and initial state s" has been provided for the counters in question: the output state to a pulse p and initial state (i.e., state at the time of the pulse) s is the first stable *interpretable* state to occur after p. The italics are important: we are only interested in those states of the counter which receive an interpretation in the program, i.e., with the relative d-c levels of the y-output lines of the flip-flops.

6. Reading "inputs" into a digital computer is an obvious case in point: the memories (some of them) are set in a certain way and computation begins. The same is true of the fanciful devices usually associated with Turing Machines. "Inputs" and "outputs" are simply the symbols initially printed on the tape and the symbols printed on the tape when the machine is in the terminal or "rest" state respectively. That the tape is part of the device, the squares of the tape being memories, is evident from the fact that there is no other provision for the storage of information—the internal states of the device having to do only with the direction of control—and from the fact that the amount of tape available greatly affects the capacities of the device. As Putnam comments in "The Mental Life of Some Machines," (1966) ". . . the tape may be thought of as physically realized in the form of any finite system

of memory storage. What we mean by a "symbol" is simply any sort of *trace* which can be placed in this memory storage and later "scanned" by some mechanism or other."

The tendency to dispense, in the sense in question, with the notion of inputs in favor of the notion of initial internal states is implicit in the psychologist's concern, not with what the subject sees, hears, etc., but with the subject's visual impressions, auditory impressions, etc. Stimuli are, for obvious reasons, identified with the information recorded, not with the information available if the subject would but pay attention—i.e., with proximal, not distal, stimuli.

7. Here, of course, it is assumed that a satisfactory definition of the relation $\underset{d}{\rightarrow}$ is available for the device d. There appears to be no general way of defining this relation in abstraction from particular facts about d. Earlier on, a definition of this relation was provided for the counters of Figure 3 and Figure 4 and this definition will also work for the counter of Figure 5. This definition depends on the fact that the counters in question reach a stable state—a state which will remain unchanged provided no further pulses are received—after each input pulse: the output to be associated with a given initial I-state and input pulse is the first stable I-output to appear after that pulse. The definition need not have been framed in this way, but given that it is, the programs given are output-adequate for the respective devices under the obvious memory-interpretations.

It is important to realize that, in actual research, failure to provide a theoretically satisfactory definition of the relation $\underset{d}{\rightarrow}$ does not necessarily render subsequent theorizing untestable, provided there is some acceptable way of gathering evidence for or against the claim that the relation holds in a given case.

8. The ith instruction, rather than the instruction x, is specified since the same instruction may appear several times in a memory-path, each time to different effect, as in the following program.

    (1) START.
    (2) SET A = A + 1.
    (3) IF A $<$ 10, GO TO (2); OTHERWISE, CONTINUE.
    (4) STOP.

9. The notion of temporal order here can easily be made precise. This will not be done, however, since no substantive point is served by complicating the definition in this direction. The intention is that, for all n, the first n-1 instructions must be executed before the changes specified (via I) in the nth instruction take place.

10. Suppose, for some memory-path p, $x_i{}^P(A) \Rightarrow (a)$. A mis-execution of x_i may result in (i) no change in the value of A, (ii) the assignment of some value $a' \neq a$ to A, or (iii) a change in the value of some memory symbol not appearing in x_i.

11. On occasion, a mis-execution may have no effect at all. For instance, the program beginning

        START.
        SET A = 1.
is not effected by a failure to execute the second instruction unless the initial
value of A is different from 1.

12. We can be sure it is a mis-exeuction of p and not the proper execution
of some other memory-path in C: we assume that d begins in I^N. M initiates
only one path in C, so a discrepancy of the sort in question must be considered
a mis-execution. Indeed, mis-execution can be defined in the following way.
Assume I is a memory-interpretation of d for C, and that p is a memory-path
in C initiated by N. d mis-executes the first instruction of p if, and only if, d
is in I^N and given an input but does not execute the first instruction of p. d
mis-executes the ith instruction of p, $i>1$, if, and only if, d executes the first
$i-1$ instructions of p but does not execute the first i instructions of p.

13. What if nothing interpretable by I transpires in d? Then, from the
point of view of I, nothing transpires in d at all. This we mirror by appending
a sequence of instructions to continue until 'STOP' is reached.

14. In practice, this assumption could easily be checked.

15. The definition is such that 'd executes C' implies 'C is ouput-adequate
for d'. Furthermore, it provides a way of defining the troublesome relation
$\overrightarrow{d} : I^N \overrightarrow{d} I^O$ just in case d executes a program C containing a memory-path p
initiated by N and terminating with the valuation O.

References

This book is, in some respects, "under-referenced." That is, specific citations of important background literature are not liberal by any standard. This is not just laziness: I discovered from comments on early drafts that a reference in a specific context often implied to a reader an interpretation of the work cited, and hence embroiled me in exegetical controversies peripheral to my main concerns. In order to compensate for my conservative use of citation in the text, the following bibliography includes many works not specifically mentioned in the text. Works actually referenced in the text are distinguished by an asterisk. Anthologies of papers central to the philosophical foundations of psychology are indicated by a dagger.

*Alston, W. (1967). "Wants, Actions, and Causal Explanations," in H. Castaneda (1967).

†Anderson, A. (1964), ed. *Minds and Machines*. Englewood Cliffs, N.J.: Prentice Hall.

Armstrong, D. (1968). *A Materialist Theory of Mind*. London: Routledge and Kegan Paul.

*Bartee, T. (1960). *Digital Computer Fundamentals*. New York: McGraw Hill.

*Bennett, J. (1973). "The Meaning–Nominalist Strategy," *Foundations of Language*, 10:141–168.

Bennett, J. (1976). *Linguistic Behavior*. Cambridge: Cambridge University Press.

*Berlyne, D. (1966). "Mediating Responses: a Note on Fodor's Criticisms," *Journal of Verbal Learning and Verbal Behavior*, 5:408–411.

†Biro, J. and R. Shahan (1982), eds. *Mind, Brain, and Function*. Norman, Oklahoma: University of Oklahoma Press.

†Block, N. (1980). *Readings in the Philosophy of Psychology*, Vol. 1. Cambridge, Mass.: Harvard University Press.

†Block, N. (1981). *Readings in the Philosophy of Psychology*, Vol. 2. Cambridge, Mass.: Harvard University Press.

†Borst, C. (1970), ed. *The Mind/Brain Identity Theory*. New York: Macmillan.

*Boyd, R. (1980). "Materialism without Reductionism: What Physicalism Does Not Entail," in N. Block (1980).

*Brandt, R. and J. Kim (1963). "Wants as Explanations of Actions," *Journal of Philosophy*, 60:425–435.

†Castaneda, H. (1967), ed. *Intentionality, Minds and Perception*. Detroit: Wayne State University Press.

*Chomsky, N. (1959). *Syntactic Structures*. The Hague: Mouton.

*Chomsky, N. (1959a). Review of B. F. Skinner, *Verbal Behavior* (1957), *Language*, 35:26–58. Reprinted in N. Block (1980).

*Chomsky, N. (1980). *Rules and Representations*. New York: Columbia University Press.

*Chomsky, N. (1980a). "Rules and Representations," *Behavioral and Brain Sciences*, 3:1–61.

*Churchland, P. and P. (1982). "Functionalism, Qualia, and Intentionality," in Biro and Shahan (1982).

Cummins, R. (1975). "The Philosophical Problem of Truth-of," *Canadian Journal of Philosophy*, 5:102–122.

*Cummins, R. (1975a). "Functional Analysis," *Journal of Philosophy*, 72:741–760.

*Cummins, R. (1976). "States, Causes, and the Law of Inertia," *Philosophical Studies*, 29:21–36.

*Cummins, R. (1977). "Programs in the Explanation of Behavior," *The Philosophy of Science*, 44:269–287.

Cummins, R. (1978). "Systems and Cognitive Capacities," *Behavioral and Brain Sciences*, 2:231–232. Comment on Haugeland (1978).

*Cummins, R. (1978a). "Subsumption and Explanation," *Proceedings of the Philosophy of Science Association*, 1:163–175.

*Cummins, R. (1979). Review of G. Pitcher, *Berkeley* (1977), *Philosophical Review*, 88:299–303.

*Cummins, R. (1981). Review of D. Dennett, *Brainstorms* (1978), *Philosophical Topics* (Spring, 1982). Reprinted as "What Can Be Learned from Brainstorms?" in Biro and Shahan (1982).

*Cummins, R., and E. Dietrich (1982). "PATHFINDER: Investigating the Acquisition of Communicative Conventions," *Proceedings of the Cognitive Science Society* (1982).

*Davidson, D. (1963). "Actions, Reasons, and Causes," *Journal of Philosophy*, 60:685–700.

*Davidson, D. (1975). "Thought and Talk," in S. Guttenplan, ed., *Mind and Language*, Oxford: Clarendon Press.

Davidson, D., and G. Harmon (1972), eds. *The Semantics of Natural Language.* New York: Reidel.

*Dennett, D. (1978). *Brainstorms.* Cambridge, Mass.: Bradford Books/M.I.T. Press.

*Dretske, F. (1981). *Knowledge and the Flow of Information.* Cambridge, Mass.: Bradford Books/M.I.T. Press.

*Fechner, G. (1860). *Elemente der Psychophysic.* Leipzig. Breitkopf und Hartel. Trans. H. Adler, *Elements of Psychophysics.* New York: Holt, Reinhart, and Winston, 1966.

*Fodor, J. (1965). "Could Meaning Be an r_m?" *Journal of Verbal Learning and Verbal Behavior,* 4:73–81.

*Fodor, J. (1966). "More about Mediators: a Reply to Berlyne and Osgood," *Journal of Verbal Learning and Verbal Behavior,* 5:412–415.

*Fodor, J. (1968). "The Appeal to Tacit Knowledge in Psychological Explanation," *Journal of Philosophy,* 65: 627–40. Reprinted in Fodor (1981).

Fodor, J. (1968a). *Psychological Explanation.* New York: Random House.

*Fodor, J. (1975). *The Language of Thought.* New York: Thomas Crowell, and Cambridge Mass.: Harvard University Press.

Fodor, J. (1981). *Representations.* Cambridge, Mass.: Bradford Books/M.I.T. Press.

*Fodor, J., T. Bever, and M. Garrett (1974). *The Psychology of Language.* New York: McGraw Hill.

Freud, S. (1920). "The Psychogenesis of a Case of Homosexuality in a Woman," in *Collected Papers,* Vol. 2. London: Hogarth Press, 1950; also *Complete Works,* Vol. 18, London: Hogarth Press, 1973.

*Freud, S. (1905). "Fragment of an Analysis of a Case of Hysteria," Monatsschrift für Psychiatrie und Neurologie, Bd. 27, Heft 4. References in the text are to the Collier edition (1974).

*Glymour, C. (1980). *Theory and Evidence.* Princeton: Princeton University Press.

*Goodman, N. (1965). *Fact, Fiction, and Forecast* 2nd ed., New York. Bobbs-Merrill. First published in 1955.

*Gregory, R. (1970). *The Intelligent Eye.* New York: McGraw Hill.

*Gregory, R. (1980). "Perceptions as Hypotheses," *Phil. Trans. of the Royal Society of London,* B, 290:181–197.

*Gregory R. (1981). *Mind in Science.* Cambridge: Cambridge University Press.

*Haugeland, J. (1978). "The Nature and Plausibility of Cognitivism," *Behavioral and Brain Sciences,* 2:215–60.

†Haugeland, J. (1981), ed. *Mind Design.* Cambridge, Mass.: Bradford Books/ M.I.T. Press.

Hempel, C. (1965). *Aspects of Scientific Explanation.* New York: Free Press.

*Hempel, C. (1966). *The Philosophy of Natural Science.* Englewood Cliffs, N.J.: Prentice Hall.

*Hempel, C. and P. Oppenheim (1948). "Studies in the Logic of Explanation," *The Philosophy of Science,* 15:135–175. Reprinted in Hempel (1965).

†Hook, S. (1960). *Dimensions of Mind: A Symposium.* New York: New York University Press.

*Hull, C. (1943). *Principles of Behavior.* New York: Appleton Century Crofts.

*Hume, D. (1888). *A Treatise of Human Nature.* Reference is to the edition edited by L. A. Selby-Bigge (1965). Oxford: The Clarendon Press.

*Kim, J. (1969). "Events and Their Descriptions: Some Considerations," in N. Rescher et al. (eds.), *Essays in Honor of Carl G. Hempel.* New York: Reidel.

*Kim, J. (1973). "Causation, Nomic Subsumption, and the Concept of *Event,*" *Journal of Philosophy,* 70:217-236.

Kim, J. (1976). "Events as Property Exemplifications," in M. Brand and D. Walton (eds.), *Action Theory.* New York: Reidel.

*Kripke, S. (1972). "Naming and Necessity," in Davidson and Harmon (1972).

Lycan, W. (181). "Form, Function, and Feel," *Journal of Philosophy,* 78:24-49.

*Meldin, A. (1961). *Free Action.* London: Routledge and Kegan Paul.

*Mill, J. S. (1843). *A System of Logic.* Reference in the text is to the abridged eighth edition reprinted as *Philosophy of Scientific Method* (1950). New York: Hafner.

*Miller, N. (1959). "Liberalization of Basic S-R Concepts: Extensions to Conflict Behavior, Motivation and Social Learning," in S. Koch, ed., *Psychology: A Study of a Science,* Study I, Vol. 2. New York: McGraw Hill.

*Nagel, T. (1974). "What Is It Like to Be a Bat?" *Philosophical Review,* 83:435-451.

*Newell, A., J. Shaw, and H. Simon (1957). "Programming the Logic Theory Machine," and "Empirical Exploration with the Logic Theory Machine," in *Proceedings of the Western Joint Computer Conference,* Vol. II.

*Osgood, C. (1966). "Meaning Cannot Be r_m?" *Journal of Verbal Learning and Verbal Behavior,* 5:402-407.

*Putnam, H. (1960). "Minds and Machines," in Hook (1960).

*Putnam, H. (1966). "The Mental Life of Some Machines," in Castaneda (1966).

Pylyshyn, Z. (1980). "Computation and Cognition: Issues in the Foundations of Cognitive Science," *Behavioral and Brain Sciences,* 3:111-169.

*Rorty, R. (1979). *Philosophy and the Mirror of Nature.* Princeton: Princeton University Press.

*Ryle, G. (1949). *The Concept of Mind.* New York: Barnes and Noble.

†Savage, C. (1978), ed. *Perception and Cognition: Issues in the Foundations of Psychology,* Minnesota Studies in the Philosophy of Science, 9. Minneapolis: University of Minnesota Press.

*Scriven, M. (1975). "Causation as Explanation," *Nous,* 9:3-16.

*Searle, J. (1979). "What Is an Intentional State?" *Mind,* 88:74-92.

*Searle, J. (1980). "Minds, Brains, and Programs," *Behavioral and Brain Sciences,* 3:417-457.

*Shannon, C. (1948). *The Mathematical Theory of Communication.* Urbana, Ill.: University of Illinois Press.

*Skinner, B. (1953). *Science and Human Behavior*. New York: Free Press.

*Skinner, B. (1957). *Verbal Behavior*. New York: Appleton Century Crofts.

*Tarski, A. (1956). "The Concept of Truth in Formalized Languages," in A. Tarski, *Logic, Semantics, and Metamathematics*. Oxford: The Clarendon Press. The paper was first published in 1933.

*Titchener. E. (1897). *An Outline of Psychology*. New York: Macmillan.

*Watson, J. (1924). *Behaviorism*. New York: People's Institute Publishing Co., 1970.

*Weber, E. H. (1934). *De Tactu*, Leipzig. Available in translation as *The Sense of Touch*, trans. E. Ross and D. Murray. New York: Academic Press, 1978.

*Wittgenstein, L. (1953). *Philosophical Investigations*. New York: Macmillan.

Index